The Solidarity Economy

AF411706

Diverse Economies and Livable Worlds

SERIES EDITORS
J. K. Gibson-Graham, Maliha Safri, Kevin St. Martin, Stephen Healy

The Solidarity Economy

Jean-Louis Laville

Diverse Economies and Livable Worlds

University of Minnesota Press

Minneapolis
London

Originally published in French as *L'économie sociale et solidaire: Pratiques, théories, débats.* Copyright Éditions du Seuil, 2010 and 2016. The present edition is a reviewed and expanded version of the work published at Le Seuil in 2010 under the title *Politique de l'association.*

The University of Minnesota Press acknowledges the work of Josh Booth and Jill Benson on the translation of this work.

Translation copyright 2023 by Jean-Louis Laville

All rights reserved. No part of this publication may be reproduced, stored in a retrieval system, or transmitted, in any form or by any means, electronic, mechanical, photocopying, recording, or otherwise, without the prior written permission of the publisher.

Published by the University of Minnesota Press
111 Third Avenue South, Suite 290
Minneapolis, MN 55401-2520
http://www.upress.umn.edu

ISBN 978-1-5179-1359-5 (hc)
ISBN 978-1-5179-1360-1 (pb)

A Cataloging-in-Publication record for this book is available from the Library of Congress.

Printed in the United States of America on acid-free paper

The University of Minnesota is an equal-opportunity educator and employer.

UMP BmB 2023

Contents

Introduction to the English Edition

STEPHEN HEALY AND MALIHA SAFRI

> Associations . . . attest to an indomitable aspiration for democracy—an aspiration whose realization requires democracy to be integrated into the economy.
> — *Jean-Louis Laville, Introduction*

WE ARE VERY EXCITED to help bring into the English-speaking world a translated contribution by Jean-Louis Laville, a major thinker whose work is widely known in the Francophone world. Jean-Louis Laville is professor at the National Conservatory of Arts and Crafts in Paris, where he holds a Chair in Solidarity Economy, a field in which he is a seminal thinker. This book, published first in 2010 as *Politique de l'association* by Seuil Press in Paris, helps bring a historical perspective to the work of constructing collective economic forms as a basis for more liveable worlds. From Laville's perspective, associations are an enduring feature of human society. Given their prevalence, the quality of these associations matters a great deal, for from them emerge durable institutions that, in turn, shape us.

The book is divided into three parts. Part I is a history of democratic associationalism in the nineteenth century. Part II focuses on contexts and examples of the social and solidarity economies in the twentieth century that emphasize the development of cooperative practices and institutions. In Part III Laville makes a major contribution to differentiating the third sector, the social economy, and the solidarity economy. Both his treatment of the concept of association and his subsequent elaboration of the solidarity economy aligns with key ideas animating the Diverse Economies and Livable Worlds series.

Most of the earlier volumes in this series are concerned with post-capitalist possibilities in the current moment. But being interested in postcapitalist possibility today requires us to pay attention to the historians of postcapitalist politics. The reasons for being interested in that history seem too obvious to bear repeating, but we find it worth reminding ourselves that the past is never simply history but is carried into the present as part of our contemporary condition (Lury 2020). It behooves us to learn from both successes and failures and to incorporate new strategies into contemporary politics. Laville's contribution helps us avoid the pitfalls and errors of the past that need not be duplicated unknowingly.

Laville's core argument is that our capacity to associate finds expression in contemporary life and persists even in societies where capitalist enterprise, private property, and ideological individualism seem to rule the day. Expanding a vision of our shared past, or in some cases actively correcting and rewriting it, produces new subjective (and therefore political) possibilities. For him, this process is not so much creating the conditions in which associations "emerge" but rather the context for them to "reappear." For example, when Laville examines the past of associationism in North America, he focuses on the many national and local women's associations that participated in the suffrage movement, and the church-based associations operated by African Americans in the pursuit of equal human rights. One only needs to think of scholarship by Jessica Gordon Nembrard (2014) or Ashantee Reese (2020) on the role that cooperatives and other related institutions have played in supporting the long (and ongoing) struggle for social and racial justice in the United States. Telling that history provides a genealogy of a contemporary postcapitalist politics of solidarity that can have important performative effects.[1]

This brief introduction describes two of the book's important theoretical contributions to thinking about postcapitalist politics: first, Laville's historical analysis and theorization of associationism, and second, his conceptualization of the solidarity economy as a transformative social movement driven by ethical imperatives. Both of these ideas correlate with the diverse economies framework and theory of community economy, respectively. Further, both association and solidarity seem particularly relevant to the current social and political milieux in the United States and elsewhere, offering a way of responding, or perhaps superseding, movement debates about the relative importance of informal versus formal institutions and their role in social change.

What Is Associationism?

In his opening pages of this book Laville writes, "the act of associating is a 'fact of society' that 'directly challenges our most basic categories of sociological analysis'" (Introduction). What this implies is both the diffuse nature of association and also the way that seeing it changes our shared understanding of sociological analysis accounts for why its meaning seems to shift depending on the political context (something he explores in part III). From the outset we can see that association is, for Laville, a term that has interrelated ontological, conceptual, and practical consequences and is the starting point for both so-called premodern and modern societies alike.

> What scholars sharing an interest in voluntary organizations and associative life as a main way of defining public engagement are doing when they study relationships of association and the prominent position in civil society of associations around which autonomous public spheres can develop. While not all associations created by free people have political objectives, in each one there is a sense of power that comes from acting together. Associations can reinforce inherited affiliations (of kinship or ethnic groups, for instance), but they also enable people—faced with the questions about how to live together—to construct new forms of belonging. (Introduction)

Two things follow from this positioning of associationism. One immediate implication of this repositioning of associationism as a transhistorical, political, and cultural constant is that it dispenses with the sharp divide between premodern societies held together by "mechanical solidarity" and modern societies where "organic solidarity" is a function of economic development and growing interdependence. In short, we are presented here with a concept where humans are always associating, and the capacity to associate carries the potential to exercise political power. Association spans both informal settings and formal institutions: in clubs and unions, in spiritual groups and churches, and in social movements, civil rights, and ecological justice groups. Associations can be both destructive and democratic, and Laville is careful to acknowledge he selectively focuses on the latter. Given the presence of associationism everywhere, the decisive questions become those of intention: what kind of associations hold us together, and how do durable forms of association—clubs, churches, enterprises—shape us? A second implication is that the capacity to associate, from seemingly pedestrian contexts like sporting clubs to global entities like transnational corporations, is for Laville connecting forms of belonging to the "question of how to live together" (Introduction). The latter question, and how forms of practice are connected to postcapitalist possibility, are central to diverse economies scholarship.

This more encompassing, protean, transcultural, and transtemporal conception of association accords with many intellectual currents in contemporary anthropology and decolonial and feminist theory that have informed diverse economies scholarship, and all of which speaks to the diversity, the plurality of economies, societies, and life itself. Laville's work aligns with the scholarship of the late David Graeber (2021) on the role of mutuality in historical anthropology, including his posthumously published *Dawn of Everything* (with David Wengrow), where he argues that the advent of agriculture and urbanization did *not* automatically come with hierarchy and inequality and, indeed, that civilizations (including neolithic ones) have had multiple and experimental ways of organizing society. This same thread runs through Laville's book: human societies are often more inventive and pliable than they are imagined to be. Evoking epistemologies of the global South from de Sousa Santos's (2015), Laville argues that Eurocentric ideas and institutions leave us ill-equipped to understand the forms of association flourishing in Central and South America (chapter 2). Finally, we note how Laville's repositioning of association at the heart of the human experience resonates with Kate Raworth's (2017) refashioning of economics around more encompassing conceptions of wellbeing, Joan Tronto's efforts to replace the individualist *homo economicus* with plural *homines curans* (caring people) (Tronto 2015), and Marie Puig de la Bellacasa's (2017) attempts to admit more-than-humans into the realm of shared social and ecological concerns.

The relationship between being and belonging and the question of how to live together are both key concerns for community economies theory as well. In this sense, associationism corresponds with Gibson-Graham's (2006) open, "minimalist" formulation of community economy inspired by the late Jean-Luc Nancy's definition of community as simply our being-in-common. Correspondingly, a community economy is simply a space where we negotiate the terms of our shared interdependence, our being-with one another in which "solidarity" is one possible expression. In both these conceptions our being in common functions as an ontological ground (Nancy 1991). Writing against the backdrop of twenty-first-century fascism (once a relic and now once more part of our contemporary condition), Nancy opposed the concept of being-in-common and imaginary coherence of common-being grounded in exclusion, and in the U.S. context one expression of common-being is the persistence of the formal and informal institutions which reproduce white supremacy.

Interdependence via associative relations with one another permeates being with one another in social, political, and economic space. Our associative relations are there, whether we affirm them as solidary bonds or deny them. Accordingly, how these relations are negotiated is of the utmost importance. For Laville this takes shape as an examination of the development of associations with their own ethos, and how that development impacts the different politics underlying the third sector, social economy, and solidarity economy movements.

What, in the Name of Solidarity?

> The desire to reinstate democratic solidarity at the very heart of the economy characterizes a new wave of initiatives that appeared in the last quarter of the twentieth century. They result from the search for new institutional regulations capable of combatting intolerable levels of social inequality and environmental damage. They thus move beyond a palliative function, fueling reflection on the nature of social solidarity and the goals of economic exchange. These tendencies, which started to emerge in self-managed and alternative collectives, are reappearances rather than entirely new phenomena. (chapter 9)

In the last third of this book Laville explores association in its contemporary forms. He does this by distinguishing the "third sector," "social economy," and "solidarity economy" in chapters 7, 8, and 9, respectively. The powers of association are at work in all three of these forms, but they are directed toward different ends. In the case of the third sector—and at least in the French context, the social economy—the goal is to ameliorate the dislocating effects of capitalist inequality and extend opportunities to those excluded from the mainstream labor market. In contrast, for Laville, solidarity economy names an intention to democratize and ultimately transform economies, societies, and ecologies.

While Laville aligns himself most with the solidarity economy, he does not discount the importance of the third sector and social economy movements, as they have found expression particularly in Europe but also elsewhere in the world, for two reasons. First, they are significant in countries around the world in terms of the numbers of people they employ. Second, as forms of association, they remain places where the capacity for association finds expression and, accordingly, are spaces where we are invited to connect forms of sociality with the question of how to live.

He begins by explaining the meaning of the third sector in more detail, given that it has different meanings even within the European context. While the term in his native France refers to any efforts directed at maintaining social cohesion, in the rest of Europe third sector refers to an organizational form "neither capitalist nor part of the state, it is a sector composed of nonprofit organizations, which are distinguished from both 'for-profit companies' and 'public services'" (chapter 7). In contrast, the social economy is composed of cooperatives and mutuals and their role in economic life (chapter 8). In both of these chapters he points out that these third secotor and social economy actors employ a significant percentage of the labor force throughout the world and that often they are involved in sectors like childcare, where the presence of the "profit motive" is seen by consumer-parents as a moral hazard.

These distinctions between the third sector and social economy become relevant in how they contrast with his reflections on the solidarity economy substantively in chapter 9 and in the conclusion. Laville begins this last chapter by stating that the central problematic of the solidarity economy is the relationship between economy and politics, something that has come into focus for social movements in the last quarter of the twentieth century as social and ecological conditions were becoming intolerable (chapter 9).

Laville opens the chapter by showing how this latest movement expands the possibilities for solidarity by blurring the boundary between the cooperative and associative forms. In Italy, for example, the concept of the "social cooperative" was developed in the early 1990s as a legal form that allows cooperatives to support (and be supported by) a community of benefit that is larger than worker-owner members. In doing so, the cooperatives escape from the confines of the third sector or the ameliorative role they are assigned in the social economy. Cooperatives want to do more for more people, and even in service to more-than-human communities, leading some diverse economies scholars to suggest that cooperatives, or at least the surplus they generate, might be better understood as commons managed for community benefit (Healy 2018).

For Laville, developments like this demonstrate how the solidarity economy repoliticizes the economy, in part by calling into question what an economy is for in the first instance. As Laville puts it:

> Once economic activities are put to work as means at the service of solidarity economy ends, the production of goods and services falls under a different logic: it is no longer determined by a quest for profit but rather by a desire to realize a common good. (chapter 9)

But precisely for this reason, the solidarity economy is pitted against a dominant ontological understanding of the "economy"—most notably what counts as economic, what gets valued, and who gets to decide this. Democratizing the economy means allowing for more input about what counts as economic. Quoting Lipietz approvingly, Laville argues that this means "why" we do it takes precedence over "how," and this reordering of the questions wrests the economy from being an object of administration and makes it into a space of ethical deliberation and political possibility (chapter 9). For Laville one consequence of repoliticizing the economy, interrogating the "why" of the association as a basis for transforming the "how" of economic organization, involves a direct confrontation with the dominant ideological and practical conception of economy.

Here is another connection between Laville's ambitions and current diverse economies scholarship, particularly in the context of the global pandemic. As many scholars have noted, one of the things the Covid-19 pandemic brought to our attention was the explosion of mutual aid practices in response to both the virus itself as well as the economic dislocations that came from public-health responses to this emergency. From practices of neighborliness to coordinated efforts to redirect food from shuttered restaurants and institutions to people who needed it, the world was awash with examples of inventive and mutualistic responses to the pandemic (Dean 2020; Sitrin et al 2020). Scholar and movement activist Lauren Hudson (2020) notes that members in Black communities in the Brooklyn borough of New York were able to respond early and effectively to the health and economic consequences of the pandemic in part because mutuality was already there at hand as a shared practice as part of Black Lives Matter mobilization. She points out that many of these "informal" (associative) efforts were better able to act swiftly to provide assistance than formally organized cooperatives whose movements and efficacy were hampered by city and state regulations. Like Laville and Lipietz, she argues that what matters is how communities, associations, cooperatives answer the "why" question in relation to economy.

For Laville part of the genius of the solidarity economy is not simply the way that it operates "outside" the state and market, but the way that it recombines elements from both while belying their illusory separation. Defined by market-oriented organizations (e.g., cooperatives) that internalize the common good as a part of their social license as well as organizations that directly provide for social and ecological well-being, with or without support from local or state government. And it's precisely for these reasons that the solidarity economy exceeds the boundaries of the social economy and third sector framings. However, this does not place the solidarity economy somehow beyond or outside of the larger societies of which it is a part. Laville reflects on the dangers of what he calls isomorphism, which we might understand as the invidious way in which the logic of dominant conceptions of economy can reoccupy spaces of solidarity so that what was once a capacious and radical space becomes just the same as everything else. Laville follows Enjolras in writing about three types of isomorphism that can undermine solidarity economies. In institutional isomorphism, norms of "professionalism" can work against solidarity, "mimetic isomorphism" too simply replicates solutions that worked elsewhere, or coercive isomorphism where state authorities work to shut down perceived threats. Laville does not idly warn us of these dangers; in his view this is precisely what has happened to well-meaning institutions of the social economy as well as the cooperative banks that followed mainstream finance right over the cliff of the global financial crisis.

There is a tendency among leftist intellectuals to regard the threat of isomorphism as an inevitability, as further confirmation of Fisher's (2009) capitalist realism. In contrast, Laville treats this as a danger to be understood and militated against through practice. He also treats it as a symptom of the confrontation between a solidarity economy and a dominant conception of the economy in which all bonds, all obligations, all interdependencies, relations of care, love, and affection give way to the "universal grammar" of transaction. One way of thinking about this is that there has been fifty years worth of effort to convince people that society "does not exist" and that there are no alternatives to capitalism, as Margaret Thatcher once put it. But this capitalist-utopianism has not erased the human capacity to associate, and how the economy is one place where solidarity is and can be expressed.

Conclusion

The aim of this introduction is to orient series readers in relation to what is valuable in this book. One tendency, particularly in the U.S. solidarity movement, is a recurrent desire to position either informal practices as more important to the solidarity economy or, in contrast, to see the emergence of cooperatives or other formal solidarity economy institutions as the necessary priority of the movement. Laville's historical and theoretical treatment of the concept of association offers us a way of bypassing this debate by subverting the distinction between the two. The capacity to associate is being exercised in both formal and informal spaces, but what becomes crucial for both solidarity and democracy is the way that it calls into question the fundamental intentions and design of the economy.

Foregrounding the politicization of the economy and illuminating how the economy exists as an object that we iteratively design opens the space for negotiation by means of democratic inclusion. This intervention is at once timely and difficult. As deepening economic inequality and ecological precarity affect people even more deeply, it is not surprising that preserving privilege (however meager for the base) takes on an ever more strident and aggressive form. It is in this context that an open, pluralist, and democratic solidarity economy becomes a political imperative.

And last, we put this in the line of the great tradition of radical historiography, but with a twist. No doubt we find deep inspiration in the "people's history" tradition that exposed and exposes the workings of exploitation (Zinn 2015). Laville's work is in a slightly different vein, the kind that exposes our great collective practices and politics as inspiration (Curl 2012). His history demonstrates how associations deeply shaped and permeated key aspects of society, in all parts of the world. We find this inspiring because it helps us recast the very notion of "success" and longevity of postcapitalist institutions and practices as comprising our past, present, and future horizons.

Bibliography

Curl, John. 2012. *For All the People: Uncovering the Hidden History of Cooperation, Cooperative Movements, and Communalism in America.* Oakland, Calif.: Pm Press.

de Sousa Santos, Boaventura. 2015. *Epistemologies of the South: Justice against Epistemicide.* London: Routledge.

Fisher, Mark. 2009. *Capitalist Realism: Is There No Alternative?.* Portland, Ore.: John Hunt Publishing.

Gibson-Graham, J. K. 2006.*A Postcapitalist Politics.* Minneapolis: University of Minnesota Press.

Graeber, David, and David Wengrow. 2021. *The Dawn of Everything: A New History of Humanity.* London: Penguin.

Healy, Stephen. 2018. "Corporate Enterprise as Commonwealth." *Journal of Law and Society* 45, no. 1: 46–63.

Hudson, Lauren. 2020. "Building Where We Are: The Solidarity-Economy Response to Crisis." In *Rethinking Marxism* Dossier, Summer.

Laville, Jean-Louis. 2013. *Politique de l'association.* Paris: Média Diffusion.

Lury, Celia. 2020. *Problem Spaces: How and Why Methodology Matters.* Hoboken, N.J.: John Wiley & Sons.

Nancy, Jean-Luc. 1991. "Of Being-in-Common." In *Community at Loose Ends,* ed. Miami Theory Collective, 1–12. Minneapolis: University of Minnesota Press.

Nembhard, Jessica Gordon. 2014. *Collective Courage: A History of African American Cooperative Economic Thought and Practice.* University Park: Penn State Press.

Puig de La Bellacasa, Maria. 2017. *Matters of Care: Speculative Ethics in More Than Human Worlds.* Minneapolis: University of Minnesota Press.

Raworth, Kate. 2017. *Doughnut Economics: Seven Ways to Think like a 21st-Century Economist.* Chelsea, Vt.: Chelsea Green Publishing.

Reese, Ashanté M. 2019. *Black Food Geographies: Race, Self-Reliance, and Food Access in Washington, DC.* Chapel Hill, N.C.: UNC Press Books.

Sitrin, Marina, and Colectiva Sembrar, eds. 2020. *Pandemic Solidarity: Mutual Aid during the COVID-19 Crisis.* London: Pluto Press.

Spade, Dean. 2020. *Mutual Aid: Building Solidarity during This Crisis (and the Next).* New York: Verso Books.

Tronto, Joan C. 2015. *Who Cares? How to Reshape a Democratic Politics.* Ithaca, N.Y.: Cornell University Press.

Zinn, Howard. 2015. *A People's History of the United States: 1492–Present.* New York: Routledge.

The Solidarity Economy

Introduction

WHILE THE END OF THE TWENTIETH CENTURY seemed to confirm a virtuous complementarity between market economy and democracy, the twenty-first began with a major upheaval that failed to deliver on promises of continued enrichment and personal fulfilment for all. Since then, what has been striking is democracy's alarming fragility, faced with the unrestricted development of the economy. This fragility cannot be resolved through minor adjustments to the existing system or a return to previous systems of regulation. It challenges the very foundations of our model of society and touches the very definition of politics and the economy. Politics goes far beyond just what politicians do, while economics cannot be reduced to the operations of the market. The thesis developed here is that in order to strengthen democracy and humanize the economy, we must turn to associationalism, that is, a project built on collective activity carried out by free and equal citizens with reference to a common good. Far from being an idealistic vision, such a thesis calls for an examination of associationalism—of why it has persisted, but also why it has encountered difficulties. The ideas about associationalism have been developed by numerous authors after Tocqueville (1843); among them: Hirst and Bader (2001), Kaufman (2003), Keane (1988), Walzer (1991). While it is important to identify the different forms that it has taken—the most recent of which have been placed under the "social and solidarity economy" banner in the international debate—this is not just to better understand what is an underestimated phenomenon; it is also because of "the need to rethink a new democratic architecture" (Rosanvallon 2004, 434).

We will begin by reviewing the end of the twentieth century in order to describe the situation we have inherited. Admittedly, there were some positive outcomes. In the last quarter of this century, the number of democracies in the world increased. Globally, average life expectancy increased, rising by seven years, and average living standards improved, with a rise in consumption over the same period corresponding to a 40 percent increase in goods and services. Nevertheless, social injustice persists far beyond anything that could be considered acceptable. International financial institutions have acknowledged an increase in income disparities both within and between countries. Since 1980, the World Bank has recorded a significant rise in inequality within the richest nations, in a reversal of previous trends. According to the International Monetary Fund, the gap between the richest and the poorest countries continued to widen throughout the 1990s. Since the beginning of the 2000s, there has been no discernible improvement. The scandal has continued: in 2008, hunger riots broke out in more than thirty countries. If the poverty line is fixed at 50 percent of median income, then in the mid-2000s one child in eight in the OECD countries was living in a poor household. In 2015, the income of the wealthiest 10 percent was 9.6 times higher than that of the poorest 10 percent, while this ratio was 7 to 1 in the 1980s and 9 to 1 in the 2000s (OECD 2015, 125–54). About 10 percent of the world population suffer from hunger, 520,000 being in a catastrophic situation of famine. With climate change, 80 million more people will be concerned in 2050, 130 million living in an extreme poverty in the next ten years.[1] And the pandemic crisis has accelerated the discriminations between rich and poor people. It is astonishing that the world has come to accept such disparities; especially as, far from diminishing over time, they persist in societies that are simultaneously obsessed with consumption and incapable of meeting everyone's basic needs. The capitalism of the early twenty-first century has compounded inequalities, which are close to the levels recorded at the beginning of the nineteenth century (Piketty 2013). The capitalist way of life (Arnsperger 2005) exacerbates the contradiction between the right to equality and actual inequality, which continually undermines the sense of belonging to a common world. At the same time, awareness of this antinomy has largely been forestalled by the failure of the system that aspired to be an alternative to capitalism: communist totalitarianism.

The twentieth-century fate of this alternative has made it necessary to renew the critical perspective. So that we do not set ourselves up for further disappointment, such a perspective needs to address the question of social change—of a democratic transition toward a more egalitarian world that can only be anchored in existing social practices. In the words of Hirschman, critique must be accompanied by "possibilism" (Hirschman 1971b, 1986). Critique of "the order of things" cannot adopt the perspective of another system endowed with a superior rationality. It has to start from the perspective of an "order of populations and people,"[2] which reintroduces democratic struggles—as experienced by the protagonists—into the analysis. It is vital not to repeat the mistakes of the last century—not to hold on to the chimeric hope that mankind will change—but rather to respond to demands that human dignity be respected. To do this, we must abandon both economic determinism and an exclusive focus on the market and the state.

Our analysis must first reexamine the place of the economy in society. The past few decades have shown us that the dual promise that poverty can be overcome through the accumulation of wealth, on the one hand, and that we will see a "trickle-down effect" from the richest to the poorest, on the other, is no longer tenable. The belief that economic growth leads to a reduction in inequalities is a legacy of the twentieth century that it is essential to cast off. To this end, we should note that behind the struggle between liberalism and Marxism that has marked the past two centuries, these opposing forces implicitly share the assumption that the economic sphere is the main explanatory factor driving social change. Orthodox Marxism has neglected legally guaranteed political freedoms, viewing them as a mere superstructural mask concealing the reality of society: the economic base. Meanwhile, liberalism distinguishes itself from Marxism by contending that the economy operates according to its own logic of individual self-interest; but this is just another form of economic determinism, radicalized by neoliberalism. Economism has therefore restricted our field of vision, even when it has originated from opposite ideological choices. In order not to give in to any of its variants, we must keep in mind the difficulty of combining the values of individual and collective freedom on the one hand, and equality and social justice on the other.

Challenging economic determinism logically leads us to question the respective roles of the market and the state. Contrary to common belief, *longue-durée* history has shown that the market is not the bulwark that protects freedom after all. Traditionally, the liberal right has advocated expanding the market, while the social-democratic left has demanded more state control. The conversion of the left to the market system has reduced this divide, but this should not lead us to forget the existence of two recurrent risks: total market domination and total state domination.[3] From the nineteenth century onward, the project of liberalizing the economy caused so much trouble that, as a reaction to this process, there were demands for the political to reassert itself. And the pendulum did not stop swinging there. In the twentieth century, attributing excessive value to the political led to totalitarianism and its mad dream of fusing society and state, the failure of which, in turn, greatly undermined state intervention in the economy. Overall, the experience of the past two centuries has shown that, behind the polite exchanges between democratic parties debating the respective virtues of the market and the state, lies violence—violence that emanates both from a self-regulating market and from a tentacular state. Both economic war and authoritarian statism are a threat to democracy. Evidently this threat has not dissipated, since the national socioeconomic compromises struck in industrial societies following the Second World War have been overtaken by the new service-based global economy.

Ultimately, while abandoning economic determinism—along with an overemphasis on the state and the market—appears necessary, doing so also seems arduous. Once we lose the reassurance provided by these conventional ways of thinking, unprecedented concerns arise about the conflict between economy and society. The current situation no longer warrants faith in a bright future in which economic and social progress will be reconciled. And yet a society without hope of individual and collective emancipation can no longer gain the support of its members.

This is no time for despair, however. This book is not intended to be a solely negative critique or a string of complaints about widespread economism. The apparent triumph of "economic man"—a subject exclusively driven by his own interests—calls for greater attention to "other forms of life and alter-life that discourses of resistance may draw on and encourage" (Laval 2007, 25). If we are to reject the way out offered by a conception of postmodernity that denies our political condition, then we must offer an alternative view of how democracy and economy should relate to one another.

To do so we cannot simply seek the right balance between state and market but must take civil society into account. For too long, delimiting the respective domains of market and state has resulted in the neglect of associations formed by people joining together in civil society. Reduced to nonprofit organizations, associations have received little attention. In most analyses, they are presented as simply adding an extra touch of color to social relations. They are given no importance when it comes to major economic and political issues. Our response to this quiet disdain will be to reclaim the history of associations and offer an insight into their current state. Although they by no means claim to be able to solve contemporary problems alone, they should nonetheless be involved in the debate about how to reformulate these problems. Offering new repertoires of action and symbolic resources, associations are a way of overcoming the recurrent, disastrous alternation between the all-powerfulness of the political and its powerlessness with respect to the economy. They help us develop a broader approach to political economy, as defined by Hirschman (1981): a political economy for society.

Beyond the legitimate—yet predictable—debate about the respective functions of the market and the state, we should remember that a more fundamental tension exists between democracy and economy. This book's main hypothesis is that over the past two centuries, associations have placed themselves at the center of controversies about this uncertain arrangement between the political and economic spheres. This is how associations bring about change, not in the limited sense that some associations engage in social activism, but in the broader sense that whole swathes of the associational domain have participated in social change.

Associationalism—which insists that self-governing associations have a vital role to play in deepening democracy, advocated by francophone theorists from Tocqueville to Mauss and anglophone authors from Cole to Dewey—has new relevance in the twenty-first century now that the limits of the market–state dualism typical of the twentieth century have become obvious. This book aims to highlight the importance of this project by reframing associationalism conceptually through a revised history. Advocating such an approach is not straightforward, as it diverges from what is widely accepted; this is why we must outline its foundations from the outset. To this end, it is helpful to begin by clarifying how the invention of democracy enabled the invention of modern solidarity. We can then situate associations in relation to this dual invention.

Politics and the Invention of Modern Democracy

The political sphere can be defined in relation to power founded on the use of legitimate violence—power that enables the establishment of an authority characterized by domination. However, the tradition of thought that approaches politics in this way—best-represented by Weber—does not provide a complete understanding of the political. The political is also what keeps societies together, and we can credit Arendt with having identified this other understanding of power as "being *together.*" Emphasizing this understanding, Arendt highlighted "the moment when the constraints of the political become the object of collective deliberation and decision-making."[4] The invention of democracy is that development of the political that is brought about by common action and dialogue about the polity. But these drivers of democracy simultaneously constitute a distinct domain of activity that threatens to occlude the political—the domain of politics.

In Greek antiquity, a public sphere distinct from the private sphere was established—a public sphere through which men recognized their state of dependence and their desire for a common world open to a multitude of perspectives. Democracy results from this fragile balance between Weber's "administrative power" and Arendt's "communicative power."[5] This balance can only be maintained through "creative action" (Joas 1996) within a nonappropriable public sphere—and it is a balance that cannot be guaranteed by a system of institutions alone. Moving away from analyses that focus exclusively on domination, we should remember that preserving and enlarging a public sphere is crucial for democracy. And achieving this depends on citizens' voluntary engagement.

Nevertheless, the continuity between the Hellenic public sphere—whose significance Arendt affirmed—and the modern public sphere that emerged via the bourgeoisie must not stop us registering what changed. We should avoid a common interpretation of Arendt that conflates the Athenian regime with the essence of democracy. The public sphere remains a structuring principle of our political system, but in Greece it remained the exclusive domain of citizens exempt from productive labor. The authority they exercised in the home spared them from the tasks linked to subsistence and the reproduction of life carried out by women and slaves. It was only possible for equals to come together in a world of freedom—a world where enlightenment was sought through discussion—because questions related to necessity and material needs were dealt with in the shadows.

The public sphere is not unchanging. The freedom of the moderns is not the freedom of the ancients (Constant 1988). With the representative system, individuals can lose themselves in the enjoyment of their private independence. But in parallel to this risk of political apathy there is a move toward equality that forms the basis for new demands for active participation and the sharing of political power. This is where modern democracy departs from ancient democracy. Modern democracy rests on the establishment of a system in which the benchmarks of justice are individual freedom and equality—thus citizenship is no longer limited to a particular social group. The difference is sizeable. Even if it is not realized in practice, the public sphere's accessibility in principle changes the conditions under which democracy operates, especially as it does so in a context where certainty about the meaning of the world has been lost. The loss of shared transcendences allows power to be de-sacralized both through the formation of citizens' collective will and through their participation, which requires them to accept conflicts of opinion and debates about rights.

Modern democracy generates the contradictions pointed out by Tocqueville. Personal freedom and independence lead to fears about the breakdown of identity, which in turn results in individuals clinging together to avert this. While public opinion is a manifestation of individual freedom of expression, it also becomes an anonymous force over and above the individual that lies beyond their control. While the law can be subjected to critique and adapts in response to new experiences, it can also become homogenizing and use the will of the people as a pretext for becoming overly intrusive. Nevertheless, these ailments of freedom and equality bring with them their own remedies. Making a distinction between the domains of power, law, and knowledge, democracy gives rise to a new "symbolic constitution of the social" (Lefort 1986, 22–29). It disentangles power and law, since the legitimacy of power rests on its conformity to law, which only an independent judiciary is in a position to decide. Ultimately the legitimacy of controversies about the legitimate and illegitimate prevents power from placing itself above society.

The ground was prepared for this development in the eighteenth century by debates initially centered on personal experiences and their literary expression, which built up into political expression. Gradually the rules governing social life were liberated from the monopoly of interpretation that church and state authorities had once granted themselves (Habermas 1991, 51–56). Questions about the social contract pervaded the modern public sphere, which diffracted into various spaces where discussions took place (cafes, salons, clubs). Together, these spaces constituted a sphere of communication that was unprecedented in two principal ways. First, its requirement of openness to everyone—considered equal insofar as they are human beings—encouraged the challenging of inherited hierarchies. Second, it affirmed "plurality as the objective of a political community that is not based on or justified by any common origin and as a matter of principle rejects any final communion" (Tassin 1992, 33).

The limits of the liberal bourgeois public sphere are thus apparent. The public sphere symbolically constitutes the matrix of the political community. But as Eley (1992) points out, it is also an arena of conflicting meanings. Various publics seek to be heard, and confront one another in clashes that may involve strategic behavior or attempts to eliminate other points of view. The public sphere cannot be reduced to the exchange of rational arguments alone; it also involves actions that depend on the conviction of those carrying them out, as well as attempts at persuasion, or even the use of pressure or seduction. Emotional and affective strategies are also used to make public issues that were previously a private matter.

The tensions between the bourgeois public sphere and an "oppositional" public sphere are evidence of this. This other sphere is both rival and complementary to the first. Habermas referred to it as "plebeian,"[6] whereas Negt, in his dialogue with Habermas, prefers the term "proletarian" to describe all the rebel human potential seeking its own mode of expression (Negt 2007, 222). In this plebeian or proletarian sphere, the working-class public stood up to the bourgeois public by forming self-determined groups. But they did this in the name of the principles established by the bourgeoisie. Popular gatherings were based on the ideal of freedom of expression for all and on the spread of a new political culture. They too embraced noncoercive social relationships, based on members volunteering, engaging in discussion, and deciding by majority rule. This is why it is possible, as Habermas himself[7] recognized, to talk about a polycentric public sphere, or plural public spheres, rather than a single public sphere. Emphasizing this plurality of public spheres discourages us from understanding the public sphere in an abstract manner. Instead, it leads us to examine how citizens whose relationships are governed by the principles of equality and freedom question the gap between the claims of democracy and everyday reality. This is how Honneth (1995) sees public spheres as gaining concrete reality: in his view, it is principally the erosion of democracy through denials of recognition that drives collective action in public spheres under constant reconstruction.

This clarification of how public spheres develop in practice sheds light on the political role of associations. The practical part they play in opinion formation has a theoretical consequence: it encourages us to move away from "atomistic" thinking. This is what scholars who share an interest in voluntary organizations and associative life as a main way of defining public engagement are doing when they study relationships of association[8] and the prominent position in civil society of associations around which autonomous public spheres can develop[9]. While not all associations created by free people have political objectives, in each one there is a sense of power that comes from acting together. Associations can reinforce inherited affiliations (of kinship or ethnic groups, for instance), but they also enable people—faced with the questions about how to live together—to construct new forms of belonging.

Economy and the Invention of Modern Solidarity

These questions would find an answer in the concept of "solidarity." During the nineteenth century, solidarity was conceived as a force for social integration in opposition to the influence of money and administrative power, according to Habermas. The philosophers who introduced this concept claimed that symbolic exchange had primacy over economic exchange but rejected any return to the former social order based on inherited affiliations. At a time when the barriers of hierarchical society had crumbled, this recourse to the language of solidarity reflected uncertainty about social cohesion as much as it denoted the renunciation of a sense of security based on religious dogma. The gradual emancipation from tradition led to an awareness that the main source of meaning was meaningful activity. But meaningful activity could not be reduced to strategic rational action any more than motives for action could be reduced to material interest. As Durkheim argued,[10] the concept of solidarity was of fundamental importance to sociology in its early stages; as Mauss observed—solidarity subjects the gift, "one of the human rocks on which societies are built" (Mauss 2001, 148), to a process of secularization; it designates not just a traditional community relationship "determined by nature" but rather includes voluntary initiatives where "human beings become fully conscious of the bonds that unite them" and construct "planned, deliberate, active solidarity."[11] This relationship—distinct from both charity and instrumental relationships—is founded on reason, and it should be understood as an acknowledged interdependence between people and groups.[12]

To think that this approach to solidarity might demarcate the social domain would be anachronistic. When it first emerged, this approach was set on an economy capable of adhering to the political principle of equality—an economy that emphasized human beings' relationships with each other and the natural environment. This definition—which Polanyi (1977) arrived at by drawing on a large body of anthropological research—led to the identification of a number of principles of economic behavior. In addition to the market, there is reciprocity, which results from the presence of symmetrically placed groups; redistribution, whereby a central authority organizes the allocation of resources; and householding, which refers to the rules of a given closed group that guarantee the production and sharing of resources in order to satisfy its members. The solidarity made possible by democratic revolutions is therefore in no way traditional; it moves beyond householding to reconstruct both reciprocity and redistribution. It introduces the idea of egalitarian reciprocity experienced through direct interaction between citizens, which will be followed by the implementation of a system of redistribution according to terms set by elected authorities. So it was indeed the invention of a new form of solidarity that resulted from the rise of democracy in the "first" nineteenth century, "the age of revolution" (Hobsbawm 1962). It long preceded the invention of the social domain, which would become a bifurcation characteristic of the "second" nineteenth century, "the age of capital and empire" (Hobsbawm 1975, 1987).[13]

Among the often-ignored debates from this "first" nineteenth century, we see the hope of achieving equality giving rise to struggles for political reform and revolts against economic subjection. Groups that are denied their dignity as citizens, or are victims of exploitation, rise up against the exclusion and disdain to which they are subjected. In this respect, as Fraser (1990) suggests, the themes addressed in popular spheres are different from those considered in the bourgeois sphere, since they integrate economic issues into public debate. According to Faure and Rancière (2007, 32), "labor's speaking out" about the "issue of power on the shop floor is by no means a hijacking of political action by workers." Instead, it expresses a desire for dignity for all that is connected to forms of resistance—a desire reiterated in demands for work that would allow the power of collective autonomy to be realized. The contradiction between the assertion of equality and the persistence of inequalities leads to the incompatibility between political freedom and economic subjugation being denounced. The solidarity invoked to justify the further opening up of the public sphere can also be invoked to justify reorganizing the economy on a more egalitarian basis. Economic behavior requires political and normative frameworks ranging from fundamental social arrangements to mental habits; it can therefore include solidarity, according to Durkheim and Mauss. The claim here is that the economy is not a given but rather an institutional creation that is part of a historical process. The existence of solidarity shows that democratic demands have an impact on the economy.

In this perspective it is crucial to underline the differences between work, labor, and action, understanding them as different types of activity as Arendt (2018) does; this is as much to avoid a disastrous political injunction being issued to the economy as to prevent the absolute power of an economic system subordinating the political system. However, the analytical distinction should not be turned into an empirical dichotomy;[14] on closer examination, the idea of a separation in lived experience between politics and economics does not seem tenable. The invention of modern solidarity during the nineteenth century supports the idea that political relationships cannot be assessed against the example of the Greeks without adopting their ideological model. In Greek democracy, it was by freeing himself from labor that man could devote himself to city life, which involved what Arendt calls action; a free man's political activity depended on him not being confined to the domestic sphere or involved in tasks related to survival and reproduction.

The economic sphere was therefore kept apart from the public sphere. But this separation cannot be transplanted into contemporary democracies. Once the principle of unlimited citizenship is established, social groups forced to take on economic duties in order to ensure their livelihood can legitimately criticize the social division of work when they believe it contradicts democratic ideals. The economy therefore cannot be considered a domain separate from political activity, governed only by the laws of efficiency and devoid of any values. The idea that it is possible to find a social balance by giving free reign to private interests remains a contentious issue, and the management of the economy has been the subject of fierce debates that have only died down temporarily over the past two centuries. In particular, these debates concern the gap between the future promise of an inclusive democracy and the present reality of increasing inequality. At the beginning of the twenty-first century, as in the nineteenth century, this discrepancy is wide enough to prompt a number of citizens to call for changes in the economy.

In these struggles, associations have contributed to a conception of the economy that has not been purged of all reference to ethics and values. They are not just platforms for public expression; they challenge the postulate that the political sphere is radically autonomous in relation to the economic sphere. While they are the concrete manifestation of positive freedom (Berlin 2002) and therefore take on a political dimension, they also assume an economic dimension through the organization of diverse production and consumption activities. Through the practices they promote, they break down the boundary between politics and economy whose existence has often been inferred from Arendt's typology of human activities.

Reconnecting with the Associationalist Tradition

Today, the expression "social and solidarity economy" (SSE) has been adopted across all continents, as though it is assumed the SSE will continue the legacy of the inventions of democracy and solidarity that we have just been discussing. Yet instead of its potential, the concept of the SSE tends to be adopted without any analysis of the underlying institutionalization process[15] from which the SSE emerges. In contrast, this book proposes to trace the genesis of the associationalism that led to this process, drawing on a variety of national contexts in Europe and the Americas. Clearly, the history of the associative movement cannot be limited to associations with nonprofit status. The act of associating is a "fact of society" that "directly challenges our most basic categories of sociological analysis." While "it cannot be reduced either to calculations of interest or to power relations and strategies, it does point toward another kind of social and political bond: that of solidarity" (Chanial and Laville 2006, 46). To elucidate current issues in the social and solidarity economy, we must return to this broader understanding of association.

This book's purpose is thus to examine associationalism, whose complexity quickly becomes apparent when we consider the interdependencies between the political and economic spheres. But major obstacles to articulating a project of this kind still need to be removed. The first relates to the multiplicity of associative forms that have existed in different eras. As it has been present in a wide variety of historical situations, the associative phenomenon's particularity risks being lost amid the kaleidoscopic effect created by its particular instantiations. The proliferation of associative forms thus obstructs our understanding of associationalism.

To overcome this difficulty, we should clarify straight away that in this book we will only consider associationalism in contemporary democracies. As Dewey (1920, 203) argued, contemporary democracy can be characterized by "a movement toward multiplying all kinds and varieties of associations: political parties, industrial corporations, scientific and artistic organizations, trade unions, churches, schools, and clubs and societies without number."

Another clarification must be made from the outset: acknowledging this proliferation does not imply any idealization of the associative movement. It is clear that not all associations are democratic. Some compound injustice. Others even try to undermine the foundations of the democratic system. Many associations also develop an autocratic form of governance, and examples of associations run by demagogues and autocrats are well known—not to mention those where power has been seized by irremovable leaders. To assert that there is a link between associations and democracy is thus not to succumb to a mythification of associations. It is simply to acknowledge that the associative framework enables social experiences that help transform the institutional order or rewrite the established normative order (Renault 2004,

188–89). Of course, businesses sometimes make use of deliberation in the workplace; but they remain institutional arrangements where shareholders are dominant. In contrast, the particularity of modern associations is that within them citizens determine their own action. By respecting legal equality among stakeholders and not obeying any external injunctions, associations at root represent a dimension of the public sphere emanating from civil society, as well as a mode of economic action that is not subordinated to the ownership of capital.

This recognition of associations' place in theory can be reconciled with observations of their empirical ambiguities in practice. Associations are rooted in their cultural, social, and ideological contexts. They thus reflect the state of power relations and social conflicts. They are subject to permanent tensions between different modes of expression and different logics, to clashes and negotiations between social classes and groups. Dominant groups maneuver within them to increase their influence, or even to gain the monopoly of legitimate public expression, while excluded or dominated groups fight for recognition. Furthermore, as Barthelemy (2000, 16 and 59) notes, associations do not simply act as the citizens' voice; they are also implicated in power relations because "they mediatize the ideological conflicts of society as a whole, help train elites and structure local power, and participate in the development of public policies, while at the same time legitimizing the politico-administrative sphere." Certain associations are so institutionalized that they have become more like appendages of the state or the business sector than independent entities. This is why associations are ambivalent. Far from being only an expression of civil society's autonomy, they can also be considered instruments of power and social control.

So it would be pointless to try to follow all the twists and turns of associations. The approach taken here limits itself to identifying what links associations to the inventions of democracy and solidarity. Both Arendt and Habermas touch on this project from a political perspective whenever they refer to the public sphere. From an economic perspective, the study of associations as institutional creations was begun by Durkheim and Mauss who, in their attempts to uncover the social foundations of economic facts, showed how different kinds of associations (professional groups, mutuals, cooperatives) constitute modern forms of giving in a secularized society. According to Mauss, they contribute to the acquisition of a solidarity-based sociality and ward off violence.

Another objective of this book is to continue this project by focusing on associationalism—that form of mobilization that, within the broader "movement toward association," claims to be the place where law and collective expression converge.[16] Associationalism is rooted both in popular collective action, driven by an impulse toward equality, and in the imaginary of a "self-government of associated citizens."[17] These emancipatory practices contrast with other practices that use associative forms of action to defend established hierarchies (see Breaugh 2007, 161–62). However, associationalism cannot be reduced—as it so often is—to short-lived movements of revolt. While it often opposes the system, it does not try to evade the test of time. Its actors seek to multiply actions inspired by democratic principles through the creation of economic institutions and new spaces for socialization.

When we adopt this perspective on associationalism, it becomes impossible to reduce associations to an agreement struck between individuals with a view to realizing what they believe to be their common interest. The interpersonal relationships in associations are not based on shared interests alone. They go beyond compacts between individuals concerned with their private interests, encompassing these compacts within a broader effort to achieve common goals, including the intersubjective conditions of justice and personal integrity. Associative relations thus cannot be analyzed exclusively through the lens of utility maximization; they require us to refer to solidarity. Hence Habermas's (1997, 53) definition of association as a "sociological concept that allows one to think of spontaneously emergent, domination-free relationships in noncontractualist terms."

The paradox of association for social theory stems from the fact that it comes under both the principle of community (*Gemeinschaft*) and the principle of society (*Gesellschaft*) (Tönnies 1987), operating at the juncture of a tight circle of interpersonal links and a broader circle of impersonal connections (Simmel 1978), at the nexus of primary and secondary socialization. In sum, association can be defined as the cooperation of a number of individuals to pool their resources, knowledge, or activity to achieve a goal that is different from—or not principally that of—sharing material benefits. Dewey's approach underlines the fact that this agreement can take various legal forms aside from nonprofit status. Indeed, the associationalist perspective aims to bring together initiatives that have been addressed separately because some have different legal forms (cooperatives, mutual societies, trade unions, and nonprofits), and others have no formal status. Associationalism characterized the "first" nineteenth century but was overshadowed from the "second" nineteenth century onward. Confused with utopianism by the proponents of "scientific" socialism, it was also stigmatized by advocates of a capitalism checked by redistribution or by "moral" commitments. Influenced by evolutionism, these different groups likened it to a primordial coating of gunge (*gangue*) (Gueslin 1998, 5 and 189) that it was necessary to scrape off for revolution or reform to occur.

Contrary to these disparaging interpretations, described in the first part of this book, understanding associationalism through its social practices provides a means of better grasping the grammar of social struggles. Doing so also frees us from an implicitly statist approach, because it revives debates on the relationship between the political and economic spheres, showing that the invention of modern solidarity came long before the invention of the welfare state. Acknowledging this history allows us to consider a reinvention—set out in the book's second part—that takes account of the welfare state's limitations. The aim of the third part is to elucidate the differences between the theoretical frameworks that have been developed to understand this complex phenomenon. As we will see in the conclusion, assessing these differences is a pre-requisite for understanding the challenges of building a social and solidarity economy.

An important characteristic of modern associationalism is that it acknowledges the political dimension of collective action. This gives it economic potential. Since it is tied to the democratic project, it can trace the outlines of an economy that will serve society. As Gide says, association can take on an "infinite diversity of forms" that are "not all very well known" and has the potential to both rival and reduce competition because it calls for individual initiative while at the same time developing solidarity-based protection.[18] In doing so, association has helped prevent the economy from becoming completely self-regulating—via an equilibrium supposed to result exclusively from the interplay of interests—and has left open the possibility of public deliberation influencing the economy's operation.

Keeping the above clarifications in mind, we can begin our history— that of an associationalism that has challenged the relationship between democracy and economy. The stages in this history have been seen as first steps—as touching, old-fashioned stories from a bygone age of an immature and naïve utopianism stamped with the seal of historic failure. But theorizing about associationalism requires us to challenge this evolutionist, linear version of history. We must describe its unfinished struggle for legitimacy, identifying some of its forgotten aspects in order to reveal the elements that still speak to us today. Finally, we must understand the revival of associationalist initiatives. Although they are destined today, as in the past, to be small or even minuscule in scale, associations nonetheless attest to an indomitable aspiration for democracy—an aspiration whose realization requires democracy to be integrated into the economy. Despite overly deterministic or simplistic characterizations, these associative practices—which seek an alternative way of combining the economic and the political spheres—are still an enigma. With the aim of resolving this enigma, the remainder of this book is arranged into three parts.

The first part examines associationalism's past. The second focuses on its present. My overall concern is to identify not just the differences but also the similarities between diverse contexts. International comparisons usually aim to emphasize the diversity of national models, but this does not exclude the possibility of finding certain convergences. The particularities of each country must not lead us to forget the challenge every political entity faces: building a common world. Thus instead of conceding the compatibility between market and democracy, it is more instructive to consider the various ways in which modern democracy and capitalism confront one another. It is by looking at the institutional framework shaped by these tensions that we can understand associationalist developments. The aim is to explain their instituting strength without thereby denying their incompleteness. In this respect, European and American initiatives may be set on the same wavelength. This, in any case, is the spirit in which I have adopted an international perspective. My intention is to compare the realities of these different continents so as to better understand what has occurred in each of them. Rather than examining associations from the perspective of what they should have become, this study will focus on the characteristics of past and present associations. It is important to guard against the neglect of associations that prevails in most theories of democracy, without thereby indulging in the excessive praise seen in texts on social capital (Putnam 2000), which establish a simplistic correlation between associationalism and the progress of democracy.

The third part therefore leaves behind these constantly shifting categorizations and turns toward conceptualizations that encompass associationalism in its entirety, with the aim of establishing its boundaries. But these boundaries remain somewhat blurred, which explains why associationalism is often given different names. The three terms that have become widely recognized internationally are "the third sector," "the social economy," and "the solidarity economy." While the notion of the third sector foregrounds association in the narrow sense of the term, reflection on this notion's limits—as well on as the complementarities between the social economy and the solidarity economy—has led to the expression "social and solidarity economy." Far from denoting an established reality, this new perspective suggests uncertainty about the future. It points to diverse forms of institutionalization that merit debate. The conclusion is largely devoted to these issues of normalization and change.

Before beginning our journey through associationalism, a few more words on the reasons for undertaking it. It principally results from observing how unsuitable specialist studies are for grasping entities such as associations. When certain disciplines, such as political science, examine engagement and participation, they mainly see economic activities as evidence of a drift toward the apolitical. Others, such as economics and sociology, often ignore their political dimension. A recurring problem in economics and social science is that, in attempting to understand associations, they tend to fall back on models of the private enterprise and of public services. One of the questions posed by South American scholars concerns the relationship between this tendency and the foundations of Eurocentric thinking that, in the words of Santos, is unfit to make sense of "the most innovative and transformative practices occurring around the world."[19] For this reason, he argues for an "epistemology of the South" that rejects these narrow, reductive categories that are only able to detect either third-rate businesses or public subservices emerging in civil society. On the contrary, as mentioned earlier, it is necessary to go back to what—according to

Hirschman (1970)—remains political economy's major task: to gain a better understanding of ongoing interactions between political and economic factors. This broader political economy is a political economy for the common good that "connects theories about economic and political principles, instead of categorically opposing them."[20] Doing so entails particular methodological choices.

The first choice is to acknowledge the imbrication of practices and ideas. This prevents us from separating off the world of ideas; on the contrary, it calls for us to accept "the nonseparation of materiality and intellectuality—of the world of ordinary things and that of philosophical and spiritual questioning" (Roche 1999, 26). It is this "intertwining of discourse and practice" (Rancière 1981, 8) that the history of ideas fails to grasp. Only a dynamic approach to the interdependencies between representations and practices reveals the extent to which representations privilege certain aspects of social reality that they thereby help reconstruct, as well as showing the extent to which social practices give rise to interpretations that influence representations of the world.

The second choice is to take on a normative approach that converges with public sociology (Burawoy 2005). What really matters here is the democratization of society. Researchers are no more in the privileged position of being able to distance themselves from their conditioning than anyone else. Against the illusion of positive knowledge free from contamination by values or ideology, it is important to remember—in line with Ricoeur (1986, 325)—that making the researcher's choices explicit "will do more to clarify and advance scholarship than will denying their existence and then surreptitiously reintroducing them." In other words, researchers are part of society and cannot extract themselves from it, even if their thought is underpinned by a historical perspective that allows for a degree of distance.

This leads us to our third choice, which is to construct a history of the present with the aim of "understanding and acting today"—and to do so by "reconstructing the system of transformations that the current situation has inherited" (Castel 1995, 12). Castel has argued for such an approach; it by no means seeks to replace the work of historians, but rather develops "another narrative" that enables experiences and debates from the past to be reinterpreted so as to recover the promises of a previous era that may resonate today. I will do this by identifying key moments, rejecting a cumulative, linear approach to knowledge, and emphasizing alternative interpretations that could modify contemporary categories or reveal new ones.

While this introduction began with an overview of the twentieth century, we must end by emphasizing that reconnecting with the associationalist tradition requires a particular effort to move away from the theories of social change that dominated the last century. Principal among these has undoubtedly been historical materialism, which reconciles economic determinism and political voluntarism: the modification of company ownership rights was supposed to usher in a new postcapitalist mode of production. This plan lost credibility over time because of how it was used by bolshevism. Rather than addressing change, post-Marxist analyses have mainly focused on explaining the power of capitalist domination, much as Bourdieu's sociology of social reproduction has tended to do. The fastening of the superstructure onto the base—which these schools of thought examine—leads less to transformation than to the existing order's permanence, along with the institutional variations through which capitalism constitutes a vast cosmos that preceded individuals, in which everyone must live without being able to change anything about it.

In reaction to this observation of inevitable domination, at the end of the twentieth century some of Arendt's followers called for a rehabilitation of politics. But they did so without having a clear idea of how this would avoid the overdeveloped state of which Durkheim warned. Meanwhile the sociology of social movements—which had more confidence in collective action—made a cultural turn that led it to neglect economic issues at a time when inequalities were soaring. Disappointment with these overly general analyses encouraged sociological and economic approaches that were more focused on networks and local communities. The sociology of translation (Callon, Lascoumes, and Barthe 2009), along with economic and pragmatic sociological approaches such the sociology of worth (Boltanski and Thévenot 2006), involve decoding the complexity of behavior and relationships: dialogic democracy, the diversity of modes of coordination, and shared references to orders of worth are all evidence of markets' constant adaptation and plasticity. Although their structures differ, markets seem able to accommodate all kinds of economic activity, allowing us to forget "the market forces" stemming from systemic mechanisms of price determination (Le Velly 2012).

With macro-approaches characterizing the capitalist universe as inescapable, and micro-approaches underestimating market forces, the question of the links between a plurality of political and economic forms is rarely addressed.[21] This study of associationalism aims to explore these links, guided by works that have all turned their attention to the interrelationships between the political and the economic spheres. Thus Mauss and Polanyi both emphasized economic plurality while also advocating the extension of democracy to the economy, failing which the "laws" of the market threaten to make citizenship meaningless. With Habermas (1985), the Frankfurt School overcame its initial pessimism to concede that there is an insurmountable tension between capitalism and democracy and, with Fraser (2015), that the public and economic spheres cannot be separated. What I examine here is a previously unnoticed complementarity between these approaches, which can be enriched by an epistemology of the South that emphasizes that the "deepening of economic democracy goes hand in hand with that of participative democracy" (Sousa Santos and Rodriguez Garavito 2013, 130–41). Transdisciplinarity and openness to North–South dialogue will help us identify the specific tensions characteristic of the twentieth century. To move beyond them, we need to go back to their origins and revisit previous controversies. This is why the book begins by returning to the history of the "first" nineteenth century. As E. P. Thompson (1988, 16) reminds us, hindsight enables us to better understand current challenges: "in some of the lost causes of the people of the Industrial Revolution we may discover insights into social evils which we have yet to cure."

PART I

Associationalism, Democracy, and Capitalism

Democracy and Solidarity-Based Associationalism

TODAY THERE IS A GREAT DEAL OF SCHOLARSHIP that, following in
E. P. Thompson's footsteps, allows us to reexamine the phenomenon
of association. This first section draws on the rich historiography as-
sembled in much of this work.[1] Rather than aiming to be exhaustive,
my goal is to gather observations that encourage us to be neither too
anecdotal nor too particularistic in how we approach the phenomenon
of association. In this respect, even if differences between countries
are considerable, two international findings stand out. First, it is amid
the frictions between democracy and the economy that new associative
forms working toward new rights and institutions based on equality
have taken shape. Second, the sociohistory of association can be organized into three periods. While the first period is that of the creation
of associations following the establishment of democracy, the second
is marked by the rise of capitalism accompanied by discrimination
against self-organized associations. The third period is that of the increase in state intervention leading to public authorities' recognition of
certain associative actions. These are the different stages that the first
three chapters attempt to recount.

The pre-industrial economy relied heavily on families' self-
production, small-scale farming, and the urban craft industry. But this
was not an autarchic economy. There were many ways in which goods
circulated, from local markets to international trade. Stimulated by
well-known trade fairs and stock exchanges, from the sixteenth century onward the acceleration of long-distance trade flows, followed by
proto-industrial development, transformed the economy into a force
for change. Political economy took this into account when advocating
for the wealth of nations and free interaction between rational individuals within civil society.

The Rise of Political Economy

Political economy promotes a particular narrative, that of commerce refining barbarous mores. It postulates both that the social order is perfectible and that individual behavior motivated by personal interest will have desirable effects.[2] When the "exercise of commerce" is considered to be "the greatest approach towards universal civilization that has yet been made by any means not immediately flowing from moral principles" (Paine 1951, 215), this is because the multiplication of decentralized arbitrations produces not just wealth but also greater social harmony. It does so by creating a type of individual who is "more honest, reliable, orderly, and disciplined, as well as more friendly and helpful, ever ready to find solutions to conflicts and a middle ground for opposed opinions" (Hirschman 1984, 14–16). If this softening is to be encouraged through the promotion of attitudes dictated by individual material interest, then the expansion of market agreements must be favored over monitoring by centralized authorities.

The pioneer mercantilists and physiocrats helped lay the foundations of democracy, as did the liberals from the classical school inaugurated by Adam Smith. The nascent discipline of political economy was therefore part of the critique of absolute monarchy in France, but this apparent openness was belied by its economistic closedness in stating that the coordination of individual interests is enough to ensure the cohesion of society. It is worth remembering these two faces of political economy, because the difficulty of reconciling them is the source of associationalism. This, in any case, is the thesis I will defend.

The Relationship between Wealth and Liberty

From the sixteenth century, mercantilists began to reflect on ways of increasing social wealth. One of their main proposals was to encourage imports of precious metals and exports of manufactured goods. They called for policies that would support trading companies in their foreign export markets, while at the same time strengthening domestic production. In their view, a modern state should promote colonial expansion while also fostering industrial development through fiscal policy. These were the suggestions that mercantilists made to governments. But while these mercantilist advisers were initially respectful, they became pugnacious. Little by little, they moved from making recommendations to criticizing nation states, challenging those in power about the legitimacy of taxes.

At first, the monarchy did not feel threatened by these economic demands, but by the end of the seventeenth century the demands had reached an entirely different scale. Certain prominent bourgeois voices began to question the omnipotence of royal power. Drawing on Montesquieu, who believed that commerce and gentle mores reinforced one another, they argued that in order to be legitimate and have a constant and lasting force, laws must be based on general, abstract norms reflecting "the necessary relations arising from the nature of things" (Montesquieu 1950, 1). Therefore, the sovereign's role was to bring about this natural order by abolishing inappropriate regulations. This line of argument was developed by the physiocrats, who believed that only public opinion could know these self-evident universal truths that all men bore within themselves. In order to comply with these truths, private property should be respected and both freedom of trade and freedom of labor promoted. The production activities that generated "net profit"—that is, a real increase in wealth—had to be carried out independently of public authorities. They thus required the limitation of the functions of the state, which should restrict its intervention to measures that could adapt supply to demand and increase both the division of labor and the accumulation of capital. Smith perpetuated the physiocrats' belief in ordered social phenomena. Like them, he thought that the natural progress of prosperity should not be hindered and reiterated Hume's eulogy on free trade. He believed in a spontaneous economic constitution that, like the life force in the body, triumphs over artificial obstacles that governments put in its way.

The Utility-Maximizing Matrix of Liberalism

Smith moderated the ideas that had so strongly influenced him. His contribution lies in his definition of a practical principle: it is the interdependence of interests that, through the market, increases both the individual's and the nation's wealth in a virtuous circle. Smith differentiates himself from his predecessors through the central importance he gives to the individual, both as a subject driven by moral sentiments and as an economic being pursuing his own interests. The attitude of the head of government matters less than the behavior of every person. Thus political economy places the individual in charge. It theorizes the need for the state to protect the autonomy of civil society. The increase in wealth through human action should free society from the horror of hunger and scarcity. The shift to a focus on individual interests is meant to avoid an outpouring of destructive passions (Hirschman 1977) in a world no longer protected by inherited hierarchies. In line with Locke, Smith emphasizes the importance of liberty based on rights that allow individuals to form relations free from both traditional hierarchies and state control.

At the same time, this doctrine reduces the social contract to the defense of economic freedoms. And political economy is positioned as the project of an economy that guarantees the regulation of society solely by itself. It does not stop at legitimizing ownership of property, whose acquisition demands time and effort. It returns to Aristotle's condemnation of chrematistics; the wealthy "are led by an invisible hand to make nearly the same distribution of the necessaries of life, which would have been made, had the earth been divided into equal portions among all its inhabitants,"[3] Finally, this approach dispenses with political deliberation in the sense that realizing the interest of society as a whole is an "unintended consequence" (Smith 2002, 184–85n5). Therefore, for economic liberalism, the conditions for prosperity do not depend on historical constructions but on a spontaneous blossoming (see Dumont 1977; Rosanvallon 1979; Gauchet 2005) of the "propensity to truck, barter, and exchange one thing for another" (Smith 1904, 15). In this way, Smith expresses a coherent anthropological vision that privileges the individual—an individual who can both assert his interests and possess moral inclinations in the form of sentiments that stem from neither discussion between political subjects nor a historical process. At the time of the French Revolution, in 1789, Bentham claimed that self-interest was the motive "whose influence is most powerful, most constant, most uniform, most lasting . . . a system of economy built on any other foundation is built upon a quicksand" (cited by Castel 2005, 31). As Say argued, political economy was designed to be a "purely theoretical and descriptive science" of spontaneous economic constitution that should be "separated from politics, which it has often been confused with, because its principles are not manmade . . . They derive from the nature of things; they are not established but found, they govern legislators and princes and they can never be violated with impunity" (Say 1814, ix; cited by Gide and Rist 1926, 128). This view marked the beginning of a growing gap between political liberalism and economic liberalism.

Through a process of simplification and separation, economic liberalism laid the foundations for the "economistic fallacy," which in Polanyi's (1977, chapter 1) view is the major problem of modernity. It consists in confounding the economy with the market alone and breaking with the substantive approach—mentioned in the introduction—that recognized the plurality of economic principles. It fails to address intersubjectivity in the economy because it only recognizes individual preferences. The importance given to human affairs, which is designed to make behavior based on interest incontestable, is coupled with an omission concerning the earth's resources: "natural resources are inexhaustible . . . since they cannot be multiplied or exhausted, they are not studied by economic sciences," Say declared (1832, 83; cited by Bonneuil and Fressoz 2013, 49)

Associationalism as an Alternative Political Economy

The fiction of a market that moderated mores was undermined by the persistence of inequalities within societies committed to equality. The controversial genesis of associationalism occurred in this context; it drew on the spirit of the Enlightenment but was set against the notion that the economy was simply part of the natural order. The elimination of protections associated with hierarchies had led to the irruption of violence in social relations. The market system, which had been adopted for its pacifying virtues, had instead exacerbated social inequality.

The political economy of associationalism was different because it exposed the power relations hidden behind contractual mechanisms. While associationalism was not afraid of insurrection, neither was it restricted to the outbreaks of violence that are too often presented as the only counterpoints to workers' misery. According to the associationalist approach, civil society could not be reduced to a system of needs, nor could it be isolated from the economy in an overly simplistic perspective. On the other hand, the public spheres of civil society needed to be strengthened in order to facilitate emancipation. Numerous associations formed to demand that the political and economic spheres should have a clear influence on one another, with the aim of ensuring that society complied with the principles of governance that it set itself. Three variants of this general approach can be observed in social practices.

The first two variants highlight the complex relationships between democratic change and economic autonomy. One comes from actors who believed in the power of mutual assistance and—thanks to an associative movement characterized by mutuality—used this power to reconfigure the economic structures that resulted from preexisting communities. The other corresponds to the collective action of people excluded from citizenship. In order to facilitate their access to civil rights, they joined forces to organize socially useful economic activities. These two distinct types of emancipation movement will be illustrated using examples from South and North America.

A third variant can be found in Europe. It allows us to understand the emergence of demands for greater recognition of associations, including their economic dimension. These demands came from workers who, refusing to have their new freedom jeopardized by subjection to capital, began to call for a politics that would recognize their growing cooperative practices.

Emancipation Movements

As early as the eighteenth century, a diversified popular economy existed in South America. Political changes influenced this economy in the inner suburbs where groupings were informally organized by street and by neighborhood; this was also the case in rural areas where a dense network of exchanges was governed by how far people could ordinarily travel during the day. These exchanges mainly consisted in the "bartering of goods and services within a limited radius" (Braudel 1980, 8). The shockwaves from distant democratic revolutions spread slowly. Nevertheless, they did end up changing this economy, where services were based more on the principle of satisfying essential needs than a calculation of profitability, where the organization of work remained inseparable from community membership, and where exchanges were often based on payment in kind.

In North America during the same period, many instances of discrimination on the basis of gender and race persisted despite the Revolution. From the moment they began to speak, the voices of women and African Americans in the United States met with resistance that the development of economic activities sought to counter. Because they were refused access to the public sphere, both women and African Americans sought to fight this injustice by demonstrating their capacity for initiative. The responsibility they assumed for implementing solutions to pressing social problems was designed to precipitate a change in mentality and pave the way for their political integration.

The democratization of the popular economy and the civil rights movement were both part of a long-running fight for equality. The fact that they are treated here in terms of distinct geographical areas should not obscure the fact that the economic and political elements considered were simultaneously present in both contexts. It is the combination of these elements that characterizes associationalism. During this period, there was a faith in free and voluntary human action that would fade when the ideology of progress became dominant during the nineteenth century. This faith defined the boundaries of the first age of associationalism.

The Existence of a Popular Economy

Anthropological studies of pre-Colombian societies have drawn attention to their rigid social hierarchy but also a community-based form of organization with a ceremonial aspect to work and an absence of individual ownership. It is clear that colonization put an end to these forms of sociality. Latin America was pillaged. Millions of Africans were reduced to slavery, torn from their countries to be used as forced labor in the production of goods destined for export to imperialist metropolises. The role played by the Catholic Church in the acculturation process reminds us of both the physical and symbolic violence of the history of colonization. But the dominated cultures were never totally eradicated. They survived through asymmetric and contradictory interrelationships with the dominant culture, with the help of some missionaries. Thus indigenous influences were embedded in famous experiments such as the Jesuit "Republic of the Guaranis," where for more than a century and a half, until 1768, the Jesuits constructed a socioeconomic order based on indigenous community-based principles. In parallel to this attempt to preserve indigenous cultures, the most deprived groups joined together in forms of self-organization. For example, in urban spaces where there was less surveillance, African Americans gathered together in mutual assistance organizations, mainly for religious celebrations and tributes to the dead. Elsewhere, poor colonists, peasants, and artisans settled in lands unwanted by the oligarchy.

This constituted the beginnings of a popular economy. Away from the big estates, popular groups initiated economic activities with the aim of using the resources available to them to satisfy their needs (see Sarria Icaza and Tiriba 2006). These activities included family farms, craft workshops, small trading companies, transport, and services and were inseparable from domestic relationships and ethnic identities affirmed in ritual events. In this subsistence economy, there was no clear separation between household and market activities, both of which were deeply rooted in social life. Production was oriented toward the basic family group, more or less extended or restricted, depending on the context. The market dimension was constantly kept in check and moderated by the density of interpersonal relationships. Customers and suppliers had ongoing relationships that became forms of socialization and cultures to which participants were attached. Use-values were determinant, as the group sought the means of ensuring its survival and affirming its identity. So the group was not driven by a logic of accumulation, nor by behavior based on the calculation of profit and individual utility; it conducted economic activity inseparable from the collectivity in which it was embedded—activity based solely on its own wealth, hard work and the "anxieties of living."[4]

This is why this "ground-floor economy," to use Braudel's image (see Verschave 1994, 20–27), comprises a market dimension yet cannot be reduced to the market. It has fallen to several South American scholars to stress how important it is not to interpret the popular economy through the categories of the market economy. Thus Coraggio has tried to identify its particular logics.[5] According to him, this popular economy is above all a labor economy, which he distinguishes from the capitalist economy. It can only be examined via its basic building block—the household unit—and the concerns of its members. Indeed, it mobilizes different forms of activity that these members have available to them: self-production serving self-consumption, market production and sales, training, and community organization. Thinking about the popular economy in this way has theoretical implications; it changes our perceptions of the economy as a whole. It demonstrates the close relationship between domestic organization and market activities, which prevents the latter from being reduced to the results of cognitive-instrumental rationality and supposedly universal utility-maximization.[6] It calls attention to the fact that the economy is not limited to material things but includes relational and symbolic dimensions that codetermine forms of production and distribution. More precisely, the relations internal to the popular economy are structured by family relationships and the neighborhood. Interpersonal relationships can therefore be violent, marked by the most brutal patriarchy. Yet the harshness of tasks associated with survival does not imply either that pride was absent or that domination was absolute.

An Economy in Transformation

This popular economy was affected by political upheaval, too. In the first half of the nineteenth century, anticolonialist social movements escalated in Latin America; they succeeded in gaining independence and in establishing national republics, with Brazil the only country remaining under imperial rule. National independence led to widespread changes in the socioeconomic order. While the popular economy in its diverse forms survived,[7] its internal structure was modified.

All the types of organization that have just been mentioned—whether indigenous, African American, or "micro-colonialist"—were part of what some scholars have called the Atlantic world. In this world, influences from America, Africa, and Europe mixed together. This is why the rise of democracy in the North caused unrest. From 1830 onward, the concern for equality was taken up by popular groups in the form of mutual organizations. They spread political ideas derived from democratic revolutions but expressed them through local forms.[8] In Colombia, for example, the Democratic Republican Society of Progressive Artisans and Laborers was created. In Brazil, slaves who escaped or who, after the abolition of slavery, were freed, found themselves with no means of support and no prospect of employment. They resorted to economic survival strategies, collectively taking possession of land. These *kilombos* were extensions of the semiformal organizations through which they tried to deal with day-to-day problems.

Chile provides particularly instructive examples.[9] Along with peonage, an unstable and insecure form of paid work in the haciendas, a new form of popular entrepreneurship was developed by the *labradores*[10] over almost 150 years—from 1700 to 1850—in agriculture, animal husbandry, preindustrial mining, and forestry operations, in the small businesses run by women, and also in artisanal production. In 1854, "modern" forms of paid work only accounted for 0.1 percent of the general labor market, the *labradores* 20.8 percent of the labor force, and artisans 29 percent, 20 percent of whom were in the countryside. In the towns, small independent businesses—although taxed from 1773 onward—were widely popular. Based on their domestic know-how, women provided people with diverse goods and services. They sometimes joined forces on a professional basis to organize festivities or to negotiate with institutions, as did the washerwomen responsible for doing the laundry for hospitals and the army. These activities went hand-in-hand with the development of the craft sector. In Santiago in the mid-nineteenth century, more than half of the population were involved, in one way or another, in the popular industry established by artisans (made up of small factories, spinning mills, dye houses, and sheet metal and printing works). Using local resources, they relied on community labor known as *la minga*. Later, those working in workshops acquired imported tools and joined together to form federated associations of entrepreneurs. The first mutual organizations emerged in 1850 in the form of societies, uniting artisans in the organization of healthcare, savings, and social protection schemes.

The popular economy is the product of particular places and historical circumstances, but it is also produced by its actors' everyday practices and political visions (Sarria Icaza and Tiriba 2006, 219). Among these visions were the reduction of dependency and the democratization of the popular economy. Achieving these goals meant applying economic logics to serve social ends, while at the same time giving them new democratic substance. Despite its harshness, the popular economy could also be a source of dignity when it allowed individuals to develop collective solutions to their food, housing, and health problems.

This was the conviction of those who, under the influence of the new democratic political climate, modified entire sectors of the popular economy. The growing demand for equality that motivated them and guided their actions transformed their practices into vital means of resisting the increasing penetration of capitalism.[11] Hoping to emancipate themselves from traditional forms of dependency, they also rejected forms of subordination inherent in an economic order governed by capital.

The form of associative organization mobilized in South America to change the popular economy was also used in North America to demand civil rights. While ways of life and popular-economic practices in South America were influenced by democratic victories, the protests against sexual and racial inequality in the developing United States of America, in turn, did not disregard economic pathways. They used these pathways to gain legitimacy and, in doing so, avoided the violent rejection of their demands for civil rights. From this perspective, the link between politics and the economy becomes apparent when we look at associations set up by African Americans and women.

Protests against Injustice

Tocqueville was the first to underline the extent to which realizing an egalitarian democracy depends on the creation of associations: "after the liberty to act alone, the most natural to man is that of combining his effort with the efforts of his fellows and of acting in common." According to him, "There are no countries in which associations are more needed to prevent the despotism of factions or the arbitrary power of a prince than those which are democratically constituted" (Tocqueville 1843, 1:208). He adds that "among the laws that rule human societies there is one which seems to be more precise and clear than all others. If men are to remain civilized or to become so, the art of associating together must grow and improve in the same ratio in which the equality of conditions is increased" (2:118).

For Tocqueville, it is precisely this art that flourished in North America. Immigrants created local organizations that combined religious devotion, mutual help, and the desire for reforms. In this still-colonial society, they patiently built an institutional infrastructure where the boundaries between private and public activities were more blurred than in Europe. Tax collection and state administrative functions were limited, which left social intervention dependent on private contributions of both time and money. In order to meet social needs for education and healthcare, nonprofit organizations were formed to set up local schools and hospitals through a combination of donations, help from volunteers, and personal dedication. In Boston and New York, these organizations possessed charters that defined them as organized extensions of public authorities, in an approach that drew on English common law.

After the American Revolution, two factors increased opportunities for citizen participation: the first was the separation between church and state; the second was the development of a political philosophy that was more stringent when it came to equality. During the 1790s, study and discussion groups got together to scrutinize draft legislation as well as the conduct of elected representatives. Democracy was enhanced by civic scrutiny but, in the words of George Washington's 1794 congressional address (cited by McCarthy 2003, 27), this did not occur without tensions arising between these "self-created societies" and the "government of our country."

The generation that included Benjamin Franklin, Thomas Jefferson, and James Madison thus experienced a real surge in associative activity. On the one hand, this prompted new alliances between civil society initiatives and governments. On the other hand, it led to a contested extension of the public sphere. This associative wave encouraged the voicing of opinions that were not necessarily based on consensus, and those excluded from democracy were to use their citizenship to fight against patriarchy and racial domination.

From the beginning of the nineteenth century, African Americans—most of whom were still enslaved—nonetheless succeeded in building their own institutions: small mutual aid groups promoting self-organization and civic virtue. Although modest, there were enough of them to ensure that their demands for slavery's abolition could no longer be ignored. They were supported by independent churches that raised funds that were then invested in the African American community. For example, in the mid-1820s, the African Methodist Episcopal Church, founded by Richard Allen in 1816, had more than a thousand members. The church not only supported its destitute or needy members; it also provided start-up capital to help small entrepreneurs. It became a seat of protest, providing African Americans with increased confidence in their mobilizing capacity and their collective strength, expressed in written petitions. Almost a century later, this stance led

W. E. B. Du Bois to conclude that this church was one of the greatest Black organizations in the world (McCarthy 2003, 120), where religious and economic activities always had a political dimension. As they published newspapers and set up national antiracist conventions, African American churches were transformed into spaces of struggle against continuing discrimination (see Brooks-Higginbotham 1990). Promoting a vision of gradual and peaceful social change, they challenged the idea of armed struggle and sought a political solution to injustice.

Women, meanwhile, were kept away from the public sphere through an established separation between the domestic and political domains, reinforced by customary law. The couple was not an association. It was a "union, that is, an organism" (Fraisse 2000, 20; see chapter 1, *"Fair society"*) in which the woman was deprived of any personal property and confined to the family space; if not a slave, she was at least her husband's servant. But although modern democracy sidelined women in practice, this was not—contrary to ancient democracy—one of its principles (Fraisse 2000, 63). Between the assertion of principles of equality and their denial in reality, there was room for the possibility of collective action—but this consistently encountered male resistance. Hence, in 1776 Abigail Adams wrote a draft proposal for political parity. Shocked by her husband's negative reaction, she responded to him as follows "I cannot say that I think you very generous to the ladies, for whilst you are proclaiming peace and good will to men, emancipating all nations, you insist upon retaining an absolute power over wives. But you must remember that arbitrary power is like most other things which are very hard, very liable to be broken—and notwithstanding all your wise laws and maxims we have it in our power not only to free ourselves but to subdue our masters, and without violence throw both your natural and legal authority at our feet."[12]

To avoid endlessly coming up against a wall of incomprehension, some women made their way toward a political existence through economic organizations—mainly refuges and forms of assistance providing daily support for poor women and their children. The commitment of these organizations' leaders helped convince the authorities that these institutions were serving republican ends. They formed part of a quasi-public register: they made use of contracts and benefited from donations from rural public authorities in North Carolina, as well as urban areas such as Philadelphia, Baltimore, New Orleans, and New

York. In New York in 1798, the Widows' Society had two hundred subscribers and provided jobs for widows who would not otherwise have found one by paying more than three hundred women to make shirts. Between 1770 and 1820, women's associations provided both jobs and assistance. They challenged misogynistic stereotypes, developing a new kind of republican sentiment where public service was connected to personal sacrifice and individual virtue. Belonging to a registered association also allowed married women to own property collectively that they could not own individually. Their contribution in terms of time and money raised explains why these economic activities addressing social needs were encouraged by local authorities. There have been many tributes to their concern for personal independence and dignity, which traditional republicanism continued to view paternalistically.

The proliferation of assemblies in the 1830s and 1840s encouraged an increase in women's participation but, as Ryan puts it, the cacophonous style of politics that was practiced there—which combined debate with insults and punches, all washed down with drink and laughter—perpetuated a male chauvinism that rejected the "effeminate" (Ryan 1992, 259–88; see also Ryan 1990). It was with the Civil War that opportunities arose to provide supplies for troops and then, beyond the 1860s, the responsibility of caring for the poor and dependent classes. By "creating institutions that provided education, vocational training, and moral guidance to the poor, women volunteers constructed a private system of public welfare" (Ryan 1992). They were less reluctant than men to seek government funding, even soliciting help from local councils and public authorities for this purpose. Progressively, they gained a reputation as "effective administrators of public services" (Ryan 1992) and influenced policies through a variety of means: public meetings, petitions, lobbying, and so on.

These historical observations lead us to reformulate Habermas's concept of the public sphere, construing it as both plural and decentralized. Indeed, for marginalized groups, the proliferation of public spheres promotes access to political discussion where established authority can be challenged. Here "the notions of interest and identity need not be antithetical to the public good" and action repertoires might include "civil disobedience and even violent acts" (Ryan 1992, 285–86) like in the New York Draft Riots in 1863.

Most of the time, African American and women's political demands were made without direct confrontation with the white male power structure, by means of economic activities with a high social value. Alleviating suffering and helping the most destitute were actions that were recognized as being useful to the community. The professed motives, which were often religious, helped to make meetings that would otherwise have been condemned by conservative attitudes more acceptable. But behind this apparent social conformism loomed a more dissenting protest movement. Participants were no longer isolated; they identified with these collective organizations that reinforced their self-esteem through personal empowerment and self-determination.[13] Economic action facilitated the emergence of political consciousness because the people concerned were involved in finding solutions to their own problems.

Democratic Solidarity in Action

In Europe, workers' associative practices—which centered on the protection of professional expertise—were experienced as an extension of their political emancipation, to such an extent that association was affirmed as an important institutional principle—one designed to realize democratic potentials. With the development of forms of solidarity among artisans and manual workers determined to collectively defend their interests, the mutually supportive alliance between political emancipation and economic independence assumed an unexpected scale. When these artisans and workers forcefully demanded that their collective forms of organization be recognized, their resistance evolved into a campaign for a politics of association.

A Political Movement Emerging from the Economic Sphere

While the French Revolution was breaking out, the 1790s also saw a kind of "English Revolution."[14] Both revolutions rapidly led to the banning of any form of association. The guild regime along with regulations governing production were abolished in France and in England. In France, the right to associate was challenged as early as 1791 with the Allarde decree abolishing guilds. The Chapelier Law reinforced this by preventing any coalitions between workers and employers. In England, the 1799 and 1800 Combination Acts made all forms of workers' association illegal. These measures extended previous legislation such as the common law against conspiracy and the Elizabethan statute of apprentices and craftsmen, and together were referred to as "the laws against combination." Until their repeal in 1824 and 1825, they were a means of intimidation and deterrence against worker gatherings. Paradoxically, however, the threat of prosecution was not always carried out. Working men's clubs and the London guilds were tolerated as long as they did not descend into "rebelliousness," emphasized mutual assistance, and gave up on any idea of national coordination and negotiation.

The labor movement was mainly composed of domestic workers and, in many towns, of "shoemakers, weavers, saddlers and harness-makers, booksellers, printers, building workers, small tradesmen, and the like." Radical London emerged "from the host of smaller trades and occupations" rather than "heavy industry." In fact, "the factory hands, far from being the eldest children of the industrial revolution, were late arrivals" (Thompson 1971, 193). The production sites, although varied in nature, were places where political views were discussed. As Thelwall writes, each one was "a sort of political society which no act of parliament could silence and no magistrate disperse" (Thelwall 1796, 1:21–24, cited by Thompson 1971, 185). Workers, craftsmen, and radical laborers kept up their own traditions, while at the same time establishing links with the illegal Jacobin and trade union movements. Their main inspiration came from a belief in the transformative power of reason and the "Socratic spirit"—in every individual's capacity for self-improvement. Equality was the benchmark that made any distinction of status unacceptable. As the mutinous sailors from HMS *Hermione* declared in 1797, they had long been seeking to become human beings. They had now become so, and they wanted to be treated as such. This demand was born out of shared experiences that constituted the basis for collectivist conceptions of society, in opposition to the bourgeoisie's individualist conceptions. It was a demand expressed in the colorful language of philanthropic societies, which made haphazard references to Christianity, fraternity, and "social man."

Indeed, during this period, philanthropy was indissociable from the dominated classes' quest for freedom. It helped establish the typical modus operandi of independent workers' organizations. In contrast to church assistance, these organizations emphasized freely accepted self-discipline and the observance of rituals demonstrating shared belonging through outings, evening events, and celebrations. Codes of conduct and rules—which were established away from the watchful eye of the authorities—resulted in new forms of sociability based on self-respect and political awareness. Friendly societies were emblematic of this self-organization and practical ethic: they brought about the creation of trade unions, sheltered them, helped them to become federations and trained their leaders, while also providing cover for clerical workers, small traders, and factory workers against illness, unemployment, and death-related expenses.[15] In 1773 they were estimated to have 648,000 members, which had increased to 925,000 by 1815. The personal effort demanded at a time when living conditions were often particularly hard was motivated by enthusiasm for self-education, free thinking, and the criticism of religion, the wealthy, and internationalism. Consequently, the principal conflicts were not only about sustaining their livelihoods; they were also fueled by demands for trade union rights, respect for local traditions, justice, autonomy, and security. Cultural conflict was inseparable from political conflict in a context where production facilities and manufacturing methods were improving only gradually.

The idea of an extension of politics to the economy could also be found in France. As Corbon states, "Democracy in the political system and near-absolute monarchy in the workshop are two things that cannot coexist for long" (cited by Chanial and Laville 2005, 54). During the 1830s, the meaning of the political was reexamined in direct relation to social inequality. For workers, "equality before the law can only become effective if the right to earn a living is guaranteed" (Gossez 1967, 195). The elites responded by suggesting that a political domain limited to the right of assembly and the right to vote should be established in exchange for the surveillance of associations from 1834. But demands that had previously remained underground were brought to light by the 1848 revolutions. In February and March, a number of decisions were quickly made regarding the right to work, the abolition of the death penalty and slavery, and the freedoms of the press, of assembly, and of association. The term "association" referred to "a large diversity of collectivities: former guilds became mutual aid societies or resistance, solidarity, mutual credit, or simply fraternal societies, whose immediate objective was to fight against the most glaring inequalities and the most hated forms of exploitation, in particular 'bargaining'"

(Riot-Sarcey 2016, 43). This practice, whereby a master workman who had bid the least for a construction project employed those who would carry out the work for the lowest price, was abolished and working hours were also reduced. Sewell describes the effervescence of groups of workers who, along with bourgeois democrats, became involved in hundreds of political clubs that had suddenly sprung up in both Paris and the provinces after the February Revolution—clubs that reflected republican thinking in all its nuances. Some founded their own newspapers; many others contributed to a wide variety of republican publications. Most importantly, they reformed and breathed new life into their professional associations (Sewell 1980). *Compagnonnages,* or French guilds—which were mutual help organizations—secularized and became associations where workers were no longer subject to a hierarchy but determined their own governance. Meanwhile mutual aid societies, which evolved from guilds, developed in a way similar to those in England; they provided unemployed or striking workers with help. These tools of struggle, which wove together corporatism, mutualism, and republicanism, laid the groundwork for trade unions.

Although England and France are emblematic examples, others can be cited, such as Spain, where the 1836 legislation against guilds did not prevent the nascent labor movement from creating groups rooted in the trades. Thus mutual aid societies came into being in 1841; in 1887 there were 664 of them, and in 1904 they numbered 1,271, with 238,351 members. They were combined with other forms of advocacy in multifunctional associative initiatives. Little by little, a patchwork of collective entities was established that borrowed from the popular economy but also demonstrated a desire for independence and collective pride. Estivill conveys the richness and diversity of this patchwork when describing its different elements, among which were "mutual assistance with sowing and harvesting, the non-monetary exchange of goods and services, collective work on common property (cutting timber, the development of land, the maintenance of paths and bridges, irrigation, fishing zones)" (2015, 356). To which we must add the networks of associations offering educational and recreational activities, the *Ateneo Encyclopedico Popular,*[16] rationalist circles, courses for adults, conferences, public debates, libraries and community sports groups, choirs, brass bands and music groups, republican brotherhoods, popular theaters and cafes. According to Melo (2005), who provides us with historical detail about Portugal, this was true across the entire Iberian Peninsula. As Leroux (1863) puts it, the idea was to replace charity—which reinforced the social hierarchy governing relationships between donors and beneficiaries—with solidarity—which united free citizens with equal rights. By going beyond professional solidarity and mutual assistance, associations became the place where these voluntary social ties countered the domination of capital.

A Political Approach to the Social Unequality

In France, association was celebrated in the name of the "democratic and social Republic." Those who aligned themselves with this Republic understood "democratic" to mean that all citizens should have the right to vote, and "social" to mean that they should be permitted to associate for work-related purposes. Drawing on Gossez's inventory, Desroche identified thirty-nine professions in Paris that had their own associations, including five worker and employer associations, two associations of master craftsmen, and forty-six workers' associations, thirty-three of which affirmed their fraternal nature in their title, and five of which mentioned solidarity. Reform projects abounded, including those centered on economic self-organization. Thus Buchez envisioned two types of institution: workers' associations for independent professional workers and trade union associations for factory workers (Buchez, cited by Desroche 1981, 31–36). But the ubiquitous appeal to association went beyond the reform of workplaces to become a societal choice—one that would see the guilds electing delegates and representatives. In 1848, the project for social workshops (*ateliers sociaux*)[17] constituted the first attempt at cross-fertilization between associations and the Republic: government representatives were called upon to support associations, whose legitimacy also had to be based on elections. The same year also provided a glimpse of a long-held dream for a deliberative assembly based on the unification of small trade federations, echoing British attempts that resulted in the creation of the British Fraternal Society in 1796 and the National Association for the Protection of Labor in 1832. At the instigation of the government commission for workers—known as the "Luxembourg" Commission, as this was where the workers' delegations converged—in May 1848, a Central Committee of Workers' Delegations (Comité Central de la Délégation Ouvrière) was established, which later became the United Trades Society (Société de Corporations Réunies). In November, a General Union of Workers' Associations (Syndicat Général des Associations de Travailleurs) was created. This was followed in 1849 by the People's Bank (la Banque du Peuple), the Workers' Mutual Association (Mutualité des Travailleurs), the Central Committee of Workers' Associations (Comité Central des Associations Ouvrières) and a Union of Workers Associations (Union des Associations de Travailleurs), because "what matters most is not to discuss method, theory, or organizational plans, but to act, to put into practice the simplest and surest ways to achieve our objectives." The union's plan of creating an association of fraternity and solidarity for all associations was drawn up by Deroin, who set out its principle: "the most complete solidarity, which requires from everyone, in the name of fraternity, the dedication of one for all, and all for one" and guarantees "equality for all" by providing, "regardless of gender, the right and the means to make a living from their work" to all members—to "them, their children and. their forebears."[18]

This desire to found politics on association marked the beginning of a new type of public sphere anchored in "an open society" where, to quote Thomas Paine, "mankind are not now to be told they shall not think, or they shall not read" (1951, 147). This popular public sphere equipped itself with institutions that consolidated day-to-day experiences of solidarity and mutuality. Within this sphere, discussion could not be separated from common action that rested on the recognition of its members' equality and sought institutional change; such was the raison d'être of self-organized economic activities. This multifunctionality was typical of these pioneer associations. They were characterized by a dual embeddedness: in the political sphere, as a collective form of expression and claim making; and in the economic sphere, as the impetus behind new forms of work organization and mutual assistance.

The Divergences between Associationalism and Utopian Writings

This combination of political and economic registers—which characterized associations in this first phase—has, however, been strangely neglected. This omission, which has become so widespread that it is no longer questioned, is largely due to the confusion between pioneer associations and the views of authors identified as utopians. Although associationalism has been inspired by utopians, it does not share their prophecies. From the plan to moralize society to the panoptic desire reminiscent of Bentham's utilitarianism, Owen, Saint-Simon, and Fourier do not have much faith in the people. According to Fourier, problems of social organization will be resolved *for* the people, "but they [the people] will remain passive and external"[19] to this resolution, won over by the path shown to them by others. When advocating association, these theoreticians are entirely focused on replacing individualism, which, according to Leroux (2007), is synonymous with "disassociation." Substituting order for this disorder, the initiatives they propose must demonstrate that, in the words of Fourier, "harmonious composition" is possible. So the act of association represents the hope of a higher level of unity, and in order to hasten its coming, the apostles of this new religion have no hesitation in requesting support from benefactors. This overgeneralizing representation of association explains Proudhon's (1924) misgivings. Utopianism evades issues related to political power and property ownership rights. As Thompson puts it, it is fair to say that Fourier, Saint-Simon, and Owen have been both the greatest proponents of Fouricrism, Saint-Simonism, and Owenism, and at the same time their worst enemies. They have placed association on too high a pedestal, forgetting that the domination of a single principle—even if it is that of association—is not desirable; they have been too quick to affirm the "disastrous" division between "material" and "ideal" motivations (Polyani 1977), the first providing the motives of economic life, and the second characterizing intellectual life.

Distancing itself from prophecies, associationalism's defining characteristic is its engagement with democracy. Workers active in associations dissent from these prophecies as much as they are proponents of them; they adapt them through debate to turn them into economic and political reforms that they then put to the test in practice. Far from the written utopias of the past, the time has come for "real utopias."[20] What solidarity-based associationalism introduces is a new approach to utopia. Instead of the dream of a reconciled society, it supports the desire for change by two related means: social experimentation and the reorientation of public policy.

As mentioned in the introduction, the misunderstanding of association mainly results from separating the history of ideas from practice.

Only by reuniting ideas and practices can we distinguish between associationalism and unrealistic systems. Even if at first it was inspired by utopian writings, the spirit of association distanced itself from these ideas to join up with popular attempts at self-organization. Pioneer associationalism demanded equal rights for all citizens, and at the same time fought against an economic system that was reinforcing inequalities. As part of a movement that was inseparable from democratic progress, associationalism refused to allow birth to confer any privileges, remaining adamant in its demand for real equality. In this way, associationalism suggested another way of instituting the economy at a time when the foundations of capitalism were not yet fully established. Associations defending the rights of workers, women, and minorities, as well as mutuals, cooperatives, and trade unions were all fundamentally opposed to the idea of a self-regulated market emerging from natural law. Their members argued for fair rewards for the working classes and consequently became the voices of these classes.

2

Capitalism and the Moralization of the Poor

THE FEAR GENERATED BY THESE MOVEMENTS demanding the implementation of universal rights led those in power to take action: they sought to contain the irruption of these popular public spheres that were beyond their control. Confronted with these spheres—which, as noted in the introduction, can be described as plebeian or proletarian—a new line of argument developed about the attributes required for the right to expression. Initially, the public sphere was supposed to limit the arbitrary use of power; the bourgeoisie praised it as they believed it would challenge abuses of authority through reason. But this approval was succeeded by a distrust of public opinion that, it was now thought, would sanction the influence of the mediocre and the reign of conformity. The extension of the democratic process was no longer advocated; instead, warnings were given against the intrusion of the uneducated mass who would not have the capacity for good judgment.

From now on the major concern was to limit citizenship to people who could demonstrate their economic independence. The immaturity of the propertyless might lead to despotism, bureaucracy, and state omnipotence. In other words, the dominant idea was no longer that political freedom would permit the construction of a more egalitarian economy but rather that economic power should be a precondition for political expression. Consequently, the opening up of the public sphere—which was proclaimed in democratic principles—was in fact restricted to people whose independence was confirmed by their exercise of the right to own property. The identification of citizens with property owners had been established. Representative government could only make decisions based on the competent reflection of a relatively limited number of people.[1] Similarly, while Tocqueville viewed associations as collective entities able to perform the roles previously played by intermediate authorities in aristocratic society, he rejected the principle of the right to work demanded by workers' associationalism. He did so on the grounds that it would lead to dictatorship by a majority devoid of judgment due to their lack of economic independence, a prerequisite for impartiality.

This elitist argument was part of a darker vision of society, influenced by the protestant ethic, which occupied an increasingly important place during the "second" nineteenth century. Success in the world of capitalism was taken to be a sign of divine reward, of which the poverty-stricken were deprived. The gap between the elect destined for heaven and the wretched of the earth was therefore justified. Liberalism became tinged with pessimism. Malthus and Ricardo noted that the laws of economics did not lead to the accumulation of wealth but to hardship among factory workers and crises of overproduction. Although capitalism was inevitable, it gave rise to upheavals in which "the greatest part of the sufferings of the lower classes of society [is attributable] exclusively to themselves."[2] Only when people changed would they attain political maturity. It was not the system that gave rise to inequalities, but rather men who revealed their own shortcomings by failing to seize the opportunities offered by an economic system that held the promise of general prosperity. Poverty was a punishment, and it was the responsibility of its victims to overcome it, helped by guides who could lead the way to moral improvement.

The Undermining of Popular Forms of Organization

The plan that was now emerging to reestablish tutelage by the social elite involved undermining popular forms of self-organization. During the second half of the nineteenth century, the devaluing of the popular economy became systematic. Demands for equal rights that had been made from within this economy were now considered misplaced by those who, against human rights, favored a return to the virtue of hierarchical orders. Once again, despite the diversity of national contexts, there were important similarities between the global North and South.

Stigmatized Ways of Life

In South America, governments viewed towns and cities as barbaric places of depravity and damnation. Female itinerant traders in particular were pursued by municipalities worried about public health. In this context, popular culture was seen as nothing more than an absence of culture—as deviance. The poor, considered to be socially maladapted, had to escape their marginality by adopting the only valid culture, a culture claimed to be universal, that of the Western bourgeoisie. As a Chilean patrician said in 1935 "these people settle down every day, here, with their whole family . . . put up their stalls . . . light fires . . . bring their chairs and benches . . . and, from dawn to dusk . . . we can often hear vulgarities and swearing, which, inevitably, threatens the morality of our families, and the salubrity of the streets . . . they behave as if the street was their property."[3]

More generally, many activities that made up the popular economy were affected by the patrician class's change in attitude. This class was not satisfied with its revenues and so turned toward industrial capitalism and the mechanization of its large agricultural properties. Using imported technologies and sponsored by the state—which granted them monopolies and subsidies—this class reduced the land available to a "productive social fabric" that had previously been established away from the grip of colonial governments. The popular economy was hobbled by a series of rules that had an adverse effect on it. Peasants were forced to sell their products through intermediaries, and the workshops and small craft businesses that had established themselves in the cities were strictly controlled.

So it was not free competition that prevailed but rather a set of regulations designed to benefit an "industry imposed from above." Faced with the increasing precarity of their members' living conditions and the emergence of a proletarian class in capitalist industries, popular movements became more radical in their stances. The leaders of mutualist and *pobladores* organizations rallied around a modernization plan that was meant to solve social problems though industrial development. In order to do so, they abandoned the institutions they had created to devote themselves more exclusively to protest action demanding both state intervention and their participation—as work-ers' representatives—in national negotiations.[4]

Since Mariategui's (1979) seminal work, Western Marxism has been accused of having contributed to this pessimism that condemned the popular economy. Quijano's deconstruction of "coloniality" takes up this criticism, arguing that the productivist ideology underlies both liberalism and historical materialism—which, according to him, consti-tutes "the most Eurocentric version of Marx's heritage," a result of the "hybridization of his theoretical propositions with positivist evolution-ism and dualism, along with the Hegelian idea of a historical macro-subject" (Quijano 2007, 160). The consequences have been deeply damaging: the differentiation of social activities has been pushed to the extreme of reifying categories such as economy, society, culture, and politics; private property and exploitation have been absolutized as if they alone embody oppression. The uniformity of the capitalist mode of production has been accepted, whereas in reality it constituted more an "articulation of all other modes of production" (Quijano 2007, 159; also see Quijano 1998). From the moment that the belief in a capitalist system replaced the analysis of a "predominantly capitalist system," to quote Mauss (1997), alternative economies, although present in Latin America, became invisible.

A Dichotomy between Sectors

A dichotomy that contrasted traditional and modern sectors became more and more widespread. The popular economy was identified as the traditional sector, which was synonymous with stagnation, and contrary to the modern sector, which was synonymous with industrial growth. The existence of a popular economy was considered proof that the countries of the South lagged behind others. This progressivist vision approached history in terms of "stages" of development;[5] from this perspective the traditional economy became a sign of economic backwardness. It was defined by what it lacked (legality, rationality, structure, social and legal protection, and a barrier to entry) and by its weaknesses (in terms of capital invested, skill levels, technological de-velopment, size). As a pool of surplus labor made use of by strategies of overexploitation, it was above all viewed in terms of its dependence on the capitalist economy. The popular economy was no longer identified as such but was defined by its shortcomings and equated to backward-looking survival—to a "reserve army" of labor for the market economy or a hindrance to the "take-off" of the least developed nations.

In the countries of the global North, too, governments began to focus on the industrial sector as the driver of a desired modernization. The popular sectors of the economy were consequently neglected. Following a process similar to that which occurred in the global South, they experienced a loss of legitimacy during the second half of the nineteenth century, despite still structuring ways of life until the mid-twentieth century. As Castel (1995, 30) reminds us, the popular economy accounted for the majority of the French working population, which numbered 4.4 million in 1848, three-quarters of whom lived in the countryside. Industrial establishments of two to five people employed 1,650,000 workers in 1906 and 1,404,000 in 1926, while establishments with more than 500 workers employed just 1,034,000 workers in 1926. At the beginning of the twentieth century, workers in large-scale industry remained a minority compared with those in small enterprises employing fewer than ten people. Following an in-depth study of the German context, Lutz concluded that what he too calls the traditional sector remained stable until the Second World War in Europe. In Germany, according to figures from 1926, this sector (including family farms; small family craft businesses; very small businesses in commerce, transport, and services; and the domestic economy) still made up half of the workforce, which in this case was 17.8 million people out of a working population of 32 million, plus 4.1 million women working full-time in domestic work who were not recorded as part of the working population (Lutz 1990, 103). In France, as in the other continental European countries, most of which were less industrialized than Germany, the popular economy was at least as important. If we include the family labor force working full-time in the domestic economy, we can estimate that in France the share of the potential national workforce represented by the traditional sector fell from 55 to 49 percent over the forty years from 1906 to 1946. The popular economy thus retained a presence in people's way of life for a very long time. But it disappeared from governments' agendas, as well as from economic analysis. According to the ideology of progress, the improvement of living standards depended on the acceleration of industrial growth.

The Assertion of an Economic Ideology

The capitalist institution of society[6] resulted from continuous efforts to identify and extend the sphere of the market economy and was achieved through a series of shifts and decisions bearing on the definition of the economy. These practices of selection and formatting were based on the presentation of the market economy and the capitalist enterprise as the very essence of progress. What had been forgotten was that this progress was partly due to the "external annexation" of economic resources taken at the expense of the South, followed by the "internal annexation"[7] of a popular sector that survived until the mid-twentieth century, but had been neglected long before then.

During the 1870s, neoclassical economics put forward the concepts of marginal utility and general equilibrium. Questions of values were excluded from the field of economic science. The narrative of modernization, which equated economic development with market expansion and capital enterprise, echoed the romantic image of bartering natives. This position was not unique to liberalism. Marxist references to a unified working class made people forget that popular routes toward social and labor-market integration had been diverse. The result was a denial of the importance of a moral economy[8] based on notions of common well-being, reciprocal obligations, and shared conceptions of rights and duties. All these notions grounded in the popular economy's concrete spaces of intersubjectivity—whether urban or rural—gradually disappeared behind the performativity of a linear view of history. Societies succumbed to the trap that Braudel warned against—that of only seeing the market economy, of "describing it with such a wealth of detail as to imply an all-pervasive presence, when it is just a piece of a larger whole" (Braudel 1985, 45). As Polanyi (1977) noted, this interpretation was incorrect but was a sign of things to come. Economic reality was created through the development of an economic belief presented as a neutral observation. From this perspective, market capitalism was an unavoidable stage; it became seen as the only way to accumulate wealth, which in turn influenced the perception of the causes of pauperism.

Pauperism versus Equality

The denial of the role and the history of popular practices went hand-in-hand with severe repression by governments. Zinn used the expression "civil war" to refer to the conflict in the United States between national authorities and associations demanding greater democracy. Here the material and symbolic disintegration of the moral economy made the project of moralizing the poor conceivable.

Opposition to Gender and Racial Equality

The strategy was to substitute a fight against poverty for the struggle against inequalities. The tension between these two objectives could already be seen during Jackson's presidency, from 1829 to 1837. At the time when Tocqueville was traveling across America, the country's civil society was dominated by the white population bound together by the prospect of future success, but excluded 60 percent of American adults. Distinctions based on gender and race were deeply rooted in the southern culture that Jackson represented (McCarthy 2003). Democratic progress was the preserve of the white male population, which was anxious to retain its privileges. Women and African Americans who participated in associative activities built a political existence rooted in collective effort and religion, the right to petition, the right of assembly and free speech. Their network of independent associations also mobilized to abolish slavery and prevent the displacement of Native Americans.

But these abolitionists and social reformers were persecuted; meanwhile charitable organizations saw their political aspirations stifled by male elites' benevolence. This process of normalization was achieved either through men taking direct control or through a paternalism that offered protection to middle class white women as long as they complied with the behaviors that men considered appropriate to their gender. Although the organizations run by these women were weakened by male pressure, the situation of African American women was much worse. Victims of overt hostility, they had to fight with their limited resources for education and assistance, as well as to assert their identity. Ryan, who studied attempts to extend public spheres to benefit the women who figured in the first chapter, notes that the services and advice provided by feminist organizations in the United States remained packages of condescension when doled out, as they were, by "protestant matrons" looking after their "worthy poor" and prefiguring a selective and moralizing welfare state (Ryan 1992, 279–80).

Admittedly, cities such as Boston, New York, and Pittsburgh began to make a concerted effort to develop social policy that relied heavily on philanthropic organizations. But public authorities reduced their support for many associations with social objectives in order to focus on those that kept the poor in specialized establishments. The geographical disparities in assistance meant that these authoritarian solutions could only ever be partial, but they were reinforced by repressive legal measures. As in England, Scotland, and Germany during the same period, more stringent legislation was passed relating to the poor, who were considered responsible for their own plight.

Opposition to Trade Union Freedoms

Contrary to promises of social advancement for all, discrimination increased. Furthermore, social concerns began to change with industrialization and urban growth. Appalling housing and working conditions gave rise to the trade union movement. Sporadic unrest broke out to the rhythm of economic crises. Reexamining the popular history of the United States, Zinn sought to reconstitute episodes that, in his view, are usually ignored by American history textbooks. To quote but a few examples, in 1834 in Boston, trade unions of laborers and workers denounced the unfairness of tax and military conscription laws: "to raise any peculiar class above their fellow citizens, by granting special privileges, is contrary to and in defiance of those primary principles" of the Declaration of Independence (Zinn 1980, 205). In 1835 in Philadelphia, fifty professional corporations organized a general strike that mobilized workers to call for a ten-hour working day. In 1837 the Flour Riot broke out in New York, where 50,000 people—a third of all workers—were unemployed. At that time, women made up a twelfth of the working population, of which 55 percent were domestic workers, 11 percent schoolteachers, and 34 percent factory workers, half of whom worked in spinning mills. In one of the biggest mills in Lowell, Massachusetts, a women workers' association was created. When it organized work stoppages, strikers were evicted from their lodgings and militant members were dismissed. In 1839, the antirent movement in the Hudson Valley rebelled against the feudal system of land allocation. Twenty-five thousand farmers signed a petition that was the basis for a decree debated in the 1845 state legislature. Another example is the 1833 call for "universal voting rights," which led to the 1841 "Dorr" revolt demanding the lifting of property ownership criteria for voting rights. Whether due to excesses of violence by insurgents, provocations, or incitement to racial hatred, these movements were halted by armed intimidation and legal sanctions. The 1830s and 1840s were among the most violent decades of American history. Murders and atrocities, coupled with the infiltration of movements and the violation of freedoms, sometimes led to their radicalization, as was the case for a part of the Black movement that opted for civil disobedience. One of the best-known figures of the activism that began to emerge during the 1840s was Frederick Douglass.[9] The Black movement put social justice before respect for the law in protecting and helping runaway slaves. Persecution led to a split among the abolitionists between those who supported the use of violence and those who continued to condemn it. The growing gap between the political cultures of the North, where a diversity of associations flourished, and of the South, governed only by representatives from the white male population, led in 1860 to the American Civil War.

Repeated appeals for patriotism and for the defense of the nation did not, however, succeed in silencing trade unionism. In 1864, 200,000 workers belonged to trade unions, which were organized into federations in some sectors and produced various publications. In parallel to this, the first ever Farmers' Alliance was established, with its 400,000 members aiming to organize cooperatives to sell their produce. Large farmers' and workers' movements emerged between 1880 and 1890; Unionist troops were mobilized. But military troops were mobilized and recent immigrants, who were prisoners of their own material distress, were used to break the strikes. In 1886 was the "big labor revolt" with 1,400 strikes mobilizing 500,000 workers. The political program of Henry George—a radical economist who was the candidate of the trade unions and their offshoot, the Labor Independent Party, for mayor of New York—encapsulated the social conflict's significance. His program demanded that "property qualifications be abolished for members of juries. That Grand Jurors be chosen from the lower-class as well as from the upper class, which dominated Grand Juries. That the police not interfere with peaceful meetings. That the sanitary inspection of buildings be enforced. That contract labor be abolished in public works. That there be equal pay for equal work for women. That the streetcars be owned by the municipal government" (Zinn 1980, 252). This state of war would only come to an end at the beginning of the twentieth century, when worker and socialist unrest was able to drive forward a reform process.

The End of the Moral Economy

In the writings of Hammond and Hammond the expression "civil war" is used in relation to nineteenth-century England. Like Zinn, they want to acknowledge the violence of the clashes between. According to Thompson, the making of the working class "was not the spontaneous generation of the factory-system. Nor should we think of an external force—the 'industrial revolution' working upon some nondescript undifferentiated raw material of humanity, and turning it out at the other end as a 'fresh race of beings.' The changing productive relations and working conditions of the Industrial Revolution were imposed, not upon raw material, but upon the free-born Englishman" (Thompson 1966, 194) the creator of "self-conscious working-class institutions—trade unions, friendly societies, educational and religious movements, political organizations, periodicals" (194). The repression of these institutions worsened during the industrial revolution. "Wherever we find outwork, factory, or large workshop industry, the repression of trade unionism was very much more severe. The larger the industrial unit or the greater the specialization of skills involved, the sharper were the animosities between capital and labor, and the greater the likelihood of a common understanding among the employers" (194). Progressively, the "industrious artisan," proud of his know-how that was once celebrated by community rituals, was forced to accept a "dependent state" that was experienced as dispossession by the worker community. "Thus it is perfectly possible to maintain two propositions which, on a casual view, appear to be contradictory. Over the period 1790–1840 there was a slight improvement in average material standards. Over the same period there was intensified exploitation, greater insecurity, and increasing human misery. By 1840 most people were 'better off' than their forerunners had been fifty years before, but they had suffered and continued to suffer this slight improvement as a catastrophic experience."[10]

Aiming for a productive system based on mutualism as an alternative to capitalism, the working class defended itself without managing to bridge the differences between skilled workers undergoing a loss of status and unskilled workers, nor managing to form an alliance with the bourgeoisie, whose inegalitarian ideology was reinforced by the fear of revolution. The separation between these "two nations" was inscribed in the 1832 electoral franchise, and the force of the counterrevolution isolated a movement toward equality—which remained a workers' movement—for which the right to vote was only part of the story and should be coupled with respect and equity at work. Under these conditions, popular radicalism was revived on a number of occasions. In 1811, Luddism appeared; its attempts to destroy machines crystallized the revolt against the advent of the industrial system and laissez-faire politics. According to Hobsbawm, this "negotiation by riot" was less a rejection of technical progress than a struggle against unemployment and for the preservation of living standards, "which included nonmonetary factors such as freedom and dignity."[11] Later, protest journalism and trade unionism spread, followed by the ten-hour-day movement, the 1831 revolutionary crisis, and various movements leading to Chartism. This activity was sustained until the end of the nineteenth century but then tailed off to make way for a form of socialism that "shifted emphasis from political to economic rights" (Thompson 1966, 183). It was really the transversality of actions that were both political and economic that was lost over time, as different forms of social action became differentiated.

This separation of activities sometimes rested on the return of charity, as in Spain, but it above all had to do with a form of nonreligious philanthropy that aimed to replace democratic solidarity. In France the momentum of 1848 was broken by the repression of the June Days, and in July a council was established to promote associations "either between workers or employers and workers." Contrary to the initial proposal made in May, this council excluded mutual aid societies, provided loans rather than grants, and had a budget of 3 million francs at its disposal for the year, the renewal of which depended on results. An "Improvement Council," according to Audiganne's slip of the tongue

(Audiganne 1860, 348), it introduced a form of project supervision that began to reestablish the tutelage that the associative movement had wanted to escape from without any violence. Under the pretext of offering assistance, this supervision's purpose was to stifle initiatives by taking corrective action against projects suspected of wrongdoing, thus providing them, as Thiers put it, with the "resounding experience that will cure you of this insanity" that is association.[12] Thus the official interpretation could be spread: the chimera of association led to economic failure; it was proof of workers' inability to organize themselves and gave credence to the belief that "the public limited company is the only true association of our time."[13] An underground network certainly continued to exist, as evidenced by a pamphlet about the Workers' Organization signed by eighty workers from various associations. But the majority of these were considered obsolete due to their corporatism. By interfering with the "force of things" dear to Saint-Simon, "they only hindered the course of history" (Riot-Sarcey 2016, 206).

The Philanthropic Turn

As we have seen, the repression of self-organized associations was inextricably linked to the separating-off of the economic sphere and the disciplining of the poor. But a discourse emphasizing the increase in freedoms made this "widespread subjugation" difficult to see.[14] In spite of the distance between political and economic liberalism mentioned above, the liberal school repeated with ever greater insistence that economic freedoms went together with political freedoms (of thought and of the press) and were therefore part of the same triumph of democracy. In this view, society's problems stemmed from the imperfect realization of these economic freedoms. Following the fight for civil rights, the economic freedoms (freedom to work, borrow, trade) that had been granted were insufficient, and their absence explained why the market system had not achieved its full potential. Furthermore, both the laws of societies' spontaneous organization and the laws of efficiency had been flouted by public interventionism. The division between the political and economic domains was fixed as a principle from the moment the economy was treated as an experiment in liberalization separate from concerns about social protection evaluated by the yardstick of individual morality.

A Disciplinarian Approach

The priority was therefore to resist the temptation of social reforms—artificial initiatives whose adverse effects would only worsen the situation of the most deprived. Making political rights conditional on people's economic position was justified, as it was made clear that everyone had the opportunity to own property. The improvement of workers' lot depended on their attitude and would only be hindered by legislative interference providing unduly generous social protection that would encourage idleness and intemperance. As a rejoinder to the meeting of associations and democracy came the disciplinarian variant of liberalism, which began with Bentham and his plan for the panopticon—that is, for surveillance that would make it possible "to set poor calculators on the right track" (Laval 2007, 315–19). This marked the beginning of a new kind of politics—what Foucault named "biopolitics."[15]

Liberalism wanted to dispense with morality, but it rediscovered a moral core with the change of direction brought about by Malthus. At the end of his essay on population, Malthus reiterated that his overall purpose was "to improve the condition and increase the happiness of the lower classes of society" (1798, 526). But in his view it was moral constraint that—by eradicating vices—would allow this goal to be achieved. Under these conditions, he recognized the positive effects of "discriminate and occasional assistance" (526), but he was strongly opposed to the principle of compulsory assistance: "it may at first appear strange, but I believe it is true, that I cannot by means of money raise a poor man and enable him to live much better than he did before, without proportionally depressing others in the same class" (295). Any systematic assistance would end up multiplying the number of beneficiaries, which would render it pointless or even harmful. He therefore called for the gradual abolition of laws for the poor and influenced their restrictive revision in 1832. He viewed poverty as a failure—as a stigmata that was the sign of a lack of responsibility that could only be tackled by promoting self-discipline. Virtue was the best way to fight poverty, and corrective action that could lead to redemption was to be encouraged by all enlightened citizens.

Distancing themselves from the participation in public affairs advocated by reformers, the liberalism of "pessimists"[16] thus invoked science to argue for an end to public solidarity so as to replace it with private solidarity. Malthus's and Ricardo's commitment to English charity banks should be understood in this light. Rather than providing generalized assistance, they preferred to offer support linked to its beneficiaries' efforts; this meant that the destitute were kept together in a way that facilitated their control and prevented fraud.

From One Form of Solidarity to Another

Previously, mutual aid societies had employed the vocabulary of philanthropy, combining religious language with references to fraternity. The Lowell Female Labor Reform Association—created in 1844 in the aftermath of the Lowell strike mentioned earlier—is another illustration of these tangled connections. It portrayed its action as philanthropic, passionate about equal rights, devoted to the elevation of mankind and the rights of the republican people. But as the nineteenth century advanced, two understandings of the concept of solidarity became clearly distinguishable.

As mentioned above, the first form was democratic solidarity. Based on mutual aid as well as on the expression of demands, it drew on both self-organization and social movement forms, which presupposed equal rights among the people committed to it. On the basis of free access to the public sphere for all citizens, it strove to deepen political democracy through economic and social democracy. In opposition to this approach to solidarity, another approach was increasingly put forward, replacing notions of equality with those of benevolence and solicitude. This second form of solidarity was philanthropic solidarity, which referred to the vision of an ethical society where citizens motivated by altruism voluntarily fulfil their duties toward one another.

It was in this second sense that solidarity was invoked by Liberals like Bastiat; it was a way of increasing individual responsibility, since as everyone was affected by the behavior of others, they all had a personal interest in promoting good deeds: "all benefit from the progress of each individual, each individual benefits from the progress of all . . . solidarity is therefore, like responsibility, a progressive force, a system beautifully designed to limit evil and promote good."[17] According to Bastiat, who agreed with Malthus and Ricardo, solidarity resulted from the aggregation of individual responsibilities, which was effective only because it was voluntary. The philanthropic version of solidarity was based on this individualistic conception. It promoted the creation of mutual aid societies insofar as they could educate the most deserving workers to plan and save, and reward them according to their merits. Associations were only justifiable as groups that brought together individuals to develop their sense of responsibility but became reprehensible when they turned into a force for social change. This is why they had to be placed under the control of social elites who could protect them from being hijacked for subversive purposes.

The Return of Tutelage by the Social Elite

The philanthropic project had been redefined. In France, too, it increasingly became a project to restore tutelage over a population that would only be helped if they demonstrated a willingness to make efforts to help themselves. An "insidious regression" was taking place; in contrast to "the image of this great fraternal and messianic people, stronger through its virtue than through its arms"—an image that provided a model of "universal exchange of care and mutual aid, a virtue supposedly shared by all citizens"—there were now "appeals by public authorities to the benevolence of the social elites" (Duprat 1993, 478). This regression was exacerbated as the prevention of disorder took precedence over concern for humanity. The moralization of the poor, which had become a priority, then led to the search for an adequate form of supervision. As Cherbuliez commented in 1853, seeking to offer a solution to the causes of poverty, it is "in the direct personal action of man towards man or, in a word, through patronage, that a solution to the problem should be sought" (Bry 2006). For Le Play, the "social economy" that Pecqueur (1838) could see developing with the growth of solidarity—in a view close to that of Leroux[18]—was sliding towards *patronage*, which Le Play defined as follows: "the set of ideas, mores and institutions that keep many families grouped together—to their complete satisfaction—under the supervision of a boss appointed as Patron" (Blais 2007, 74). According to these authors, rather than generalized philanthropy that fueled poverty, a more targeted, selective, and austere form of philanthropy needed to be promoted. This form of philanthropy continued toward the end of the nineteenth century in the form of corporate paternalism. Considered a cure worse than the disease, any form of compulsory legal solidarity was to be vigorously opposed.

The decision to back associations was restricted to support for the moralism of philanthropic associations for fear of the unrest that more politicized groups might cause. Seen through this lens, voluntary association stymied the formation of a central administration in the United States. This was also the case in the United Kingdom, where, according to Thane (1982, 1), the role of the state was until 1914 merely to provide a clear and firmly established framework within which society could govern itself.

During this period, discourse did not necessarily reflect reality. In its discourse, liberalism stood against any form of public intervention. In reality, the vision that it defended benefited from strong state support. By repressing and controlling independent associations, by discouraging workers' associations and the concomitant promotion of charitable organizations and patronage structures, it redefined the contours of the associative map in favor of the social elites. This distortion of association can be seen in France where the crushing of attempts at emancipation in 1848 gave way to a "fragmented" social economy that had given up on the idea of a "shared vision of change and comprised diverse movements protesting against the separation of morality and the economy" (Vienney 1994, 76).

But despite all the advantages conferred on philanthropic solidarity, social problems persisted. Their threat to social stability made the philanthropic solution—which attributed inequalities of condition solely to individual responsibility—untenable. At the end of the nineteenth century, the philanthropic approach had been largely left behind. Associations contributed to this and, despite action taken against them, they remained democratic actors, establishing themselves as the crucibles of left-wing parties and trade unions.

3

The Welfare State and the Social Economy

IN THE FIRST HALF OF THE NINETEENTH CENTURY, the proliferation of associations—one of whose main demands concerned the organization of work—attested to the existence of popular public spheres (See Chanial 2001; Laville 2008a). In workers' and peasants' associations, joint production, mutual aid, and collective demands were intertwined. They laid the groundwork for an economy that could be based on fraternity and solidarity, discrediting the idea of a discontinuity between the economy and the public sphere. In response to these attempts, where political questions blended into economic questions, the liberal prophecy strengthened its arguments. For its propagandists, the solution was not a political one. It lay in the establishment of a market that would naturally balance labor supply and demand. Advocacy for free trade was also linked to the desire to limit the issue of inequality to the alleviation of poverty. Concerned about revolutionary intrigue, the authorities adopted these recommendations and devised institutional regulations favorable to the market. Economic liberalism "must and will unhesitatingly call for the intervention of the state in order to establish it, and once established, in order to maintain it" (Polanyi 1944, 149). The nation-state played a major role in promoting the market. However, despite philanthropists' denials, the destructive effects of capitalist industrialization could not be masked.

The Institution of the Social

To counter these destructive effects, both the market and the welfare state were embraced simultaneously at the end of the nineteenth century: social rights would gradually reduce the depth of the chasm separating the owners of capital and the proletarians, who only owned their labor power. A great transformation had begun.

A Legal Form of Solidarity

Confronted with the destitution produced by the industrial revolution, the need for social norms of justice became apparent. In view of the importance given to the market economy, its undesirable effects needed to be corrected through the restorative intervention of a protective state. This led to the creation of social legislation composed of labor laws for the workplace and social protection covering the principal risks. The prohibition of child labor and the limitation of working hours were enacted by governments under pressure from workers. The state, as the expression of the general will, became guardian of the public interest, which it was able to implement through the work of the civil service. A specific, social mode of organization made the extension of the market economy possible by reconciling it with the citizenship of workers. New forms of protection became accessible to workers. But this institution of the social was dependent on a particular conception of the economy. Questions about the organization of work were replaced by an equivalence between the economy and the market, which attributed to the market the monopoly over wealth creation. In other words, the state's ability to further social justice depended on the volume of resources it could deduct from the market economy.

In contrast to the benevolence of philanthropic solidarity, democratic solidarity laid claim to a legal obligation. Proponents of the latter asserted this increasingly clearly: the interests of the whole should prevail over contractual arrangements, which it both preceded and made possible. Sociology contributed to this development. This "science of society" replaced the language of individual responsibility with that of social cohesion. It argued that a contract required preexisting trust between the contracting parties, and that market capitalism was not a form of spontaneous order. As a consequence, the increase in inequalities due to the development of industry was no longer attributed to the carelessness of the poor.

By the dawn of the twentieth century, there had been a significant inversion in perspective. As Bouglé argues, the liberal doctrine that "let men crash against each other in universal competition" appeared "dead and buried," since "no government, no party would dare to push optimism or fatalism to the point of proclaiming that it was abandoning any kind of intervention in the economic order" (Bouglé 2007, 39–40). Notions of accident and social risk (Borgetto and Lafore 2000) took over from that of individual responsibility. They made the idea of a welfare state conceivable. The state became the guarantor of social cohesion by establishing a form of solidarity that was no longer just the expression of concern but was also translated into rights. Solidarity based solely on subjective involvement diminished and gave way to solidarity based on the rights of citizens, to the point where it became accepted that compromise between employers and workers—achieved through collective bargaining—was necessary.

The ways in which the social domain was instituted were nevertheless linked to earlier power relations between philanthropic and democratic forms of solidarity. Varying from country to country, these relations resulted in different arrangements between associations and public authorities. A typology can therefore be established based on the respective impact of different forms of solidarity and different ways of managing social services.

Weak State and Philanthropic Primacy

In America, as well as in many southern European countries, public intervention was limited by a lack of resources and corrupted by political clientelism. Nonmarket services remained overwhelmingly entrusted to women, assisted by the Church. Centered on the issue of monetary transfers, the welfare state neglected services and provided protections for people who were well integrated into the labor market to the detriment of groups trapped by precarity: access to rights was neither universal nor egalitarian but instead operated on the basis of selection and patronage (Ferrara 1996). In all these countries, association was still primarily conceived of as philanthropy, and state intervention was only subsidiary.

Furthermore, in the United States, middle-class women had acquired organizational know-how through the management of their associations, which, in spite of takeover attempts, gave them the capacity for action. As they lacked resources, expertise, and political will, public authorities established partnerships with the social services initiated by these women. This has prompted Kish Sklar to remark that, in America, educated middle-class women carried out tasks that in Europe were monopolized by male civil servants and public bureaucracies. Repression of the most socially and politically engaged movements resulted in "public–private" cooperation, which favored "more responsible" philanthropy but excluded women who, for example, displayed "unladylike" and "wicked" behavior (Kish Sklar 1973, xiv). These boundaries, established through the designation of legitimate forms of expression within the public sphere, led to what still distinguishes the United States from continental Europe today: reactive and flexible social interventions that are sensitive to structures created in civil society but which are patchy and unequally spread across populations and territories because certain forms of collective organization with more political overtones are invalidated. In this context, associations were identified as private initiatives within civil society, and they remained an alternative to the intervention of public authorities. As noted above, traces of this emphasis on individual morality and the valorization of philanthropy—which characterized the English-speaking world's approach from an early stage—can be found in the residual model of public intervention.

This American tradition was inspired by British practices: in the United Kingdom, state social security benefits had long been financed and managed locally. The limitation of central government meant there was greater emphasis on the role of associations and reference to the idea of society's self-government. Thus, at the end of the nineteenth century, the size of the voluntary sector "is hard to measure, but if the medical charities are included as well as those relieving poverty, then the amount of money passing through it was probably greater than that passing through the state poor law."[1] Affirmative action in favor of philanthropic solidarity therefore characterized countries that gave priority to the market and restricted the welfare state to protecting the weakest, at the risk of stigmatizing them.

Strong State and Democratic Primacy

Conversely, the countries of continental Europe experienced the most significant development of the welfare state. Here the relationship between the welfare state and associations was regulated by democratic solidarity. In contrast to the United Kingdom and United States, where associations were often a substitute for public intervention, associations and public authorities were generally complementary. This difference is important. The history of continental Europe refutes analyses that suggest that the presence of associations implies a withdrawal of the state. On the contrary, the European experience was one of mutual reinforcement.

Nevertheless, the spaces in which these associations developed also depended on different degrees of "defamilialization" (Hernes 1987; O'Connor 1996), that is, the collectivization of responsibilities traditionally assigned to the family. After the Second World War, associations sought recognition for the work done by women as part of the domestic economy. Their impact depended on how they were supported by public authorities. In those national contexts where they *were* supported, the collectivization of domestic tasks was encouraged by the creation of public childcare services. By making it easier for women to access employment and by guaranteeing them financial independence through social protection, the welfare state reduced the oppressiveness of patriarchy, which remained more significant in other national contexts where a lack of childcare resulted in women being obliged to work part-time (Lewis 1992).

Different Legal Statuses

At the same time, during the second half of the nineteenth century, associations acquired different legal statuses. This was evidence that the social economy had freed itself from its moralizing frame of reference and was now seen as a noncapitalist sector composed of cooperatives, mutuals, and nonprofit organizations. Popular struggles and philanthropic concern led to the recognition of so-called social economy organizations in which a category of stakeholders other than investors was given beneficiary status. That said, these legal statutes introduced distinctions contrary to the initial associationalist impulse. Cooperatives were distinguished from mutuals, with the former becoming a specific type of capital company focused on production or consumption, while the latter focused on providing assistance. Initiatives established to defend a collective identity, in turn, profoundly modified what were originally mutual-aid relationships by adjusting to the rules of the system of which they were part. As for nonprofit status, this only applied to a small part of the associative movement. Mainly intended for voluntary groups that had no productive purpose, its limits became apparent whenever economic activity was involved.[2] As a result, the different organizational structures of the social economy that emerged from pioneer associationalism appeared to be increasingly distinct. Overall, it is this compartmentalization that characterized the period.

The Autonomy of Cooperatives and Mutuals

In its pioneering period, associationalism led to a political questioning of the economy; then in the nineteenth century it was caught up in the mechanisms of tutelage; and in the twentieth century it became weakened in subsectors isolated by the separation between market and state. The social economy struggled to assert its distinctiveness as a separate sector. Cooperatives followed their own trajectory as companies active in the market, while mutuals were linked to state protection systems.

With the arrival of the social economy, the multiple types of workers' associations were displaced by cooperatives, which became part of the market economy and were engaged in sectors of activity with low capital intensity. They allowed different actors to mobilize resources themselves for activities that had been neglected by investors. While cooperatives such as agricultural cooperatives sprang up everywhere—taking off in Brazil in particular—other types of cooperative became more established in certain national contexts: in England, for example, consumer and housing cooperatives gained a particularly strong foothold. In countries with less rapid industrialization, such as France, cooperatives were regarded as a specific type of commercial company. Although they were able to benefit from certain arrangements negotiated with the state, all cooperatives were in principle subject to competition. As a result, the general logic of concentration of the means of production forced them to specialize in one core activity related to their members' identity. Concerns about survival weakened their broader project and this transformation continued to the point where they became "veritable financial groups that gradually emerged as the cooperative institution typical of developed capitalist economies" (Vienney 1980–1982, 2:108).

The emergence of the welfare state in turn modified the role played by mutuals. As noted previously, many initiatives were organized in the nineteenth century to deal with the problems of work incapacity, sickness, and old age on a solidary basis by bringing together the members of a profession, sector, or locality. Considered by socialists as means of worker emancipation, and by liberals and conservatives as barriers against social unrest, from the middle of the century these mutuals were tolerated and supervised by the authorities—as in Belgium and France. Later, the levels and modalities of contributions and benefits were standardized at national level. With the help of statistical techniques, the risks inherent in these benefits could be better managed through the inclusion of a large number of members: this system was thus securitized with the introduction of compulsory insurance. After the end of the Second World War, the types of economic activity these mutuals were engaged in led to their interdependence with social security systems, and mutual health insurance societies became social protection organizations that complemented compulsory schemes. They complied with state standards to supplement social transfers, even amending the principle of voluntary membership so they were able to provide supplementary group insurance protection. In European countries, mutuals combined their health insurance activities with activities such as the management of healthcare and social facilities. But increasing competition in the insurance sector put them under severe strain, similar to that experienced by mutual insurance companies covering property-related risks.

The Restructuring of Associations

In America the weak development of the state largely left social services in the hands of families, resulting in gender inequalities that philanthropic associations barely questioned. However, in Europe, where the state's functions were more expansive, associations participated in the development and delivery of social services. When we examine the role of associations in continental Europe, where they were incorporated into the most established welfare state regimes, two configurations stand out clearly.

In the first configuration, the universal regime of welfare state corresponding to the Scandinavian countries, extensive reliance on the state as organizer of the social domain resulted in a "collectivization of needs" (Leira 1992) in social services, which gave priority to social integration and gender equality. In Sweden, the dissolution of the guilds took place in 1846, and freedom of association was introduced in 1864. These two events reinforced efforts at self-organization, and in the last part of the nineteenth century were linked to the outbreak of "popular movements." These movements' purpose was mutual aid, contrasting with that of philanthropy, which they condemned as class oppression. With their allies, which included social democrats, temperance movements, and nonconformist churches, they gained a high degree of legitimacy in society. They were seen as "schools of democracy" for the working class. Through the internal training they provided, they worked toward and demanded universal suffrage, which was obtained in 1921. In this context, associations applied social pressure by allowing demands to be voiced. They mobilized networks to promote the creation of services delivered by the public sector. Thus the role of associations with democratic goals was important for both expressing social needs and challenging public authorities. However, their role as producers of goods and services was very limited, as it was significantly expanded public services—and not associations themselves—that took over tasks previously carried out in the private sphere.

Meanwhile the second configuration, the corporatist regime of welfare state, gave associations a major role in service provision. Hence, in Germany, different areas of activity were shared between philanthropic and democratic organizations. The former were dominated by the churches and the bourgeoisie; the latter were linked to the labor movement and were recognized as privileged partners of governments when social services financed by public budgets and insurance were set up. Under the Weimar Republic, they were grouped together in national organizations, especially those linked to churches, such as Caritas and Diakronie. Similarly, in Belgium and the Netherlands, these clusters underwent "pillarization"—a vertical division of associations according to their religious or political affiliation. In these countries, association-based services were considered part of social policies financed by taxes or social security funds. A tutelary form of regulation governed the relationship between associations and public authorities. The state established rules about how services should be delivered and regulated the professions of those who provided them. Respecting these rules opened up funding through taxation. In Germany, Austria,

Belgium, and France, associations began to tackle new social demands, which then continued to be managed by associations under state supervision. Tutelary regulation brought them closer to administrations and led them to form large national federations. These federations were linked to political parties, the Church, and the Red Cross—and were nonaligned in Germany, both secular and Catholic in France, and both socialist and Christian in Belgium.[3]

Increasing Compartmentalization

Compartmentalization thus affected associations, cooperatives, and mutuals alike. In the United Kingdom, it occurred to the extent that the idea of a common belonging became unthinkable. Associations were seen as charitable organizations, whereas cooperatives and mutuals were regarded as spearheads of the labor movement. In fact, the latter experienced an upturn in the first half of the twentieth century. In the United Kingdom, despite the repression described earlier, they reached their peak between 1890 and 1910—but they remained the preserve of craftsmen and failed to reach poorer workers and women, despite the existence of the Women's Cooperative Guild. They proved crucial to the rise of the Labour Party and the unions, but both of these formations later left their local roots behind. Germany witnessed similar developments, alternating between forward and backward steps. Cooperatives underwent dramatic expansion at the beginning of the twentieth century. By 1930, consumer cooperatives had four million members, while housing cooperatives were at the forefront of housing provision, in terms of both responding to social needs and architectural design. Undermined by fascism, they declined after the Second World War. As in the United Kingdom, social protection became a state matter more than a mutual matter.

A final—but no less important—division was that between associations and unions, which in France could amount to as much as a complete rupture. However, as Moss reminds us, the French labor movement was linked to both republicanism and to associations up until the Third Republic (Moss 1976, 31–70). Referring to what he calls "the socialism of skilled workers," he underlines the artisanal nature of the organized urban working class until after 1900 (156). During the nineteenth century, industrialization sufficiently disrupted the

security, income, and integrity of many artisans to provoke their protests, but not enough to destroy their resistance. Despite their relative
proletarianization, most activists kept the trades they had learned
through apprenticeship, which contributed to workers' control and solidarity. These assets gave them the professional and organizational capacity to resist exploitation and propose an alternative to capitalism.
Two strategies followed one after the other. The first was the federative
socialism advocated by Brousse, Malon, and Fournière; empathizing
with worker cooperatives and mutuals, it counted on trade unionism,
public services, and local politics, as well as on an alliance with Re-
publicans and middle-class reformers. Disillusionment with social reforms then led to the development of a different strategy in the form
of Guesdism and Allemanism:[4] that of revolutionary trade unionism
fighting for immediate change, but also planning the complete emancipation of the working class through the expropriation of the capitalist
class. The cooperative option was no longer considered relevant (Moss
1976, 156–160).

In more general terms, from this quick international overview—as
brief as it has been—it appears that associationalism was no longer valued. The divides between—and fragmentation of—associations, cooperatives, and mutuals were exacerbated by legal distinctions and forms
of integration into an economic system structured by state–market dualism. The selection of members on the basis of their competences con-
siderably limited the sense of belonging on which pioneer initiatives
drew. The assessment of cooperatives' productive efficiency compared
to other businesses, the incorporation of mutuals into social security
systems, and the integration of associations into social policies all led
to their specialization and technicization.

Democratic Solidarity Redefined

A democratic solidarity perspective came back after the wave of philanthropic solidarity in the second half of the twentieth century. But it
only became established in countries where social protection had become widespread, and where social services were regarded as a public
responsibility. But sometimes, as we can see in France, the foundations
for its success had been laid over the previous century through the rise
of solidarist theories supported by politicians, lawyers, and sociologists

(including Bouglé and Durkheim, as already mentioned). These theories were based on the idea of a social debt that all individuals incur as members of society, leading them to enter into a quasi-contract with their fellow men. This takes the form of a commitment to the community that the state must enforce. As Bourgeois points out, "social duty is not purely a moral obligation, it is an obligation that has a legal basis, the execution of which cannot be avoided without a breach of a specific law," and the state can enforce this law "if necessary by force" in order to ensure "a fair share of work and goods for everyone" (Bourgeois 2008, 22–23; see also Audier 2007).

Contrary to the "exaggerations of Bastiat," who, forgetting the "antinomies" recalled by Proudhon, only saw harmony in solidarity-based interests, emphasis was placed on the implicit contract. This was both voluntary and guaranteed by law, and bound man to society. In line with Leroux, who wanted to replace "Christian charity with human solidarity" (Leroux 1863, 244, quoted by Blais 2007, 84), legal rules were devised to achieve this moral solidarity that could not be confined within the limits of philanthropy or charity. Indeed, "the unfettered freedom of charity is a religious and moral prejudgment that comes from an insufficient analysis of rights," given that "the restorative function in the social order cannot be the responsibility of one man alone, nor of a few, it is the responsibility of all members of society; it is a matter for collective action" (Fouillee 1928). The challenge was to replace one-sided giving, which was a vehicle of domination, with giving between equals. In sum, the relative democratization of society—achieved at the national level after many struggles—was brought about in the name of democratic solidarity. This concept, which was linked to the emergence of the French school of sociology insofar as it broke with the liberal imaginary and its contractarian individualism, made the invention of the social domain possible.

A Delegated Solidarity

The overall picture was nevertheless more mixed than it appeared at first. Democratic solidarity had indeed historically prevailed over philanthropic solidarity, but in ways that involved this notion's transformation. The utopians of the first half of the nineteenth century had envisaged a principle of solidarity that would constitute a new religion.

This blind belief in solidarity was held "in search of a lost unity."[5] With sociology, the science of social cohesion, the point of view of society itself was adopted: its unity depended on the integration of individuals into social groups and also on the regulation of social activities through public authority. According to Durkheim (1997), solidarity is a moral phenomenon—a vehicle of mutual trust that preexists contractual relations, which is represented by the external reality of a set of legal rules and the sanctions related to them. But the state is not sufficient to maintain social ties. In addition to the protection conferred on them by law, workers must be able to join associations such as guilds to benefit from solidarity. Mauss extended this idea to other organizations that, in addition to the state, included "municipalities, public welfare institutions, pension and savings funds, and mutual societies," permitting a return to a "group morality" capable of counterbalancing "constant, icy utilitarian calculation" with "social insurance, solicitude in mutuality or cooperation" (Mauss 2001, 262–72). Mauss joins with Rousseau in stating that economic institutions are not natural structures, and that the shape they take on influences the future of society (see, for example, Rousseau 1964, 569). Solidarity, which had to be promoted by the state, nonetheless continued to be thought of in terms of mutuality. As Duguit put it, "in a way, the state treasury is a mutual insurance fund for the benefit of society" (Duguit 1922, 167–68). Fouillee also warns against a conception of solidarity that confuses it with something that necessarily exists, when in fact it is reliant on the intentional actions of morally constituted social individuals (Fouillee 1928, 312–14). This position is in line with an anglophone approach, which, from Dewey to Walzer, has stressed the importance of association as a bulwark against the breakdown of social ties and as an expression of civic republicanism. Nevertheless, despite these stances, positivism took hold in the second half of the nineteenth century. Positive science increased its influence by using the metaphor of organs in the body, and it was up to social scientists like Durkheim to diagnose the level of cohesion or "anomie" so that an enlightened government could then convert the findings into juridical means of strengthening solidarity. What faded was the awareness of the two facets of democratic solidarity: the voluntary link between free and equal citizens, on the one hand, and the norms and services established by the state to redress inequalities, on the other. In other words, solidarity was delegated to public authorities.

The democratic solidarity that triumphed was that of the same unilateral state action that we find in theories of the welfare state, where the symbiosis between associational action and action oriented toward the public interest is passed over in silence and only the action of public authorities is recognized.

The Dominance of the Ideology of Progress

Despite a bitter struggle during the nineteenth century, a tacit consensus now existed between many liberals and their opponents: they shared a progressivist reference to a reconciled future in which an original natural order would be restored. This common reference resulted in a conception of solidarity that was more about "the unity of nature" than "a living, inventive culture or practice."[6] The political activity of continuously constructing solidarity was reduced to the implementation of the "state solidarity system."[7] The state's intervention emancipated people from personal dependencies through access to rights but also reinforced "its tutelary power" and "its central role in shaping society" (Lafore 1992). The administration, which derived its legitimacy from political representation just as companies derive their legitimacy from capital, could only see users as subjects of the social security system: they were provided with benefits in a downward movement from the state to the citizen, which alone guaranteed respect for the common good. It was because a solidarity based on nature existed that the democratic state could make this happen.

This vocabulary of the natural order was also found in the segment of the labor movement that rejected an institutional architecture based on the complementarity between market and state, and opted instead for a revolutionary rupture. Communist society was understood to be the time of reconciliation that would logically follow capitalism, which would end up as the victim of its internal contradictions. "Implicitly, socialistically emancipated public opinion was still viewed by Marx as it had once been viewed by the physiocrats: as an insight into the 'ordre naturel'" (Habermas 1991, 140). More precisely, as Honneth (1995, 173–181) shows, there are two models in Marx's work. The expressivist model found in his historical analysis relates social conflict to different social groups' axiomatic beliefs, which emerge from the ways of life that these groups seek to defend;[8] classes seek to uphold the values and cultures to which they are attached because otherwise their identity is put at risk. However, in his economic writings, this struggle for recognition is limited to emancipation from work, in a second utility-maximizing model emphasized by Engels.[9] Here moral conflict is replaced by the competing interests inherent in the structure of social relations. Marxism considered as scientific socialism drew on economic writings in order to "abstract from all the political concerns stemming from the violation of moral claims" (Honneth 1995, 149) It does not make any proposals, but reveals the truth about history, accusing competing interpretations of delusion. The truth about the world comes from the analysis of the economic base, in which the development of productive forces is fettered by property relations. This economism is rooted in a notion of class struggle as a clash of conflicting interests that no longer centers on moral revolt against injustice. Consciousness is therefore an exogenous phenomenon that allows subjects to see the reality of the social relations in which they are embedded. The resulting reductionism justifies the priority given to the seizure of state power, which is alone capable of transforming social relations by attacking the foundations of capitalist domination. In this approach to social change,[10] freedom of association is neglected and treated as a formal freedom, even though it has managed to change the condition of both men and women through collective protest leading to the establishment of rights (workers' freedom of association, the right to strike, votes for women).[11]

So-called scientific socialism, obsessed with questions about the state and class struggle, forgot the combination of political conquests, social action, and economic organizations that had characterized previous worker action. The union–party relationship became fundamental within a hierarchical organization of collective actions whose objective was to establish the ruling power of the working class. For Mauss, scientific socialism "is seriously damaged by not giving enough attention" to this third pillar of cooperative action, which stands alongside political and union action. It leaves out these "essential, fundamental, central" workers' economic organizations, without which "there is no sound basis for political action" (Mauss 1899, 449–62; reprinted in Mauss 1997, 72–82). As a Marxist humanist, Thompson agrees, pointing out the loss of relational resources caused by the decline of the craft-based popular economy, which involved established and passionately defended notions of common well-being. As the weapon of the weak, this moral economy acted as a reservoir of meaning: it depended on shared norms and obligations and gave rise to demands for rights and social justice that fueled a democratic impulse that collided with capitalism. But it was destroyed by the advance of industrialization. As mentioned earlier, this was a turning point. The moral economy was subsequently replaced by a project to moralize the poor. With the loss of that pride that came from their economic power, the various groups that made up a composite working class saw any project of political self-organization fade away. For the historian, the twentieth-century labor movement's neglect of the link between economy and politics defended by "Jacobin virtues" explains "the strength of distinctions of class and status in 20th-century England" (Thompson 1988, 183).

The Decline of Associationalism

The first part of this book has summarized the paths taken by associations over the past two centuries. Doing so seemed necessary in order to identify both the origins of associationalism and the distortions of its purpose. By distinguishing between the three periods covered in these first three chapters, we can discern the issues faced by this challenge to the relationship between the political and economic spheres—a challenge that clashed with the weight of established powers, but which also contributed to their relative democratization. A linear narrative emerged. In their most influential versions, liberalism and marxism postulated a historical continuity, that of a capitalism synonymous with industrial progress or the development of productive forces. Whether this meant the end of history or laid the foundations for the coming of communism, its inevitability precluded the practices of associations, which operated "under the fearsome influence of socialist utopias," according to Tocqueville, or were considered "immature" (Riot-Sarcey 2016, 19) by Engels. Harvey's comments illustrate how associationalist experiments can be reduced to naive and outdated reveries: "before, there was utopianism and romanticism; and after there was hard-headed managerialism and scientific socialism" (Harvey 2012, 21, quoted by Riot-Sarcey 2016, 73). This vision of history bears the traces of amnesia about these associationalist initiatives' "ideas in action" and "power to act." These attributes disappeared behind prophetic discourses that obscured the fact that the utopian writers spoke on behalf of the people but were not of the people, and led to the "socialism of intellectuals" (Makhaiski 1979). Meanwhile the people themselves were from now on only referred to in two ways: as "an uncontrollable and violent mass" or conversely as "heroic, generous, selfless" (Riot-Sarcey 2016, 127). The decline of solidarity-based associationalism began with its confusion with utopianism. It then continued with the social economy, which was considered an extension of associationalism when in fact it led to the neglect of associations' political dimension. Finally, despite its economic importance, the social economy was itself largely overlooked in a twentieth century during which debate focused on the respective roles of the market and the state. By comparing southern Latin America with southern Europe and North America we can begin to revive a history that had disappeared. Numerous works inspired by Benjamin (2006) have rediscovered "an underground history of the nineteenth century."[12] The steps in this direction initiated in France[13] thus join up with the sociology of absences—proposed by the episte-mology of the South—which consists in rediscovering what has been considered unimportant or nonexistent.[14]

Since the end of the nineteenth century, the compromise based on the separation and complementarity between market and welfare state has been remarkably resilient. It was continually reinforced throughout most of the twentieth century. Two-thirds of this latter century saw the topic of association disappear from social debate. Communism forced a rupture, while the welfare state grew stronger in capitalist countries. However, after the Second World War, conditions conspired in both systems to marginalize anything that might recall the associationalist project.

On one side of the Berlin Wall, communism asserted the need to overcome capitalism. It only envisaged associations in a postcapital-ism where the free flourishing of each and every person would become possible through the development of productive forces. But this fu-ture association—where the labor force, freed from constraints, will automatically nourish higher activities[15]—actually devalued existing associations and cooperations, which were trapped in historical forms specific to a capitalist mode of production. On the other side of the wall, during the postwar economic boom, the processes of integration just described accelerated; this confined association to subsidiary roles corresponding to the different statuses through which it had been segmented. The size and the volume of activity carried out by cooperatives, mutual organizations, and associations may have increased, but their role was still limited. Something more important was taking place elsewhere, in the synergy between market and state that reinforced the belief in both economic and social progress. But then the wall dividing East and West came down, and events allowed associationalism to regain the place it had lost. The following chapters show why it is important—and how important it is—to reintroduce associationalism into debates about the future of democracy, while highlighting the obstacles it faces.

PART II

The Revival of Democratic Solidarity and the New Capitalism

{ 4 }

Associative Metamorphoses

THE ISSUES THAT WE EXAMINED IN THE FIRST PART of this book are now generally considered to be merely of historical interest. This is particularly true of associationalism, which was largely forgotten during the twentieth century because commitment to the collective was thought to symbolize a bygone era. According to this widely held view, such commitment has now disappeared in an age when self-interest to the point of narcissism has become the order of the day. This neglect of the common good is, allegedly, largely the result of the "new spirit of capitalism" (Boltanski and Chiapello 2018), which internalized the existential demands of the 1960s. The desire for self-expression and self-realization supposedly resulted in the triumph of the market, magnifying hedonism and egotism.

The various proponents of this view cover a broad ideological spectrum. The critical view of neocapitalism just mentioned underlines the system's capacity to regenerate itself on the basis of the challenges that it faces. A more reactionary view calls for the respect for authority lost after May 1968 to be restored (Audier 2008). But, despite their differences, one thing that analysts of democratic erosion have in common is that they seek to reveal effects of the system that are not directly perceived by those involved. As a corollary, if revolt leads to improved integration in the society being attacked, then the prospect of genuine social change becomes a logical impossibility. We can only celebrate lost illusions or turn to the state—or even a republican myth (Genestier and Laville 1994)—to counteract the market, as civic engagement has shown itself to be derisory.

It is clear that individualism has shifted towards a "privatism" that cuts the subject off from its "public sphere of action, the intersubjective conditions of reflexivity, in short, its public nature" (Leonardis 1997, 178). But do the risks posed by the spread of privatism allow us to diagnose democratic decline? Certainly, there are many "pathologies of democracy" that are largely attributable to a "histrionism" that refuses to "move beyond the register of frustration"—to an "identitarian and differentialist trend" that "undermines the foundations of a common world" (Fleury 2005, 122 and 133). It is nonetheless important to put the discourse about the democratic crisis into perspective. Its strength lies in its element of truth, while its weakness lies in paying insufficient attention to everyday practices.

This will be the focus of the following pages. This second section will question the pessimistic interpretation that one-sidedly stresses the refusal to engage and the futility of collective action. We will be using the same methodology as for the historical review. The shift of perspective will be the same, based on the evolution of ideas and social experiences rather than on abstract intellectual debate. From this point of view, there is a pressing fact that throws the disillusioned or nostalgic writings of yesterday's activists into question: we are experiencing a significant revival of solidarity around the globe. This is manifested in a wave of new cooperatives, but above all by an increase in the number of associations. Confronted by this phenomenon, many observers have rushed to interpret it as either an indication of state disengagement or a sign of consumerist drift. Such explanations are not wrong, but they are only partial. Reality is richer than this, and we can examine it properly by bearing in mind the lessons learned in the first part of this book: on the one hand, the theoretical differentiation at the heart of associations between philanthropic and democratic logics, and on the other, the need for a transversal analysis of actions relating to democratic solidarity. By remaining faithful to these methodological tenets, it becomes possible to come up with a different reading of our present age— one that examines the new associationalist tendencies without denying the simultaneous intensification of associations' cooptation mentioned earlier. Social struggles have not all been abandoned, but nor have they all been revived. In short, it is reductive to postulate a decline of politics and the total domination of market capitalism. Today, as in the past, it is rather a question of examining the relationship between democracy and the economy in more detail based on the history presented in the previous section—but also of showing how things have changed.

In 2010, the social economy as a whole accounted for 6.5 percent of jobs in the European Union, with an increase of 26 percent since 2003.

The majority of these jobs—65 percent—were in associations (CIRIEC 2013). The revival of associations therefore deserves our attention. It began to be highlighted by the statistics that were gathered for the first time in the final decades of the twentieth century. In France, national data reveals an explosion in the creation of associations, estimated to number 70,000 per year. Twenty-four percent of French people were involved in voluntary work in 2013. Other countries are experiencing a similar or even stronger trend—for example Germany has a volunteering rate of 34 percent, Denmark 43 percent and the Netherlands 57 percent. However, this quantitative increase may be accompanied by a qualitative decline. This has been demonstrated by a number of studies, which argue that the rise of associations has been balanced out by a dilution of their identity in terms of both their activities and actors. Their activities may become imitative when they adopt management practices imported from private companies or rules imposed by public authorities. As far as the actors are concerned, general activism—that is, activism linked to a societal project involving long-term action and strong delegations of power within federal structures—is weakening, as shown by the decline in certain trade union and ideological affiliations. On the other hand, a growing number of groups are focused on meeting the needs of their members and taking action to help the excluded who find themselves in dire need.[1] The literature therefore reveals that this new associative activity juxtaposes the provision of services for the middle classes with waves of generosity toward the most disadvantaged. The combination of the two confirms that politics has been abandoned in favor of generosity and compassion. In this context, volunteering is required to prove its competence and engagement to demonstrate its professionalism. This managerial discourse does not prevent associations from also playing a palliative role when faced with social problems, so long as they do not have pretensions to be part of the economy. The conventional view of associations is to see them as instruments of social policy that should enhance its performance. In the fight against poverty, the vocabulary of efficiency borrowed from business may be combined with an acceptance of job insecurity under the guise of social measures to address unemployment.

In which case the increase in the number of associations would be a red herring. Far from negating the thesis of democratic decline, it would be a manifestation of one of the forms this decline is taking.

But while this observation may well be true in some cases, it does not reflect every kind of social practice. The phenomenon of association cannot be fully understood if we simply highlight a qualitative normalization that belies its quantitative development. So here we will reverse the perspective. While acknowledging the equivocations of associations that lead them to align their practices with those of private companies or establish a public subsector, we must first of all focus on the revival of engagement. While indicators may suggest a weakening of democracy, they must be "placed back into a broader understanding of changes in citizen participation" (Rosanvallon 2006, 24). We will therefore emphasize both the potentials and the ambiguities of associations, bringing us closer to authors such as Bouvier and Rosanvallon, who acknowledge these two aspects of contemporary reality. Bouvier notes that the "aphasia of expectations" coexists with "new social bonds" woven into "singular" groups that are not a given but that build "a special us, a conjugation that accepts and speaks of both identity and otherness" (2005, 304–6). These groups are seeking "a feeling or desire for being together," but they are "a response, often more latent than proclaimed" (331) to an intensification of individualism. For his part, Rosanvallon highlights the vitality of counterdemocracy based on the powers of monitoring, sanctioning, and prevention through the rise of public scrutiny; he also points out that the various figures of counterdemocracy focus on "control, opposition, the downgrading of powers that are no longer a priority to obtain." Consequently, they may go so far as to "dissolve expressions of belonging to a common world," and in any event, "cannot be used to structure and support a collective proposal" (Rosanvallon 2006, 28).

This second section follows these authors' approach by examining revived forms of engagement and their limitations, but it differs in that it does not see them in a solely defensive light. While they may have been obscured behind actions guided more by necessity than by the desire for change, the struggles that commenced in the 1960s have not disappeared. A complex approach to institutionalization—one that reduces it neither to "cooptation" by institutions nor to "renunciation" by social actors—suggests that, despite its apparent decline, the democratization movement continues. In a search for credibility, it balances between the two poles of proposing another world and protesting against the existing order. This oscillation is characteristic of a multitude of local and international initiatives, as described in chapter 5. As explained in chapter 6, these initiatives are therefore caught between a strong assertiveness that requires them not to evade the "political question in economics," on the one hand, and a progressive depoliticization through participation in a functionalized associative group confined within the "apolitical," on the other (Rosanvallon 2006, 292).

Before addressing these thematics, however, this fourth chapter insists on the contemporary relevance of the associationalist perspective. Far from being a thing of the past, it has unexpectedly been gaining new currency over recent decades. Identifying this perspective requires us to move beyond the legal categorizations that, as we have seen, have been introduced since the late nineteenth century. In order to define our object of study without endorsing political and administrative divisions, we must acknowledge the links between different statuses that historically have been separated, in particular those of associations and cooperatives. To take just one example in more detail, various initiatives born into the associative framework have developed through the cooperative framework, initiating what is now known as "social" cooperation. It is therefore important to examine and describe how associations have developed.

Self-management and Radical Alternative Movements

After the Second World War, Western countries began building wage-based societies in which employment was the "great integrator" (Barel 1990). The synergy between market and state was manifested in particular by the spread of wage-earning status. High productivity gains allowed a steady flow of job creation, and periodic negotiations between management and labor led to regular pay increases. These wage-based societies were to be confronted by two "crises": the crisis of values that began in the 1970s, followed by what was known as the "economic crisis." The first crisis weakened Western societies, but the second crisis, which could have accelerated their destabilization, in fact had the opposite effect, because it occurred when the Soviet empire collapsed. Capitalism—which was beginning to be seriously questioned—regained its credibility, because "there is no alternative," to use Margaret Thatcher's expression. The renewed relevance of associationalism is thus inseparable from the weakening of wage-based societies, but also from the collapse of communist countries. A reversal therefore occurred with the transition from the first to the second crisis, but this did not prevent ongoing social conflicts. It is this immediate history that must be restored, without suggesting that there has been a linear evolution since the 1960s. In most analyses, the recent development of associations is only associated with the second crisis. It is necessary to go back to the first crisis to see the problems with these biased narratives in which the growth of associations is perceived solely as a reaction to mass unemployment and growing exclusion.

The First Crisis

The first crisis affected both the market and the state. Their respective effects were suddenly called into question, as was the synergy between the two. The crisis led to a questioning of how private companies organized themselves and criticism of the lack of opportunities for their workers to have a say. This exploitation of workers in the production process was not compensated for by their admission into consumer society. The lack of direct employee involvement in all aspects of the organization of work was coupled with passivity on the part of consumers, which led to the critique being extended to consumption and lifestyles. Behind the recognized benefits of access to goods, the limitations of the market system emerged.

This challenging of the growth model did not spare state intervention. Criticism of consumer society was also aimed at the bureaucratic and centralizing logics of public institutions. If the market made us forget the people behind "things," the state restricted itself to a "welfare-statism" where "citizens were not active subjects" but "the administered, objects, insofar as they were recipients, contributors, and taxpayers" (Gorz 1988, 227). The homogenizing approach in which demand directed supply toward mass goods and standardized services allowed extreme inequality to persist under the guise of egalitarian normalization.[2] Cracks gradually appeared in the progressive consensus, the glue that held society together based on a belief that the market and the state complemented one another to produce beneficial effects. Experts questioned whether the increase in wealth calculated by national accounts actually guaranteed a higher standard of living. The demand for a better quality of life began to emerge, partly due to socio-demographic change: an aging population, a diversification of household profiles, and more working women.

Social conflict did not merely play out as the struggle between bourgeois and proletarian classes. New social movements began to emerge.[3] Antinuclear, environmental, and feminist protests helped formulate new questions by popularizing issues such as zero growth, the damage caused by progress, and the links between private life and the public sphere. Despite their differences, those making these demands all began to think—however vaguely—about how to escape from an economic society, that is, a society structured by the fight against scarcity. They raised questions that Keynes, back in 1930, predicted would be unavoidable. It was necessary to "substitute a way-of-life politics for a standard-of-living politics" (Roustang 1998). This led a whole generation of associations and cooperatives to set up new collective-action projects in the name of self-management and an alternative society.

The Model of Society in Question

During the "Thirty Glorious years," from 1945 to 1975, the use of collective bargaining was the institutional spring through which class conflict could be absorbed by making growth and solidarity compatible at a macrosocial level. Trade unions were an expression of workers' collective power. In most European countries, the allocation of elected employee representatives led to the recognition of a form of consultation restricted to the social domain—consultation over working conditions, health and safety, vocational training, remuneration, and social services. These representatives' powers were only rarely extended to include consultation on economic issues, for example with works councils in Germany or advisory committees in the United Kingdom. In short, in the Fordist compromise, trade union counterpower simultaneously facilitated humanization and the acceptance of Taylorism. The "instrumentalization of the class conflict" (Dahrendorf 1959) allowed forms of indirect employee participation to be legally permitted. But this exclusively representative democracy was the expression of an elitist conception of democracy established in companies.[4] This attracted criticism, which became particularly strong in the wake of 1968.

The movements led by skilled workers—which brought together immigrants and young workers who were often far removed from the structures that were supposed to represent them—did not stop at demands for higher wages. Outside the system of employment relations, protests erupted that challenged the "scientific" organization of work. They condemned repetitive, fragmented work—"*Le travail en miettes*"[5]—and trade unionists and politicians took up the demands for direct participation that had been made by the workers themselves. The trend toward self-management had now taken hold among intellectuals. In the early 1960s, they began critically analyzing the mechanisms of domination and social control. From the outset, the desire for self-management played out through action. According to Mellucci, after the expropriation of the industrial revolution, the desire for self-management expressed the rejection of a second cultural and symbolic expropriation by modern capitalism. The challenge by proponents of self-management echoed that of the pioneer associations, distancing itself from the representation granted to the labor movement in industrial society (see Dalton and Knechler 1990). It questioned the meaning of production and, in doing so, took issue with the identification of growth with human progress.

In a complementary way, antiauthoritarian and environmental movements did not solely focus on the distribution of wealth, nor did they approach social relations on the basis of class alone. They began demanding political rights of participation, which Bell (1998) saw as a sign of a "post-industrial society," and Inglehart (1977) as "postmaterialism" (both cited in Neveu 1996, 66–74). Meanwhile feminism was challenging hierarchies and the patriarchy. All these new movements encouraged the formulation of original projects for social transformation, in which "political activists" were increasingly distinguished from "alternative practitioners."[6] Activists remained loyal to the prioritization of political action. It is true that they proposed a return to the roots of socialism, stating that the abolition of private property was insufficient to achieve the socialist project's aims. However, while they criticized bureaucracy, they subordinated the adoption of self-management to the conquest of state power. By contrast, the nonconformists quickly tried to create spheres of "drip-by-drip self-management."[7] This rift between activists and nonconformists is illustrated by the antinuclear movement. Some of its supporters focused on organizing large demonstrations while others also tried to prove the viability of renewable energy. From the 1970s onward, the desire to change the "here and now" through experimentation explains the craze for practices that were supposed to pave the way for an alternative society (See Gendron 2006, 479–89).

Campaigning for Social Transformation

Reconnecting with a sense of communal messianism, the people involved in this quest were convinced of the exemplary nature of lifestyles that broke away from the "system." They believed the legitimacy of their counterculture was sufficient for it to spread. But for all the collective approaches that rejected the sectarian drift of certain communities, the sustainability of the initiatives proved to be inversely proportional to the extremism of their objectives. The supporters of those who had been willing or able to eke out a living gave up their dream of an alternative society, and many moved toward more modest projects for living and working "differently." The self-management proponents' critique of how work was organized in a capitalist society and the alternative desire to establish a liberated society came together in attempts to create change by setting up different economic mechanisms: the idea of an alternative society gave way to the idea of alternative enterprises.

Originating in the "imaginary projects of alternative societies" (Desroche 1976) through an "associationalist" ideology that reflected some of the aspirations expressed in the previous century by Owen, Saint-Simon, and Fourier, alternative enterprises aimed to prefigure an alternative economy capable of "perfectly uniting what contemporary society divides" (Vienney 1980, 7–149). But just as the alternative society was confronted with the challenge of individual behavior, so the alternative economy had to confront the harshness of competition. The emphasis on flexibility, equal pay, discussion, and mutual information could not drown out the issue of low wages and long working hours (Sainsaulieu, Tixier, and Marty 1983). The failure rate was high. The majority of groups that subverted the notions of work and employment disappeared. Those that persisted devoted themselves to a more limited objective: empowering their members within collectively managed economic entities. They often chose the cooperative status as suitable for establishing and managing companies controlled by their employees.

Though far from its initial objective, the alternative movement above all resulted in new forms of associative work in the postindustrial tertiary sector (Huber 1981). It was under this movement's impetus that the cooperative labor movement in many countries opened up to the provision of intellectual and cultural services. In 1985, these service cooperatives accounted for 45 percent of worker cooperatives and 32 percent of jobs in the United Kingdom, 13.5 percent of cooperatives in Quebec, and 18.1 percent of cooperatives and 6.5 percent of jobs in France. They gained access to niche markets thanks to the fact that their managers were already embedded in political and social networks. In the area of training, consulting, technical studies, media, arts and leisure, small groups of young graduates—often united by previous work experience in companies where they learned about customer relations—contributed to an increase in the number of new cooperatives and a reduction in their average size. Brazil was also affected by "a strong associationalist movement among highly skilled workers and professionals, especially in the health sector" with, for example, "more than 100 medical service cooperatives at the end of the 1970s, nearly 15,000 affiliated doctors, 900 hospitals and 1,500 laboratories meeting the needs of more than 4 million users" (Benevides Pinho 1979, 42–56). In the 1970s, the collective entrepreneurs who created the first worker cooperatives prefigured a rehabilitation of the enterprise that would assert itself over the next decade. The new cooperatives formed part of a landscape of production in which different types of employee participation and profit-sharing were proliferating. This is illustrated by the example of the United States, where 1,200 small businesses are companies—including worker cooperatives—where workers hold the majority of the capital, and where shares are relatively equally distributed, employing an estimated 15,000 people. Many of them have been created since the 1970s, though some are older. However, they can be difficult to discern amongst the mass of companies that have a wide range of financial participation programs involving more than 40 million employees.[8] Collectives strongly committed to equality get lost in a sea of employee equity participation, whose aim is to increase employees' identification with their company.

In short, the desire for self-management and alternative ways of living and working was unable to escape a gradual dilution. It was fueled by the social upheaval that came in the wake of the May 1968 protests. But since the early 1980s, the radical critique of the concentration of power, of professionalization, of the specialization of social functions, and of the red tape around delegation procedures have all waned. It is no longer accepted at a grassroots level. The difficulties and ambiguities faced by collectives isolated in an unfavorable environment have increased, and collective action has declined. It is likely that neglect of political mediation and the belief that pioneering experiments can be spread simply through their exemplary value have been crippling weaknesses.

This apparent failure should not, however, obscure the wide variety of experiments that have been conducted. Despite the setbacks in achieving their initial aims, concern for the future of society has become a strong motivation for collective engagement. The question of the ends of production—which was not considered by the earlier cooperative movement—is now being raised and linked back to questions about the means by which production is achieved. The egalitarianism advocated in the organization of work and day-to-day operations is considered the best guarantee that production collectives' economic means will converge with their social and environmental ends. These collectives' main contribution lies in the fact that they are not focused solely on their internal operations but aim to have a wider impact on society by positing a link between the self-organization of work and a broader democratization. They wish to practice forms of direct democracy rather than contenting themselves with the forms of representative democracy guaranteed in cooperative statutes. But they are also committed to reducing inequalities via the goods and services they offer. Research associations, law and management firms, and consulting and training cooperatives all aim to make the knowledge that is usually the preserve of experts available to as many people as possible, in order to combat what de Certeau (1984) calls the "abuse of knowledge." This social engagement is accompanied by environmental awareness; for example, research and development departments are focusing on new forms of energy, and stores are selling organic products.

In sum, the originality of all these initiatives lies in their "internal modes of operation," on the one hand (they are generally based on cooperative and self-management models), and in the "specific populations that constitute their domain of intervention," on the other. Infused with egalitarian demands and "environmentalist ideas," they can be grouped together "under the term 'alternative movements'" (Corpet 1982, 32–72; see also Corpet, Hersent, and Laville 1986). While they may not have given shape to an alternative economy, the production collectives that multiplied in the 1970s did open up new areas of transformation. In the years that followed, their efforts moved into the background as the restructuring of production began to take effect. But this effervescence was not just a passing phenomenon. Although the challenge it left behind was covered over by the neoliberal wave, it would nonetheless influence later initiatives, hybrids of the impulse toward self-management and the fight for jobs.

Company Restructuring and Worker Takeovers

In any case, the situation was disrupted by rising unemployment. The voluntary collectives described above were linked to the crisis of values that affected the growth model of the *Trente Glorieuses*. From the 1980s onward, it was involuntary collectives emerging from the economic crisis that came to the forefront.

A Second Crisis

The relationship between the first and second crises should be clarified. The 1944 Declaration of Philadelphia symbolized the triumph of an ideology of progress, reformulated after the disasters of war, in which the economy was nothing but a means at the service of social progress. The cultural crisis demonstrated that this ideology had run out of steam, as social movements like environmentalism and feminism challenged the legitimacy of maximum growth as well as the paternalism that persisted in the traditional welfare state. But these protests were not libertarian forces that paved the way for neoliberalism. On the contrary, neoliberalism presented itself as a strong reaction to the "excesses of democracy" and invoked the dangers of disorder to promote a new orthodoxy. The scale of the movements within civil society stirred up fear among those in power, as summarized in the famous report for the Trilateral Commission coauthored by Crozier, Huntington, and Watanuki (1975). This argued for the need to establish the "potentially desirable limits to the indefinite extension of political democracy." This line of argument condemning the "unlimited character of present democracy" is at the heart of Hayek's writings. The neoliberal program elaborated by Hayek (1973) and his fellow economist Friedman (2020)—the main theorists of monetarism—is primarily political, aiming to restrict the role of the state and turn associations into mere service providers. What they dread is any teleological project, whether it emanates from popular sovereignty or autonomous public spheres. All organized collective action hinders the interplay of spontaneous market forces; this is why associations and state power have to be weakened in order to restore the conditions for widespread competition, which, according to these authors, means renewed effectiveness and efficiency.[9]

The parallel with the nineteenth century is striking. This was a time when the democratic dynamic triggered a renewed appeal to the market system, which was presented as being beyond question. The arguments put forward in an effort to find a way out of the economic crisis led to the invalidation of the calls for democratization made during the cultural crisis.

The second crisis—the economic crisis—can be interpreted as a resurgence of questions raised by the first crisis, which concerned the model of development. At least this was the argument put forward by Viveret, for whom "it is so difficult to organize social relations and produce a culture beyond work in a society of abundance that it is plausible to think that societies artificially recreate conditions of scarcity and poverty, thus placing the question of subsistence and work back at the heart of social ties" (1989, 8–12). Whatever the validity of this hypothesis, the 1980s enshrined the imperative of competitiveness. In this context, associative resistance sought to fight against precarity and exclusion; utopia in action was succeeded by the need to protect jobs, with companies being turned into cooperatives and the rediscovery of the popular economy. In this respect, the experience of crisis reinforced the valorization of work[10] within collectives confronted by the increased demands of capital.

Reluctant Entrepreneurs[11]

After the revival rooted in alternativist ideology, the cooperative movement was deeply affected by another wave of cooperatives, which this time emerged not out of choice but rather necessity: company takeovers. In Italy, we can identify around one thousand takeovers before 1985—although the statistics are imprecise. These mostly occurred in the north of the country and involved companies in the textile and clothing, printing, light engineering, wood, and transport sectors with an average of 30 to 100 employees. In Spain, takeovers saw companies restructured not only as cooperatives but also as public limited-liability companies whose employees were the majority shareholders. Their precise number is not known, but was at least 1,300, accounting for 50,000 jobs (see Garcia Jané 2009). In France, between 1978 and 1983—a period in which the cooperative movement expanded—takeovers accounted for between 37 percent and 61 percent of all new jobs created inside cooperatives, depending on the year.

With financial deregulation, capital was placed on the international markets and shareholders demanded a return on investment of 12–15 percent. This led to an increase in attempts to save production that workers considered to be viable, even if it did not meet the requirements of the international capital market. Indeed, there were a variety of circumstances in which businesses could still be profitable without attracting private investors. Workers were then in a position to reorganize and run these operations, sometimes also carrying out industrial conversion projects. Worker takeovers were therefore a logical reaction to more selective choices on the part of capital owners, but they suffered from a poor "brand image" as a result of huge media attention and the politicization of certain cases. For the most part, these cases related to companies with more than a hundred employees with a strong delegation of power from workers to trade unions.[12] They diverted attention from successful takeovers involving smaller companies in sectors with highly skilled workers and low capital intensity where performance was primarily linked to the quality of the work. In these takeovers, workers were more directly involved in the takeover decision—a decision that was not solely the result of trade union or political voluntarism. To take just one example, in France, 63 percent of takeovers by cooperatives in 1981 were still in business five years later, a higher percentage than all small and medium-sized enterprises, more than half of which went under in their first three years. However, most of the recovered companies were still considered failures because public opinion had been influenced by massive bankruptcies such as Manufrance.[13]

The bad reputation that takeovers had in many countries did not prevent some changes being made to legislation. These included changes in social security and unemployment insurance regulations designed to encourage the unemployed to start their own businesses, and laws for "unemployed business creators" that favored company takeovers in France, Spain, and the United Kingdom. Strategies aimed at using worker cooperatives as a means of safeguarding large-scale employment may have been short-lived, but more ad hoc support came from local authorities and trade unions. For example, in the United Kingdom in 1986, close to eighty support agencies for cooperatives received local authority funding, particularly from councils run by the Labour Party. In France, decentralization facilitated economic intervention by local authorities. In Italy, the number of takeovers carried out is also linked to the fact that the main trade unions already associated with the various cooperative federations—according to their political leanings—made a further commitment. In 1985 they signed an agreement with these federations on the nature and extent of public support needed, as well as the joint efforts that should be made to achieve this. In Quebec, in 1986, the Centrale des syndicats nationaux set up a consulting group to provide management support for cooperative projects and also to facilitate the transition from formal democracy to the participatory management of day-to-day operations. This support from public authorities and trade unions allowed a degree of progress, but it tended to remain almost clandestine or only discernible at the local level. In a public imaginary marked by the highly publicized failure of a few companies, takeovers were still synonymous with a dead end (see Paton 1989).

Resistances to Protect Jobs

This may have been the dominant view in most countries of the global North, but company takeovers were also happening elsewhere. South American countries affected by plant closures as part of the strategic reorientation of multinationals experienced the same phenomenon, but with additional difficulties. Many of the companies concerned suffered from undercapitalization and technological obsolescence, for example in traditional industries such as textiles and footwear. However, their economic problems were accompanied by a particular social enthusiasm, on which reference to workers' control drew. Without solving the problems, this reference gave a distinctive dynamic to these "recovered companies," as they are known in Argentina, one of the countries where the phenomenon is most prevalent (see, among others, Caffaratti

2003; Magnani 2003; Rizza and Sermasi, 2008). While in Europe takeovers replaced the credo of self-management with the sole aim of safeguarding jobs, in South America they were inseparable from memories of earlier experiments in self-management. This is borne out by some emblematic examples, such as the Catense cooperative and its 12,000 worker-members whose presence in the sugar cane industry is crucial to the economy of northeastern Brazil. There was clear trade union involvement in this phenomenon of workers taking over companies that had been abandoned by their former owners. The unions believed that outsourcing went against the spread of democracy in South America, a continent that had long been under the yoke of authoritarian regimes. As a result, self-management and worker takeovers were more likely to merge than succeed one another like in Europe. However, this period of worker takeovers through necessity did not exclude the possibility of these recovered companies being overvalued, which could lead to disillusionment similar to that mentioned above. Thus emphasis was placed on these companies in the policies of the State of Rio Grande do Sul in Brazil, highlighting an industrialist inclination on the part of those public officials who made self-management the "conceptual basis" of their program (See Sarria Icaza 2005). The corollary of this preference was a lack of interest in many other collective initiatives in services and small businesses. It raised the question of the relationship with a popular economy with strong roots in family and community, especially as this was growing due to the unfulfilled promises of job creation by companies in the private sector.

Rediscovering the Popular Economy

While the popular economy had disappeared from the debate in Europe, takeovers in the name of self-management were sometimes seen in South America as an expression of a workers' vanguard. But they could also be seen as the submerged portion of a much bigger set of grassroots activities. This view is also justified by the fact that the export-oriented market has never allowed such high employment as in the global North; entire sections of the population are deprived of access to formal employment channels. In South America the creation of non-agricultural jobs between 1950 and 1970 was lower than the increase in the urban population: the respective percentages were 46 percent and 59 percent from 1950 to 1960, reaching 40 percent and 47 percent from 1960 to 1970.[14] Thus the rural exodus translated into an increase in the number of people in the working population who were unable to find formal employment. With the dictatorships that interrupted the democracy of the 1950s and 1960s, and the debt crisis and social deregulation that followed, up to half of the working population were excluded from the formal economy in countries like Brazil. As in the nineteenth century, they survived thanks to forms of solidarity embedded in community networks.

The second chapter described how these forms have long been neglected. The dichotomy between the formal and informal sectors attests to this neglect. While the concept of the informal sector was initially intended to designate an economy ignored by public decision-makers,[15] it has gradually gained a pejorative connotation, coming to be defined by three criteria: small size, noncompliance with legislation, and "noncapitalist production methods" (Lautier 2006, 210). Yet the informal economy—which, according to estimates for Latin America, serves as a refuge for 35 percent of the working population—was a heterogeneous whole. One part is composed of market activities linked to capitalist companies' outsourcing strategies, not to mention illegal trafficking sometimes accompanied by extreme violence. But another part is a grassroots response to a difficult economic situation. It is based on the domestic unit, a group of people who interact on a daily, regular, and permanent basis in order to achieve the objectives of reproducing and protecting life by carrying out activities, economic or otherwise, that are essential for improving their lives (Hillenkamp and Laville 2013). This orientation, which corresponds to Polanyi's principle of the economic behavior of household management—or domestic sharing, as Hillenkamp prefers to call it—does not imply equality or even fairness. Starting from this kind of comprehensive approach, Coraggio, Quijano, Razetto, and Sousa Santos's work focuses on extensions that are able to transfer the habits rooted in the domestic sphere onto a broader and more egalitarian basis, so that they become the source of reciprocal relationships that address inequalities. Their innovative move consists in no longer restricting the popular economy to dependence on capitalism or the market. They start from a place of deep familiarity with its tangled operation—which mixes together different logics—in order to examine the conditions for its mobilization from the perspective of economic alternatives.

As was the case nearly two centuries earlier, the rise of more associative forms corresponds to an affirmation of solidarity in the extension of ordinary cooperation within primary social groups. The democratic management of projects and the mode of work organization based on collective action are inextricably linked to resolving the problems of survival.

Based on mutual aid and common ownership of the means of production, these grassroots associations include: production workshops;[16] organizations of unemployed people coming together to seek employment; community food groups, including collective kitchens and vegetable gardens; organizations dedicated to housing, electricity, and drinking-water issues; precooperative self-build organizations; and community service associations in the areas of health and culture. A ten-year survey in Santiago de Chile, where 25 percent of the labor force are involved in the popular economy, reveals a decline in food groups (from 54 to 9 percent of popular economic organizations), a rise in production workshops (from 53 to 68 percent), and growth in the fulfilment of needs that go beyond survival (housing, health, education), with horizontal and vertical integration reducing their isolation. Studies conducted throughout Chile show that, at the end of the twentieth century, the popular economy accounted for almost half of the working population. Initiatives also exist in Argentina, Brazil, Colombia, Ecuador, Mexico, Peru, and Uruguay. They are based on black and indigenous movements (see Alvarez, Dagnino, and Escobar 1998, 333), such as in the Andean countries, where indigenous principles of organization were reactivated to generate original models of development. The example of Bolivia is particularly illustrative from this point of view (Hillenkamp 2009), as is the local Nasa project in Colombia, which won an award from the United Nations.

Mobilizing against Contempt

In Colombia, as in other countries, one of the most illustrative examples is that of waste recycling cooperatives. Nearly 300,000 people, or 1 percent of the population, live off waste picking, including 50,000 in

Bogotá. These people are victims of the official and unofficial intermediaries to whom they sell the waste, and also of the contempt of the public, who equate them with the waste they collect from the street. The creation of cooperatives in 1987 was a reaction to this ostracism. Its purpose was to combat dispersion and head-to-head competition with intermediaries through an economic organization that would create a less unfavorable balance of power. It also sought to combat exclusion through a social, political, and cultural arrangement that provided access to rights. The year 1990 saw the formation of the Recyclers' Association of Bogotá, and, at regional level, the North Coast Association; in 1991 the National Recyclers' Association was established, bringing together eighty-eight of the country's ninety-four cooperatives, representing 10 percent of the people who lived from waste picking.

Another typical example is that of the Landless Workers' Movement (Movimento dos Trabalhadores Rurais Sem Terra, or MST) in Brazil, established in 1984. In 2000, 250,000 families reclaimed unoccupied land. Some fifty agricultural and livestock production cooperatives were set up to compensate for the lack of resources. These bring together 2,300 families, and around thirty service cooperatives benefit 12,000 families.[17] At the same time, hundreds of producer associations are able to receive loans. There are 1,800 elementary schools, with 3,800 teachers and 150,000 students, 1,200 youth educators, and 250 nurseries.

These examples are very different, but they both show the link between economics and politics. They have also been the subject of detailed evaluation. In Colombia's recycling cooperatives, the workers' status as employees enables them to access social security and insurance. These gains—like their integration into a collective, which is materialized in the uniform they wear—leads to improvements in both their living and working conditions, helping them escape from a true social apartheid. Cooperatives nonetheless have to overcome many obstacles. These include the traditional individualism of the sector in which they operate; the division of responsibilities with nongovernmental organizations, whose support is essential but whose involvement is sometimes perceived as interference by members; and confrontation with the privatization and rationalization of the salvage sector, which offers opportunities yet at the same time favors larger companies. Meanwhile the need for alliances with the private sector creates the risk of absorption. At a national conference, an executive from Rescatar, one of the main cooperatives, commented: "It is a global and universal economy. The same privatizations that we see in Colombia are taking place in Venezuela, Ecuador, and Peru. We're in the twenty-first century but still working like we did in 1900. We're a hundred years behind! We are competing under unequal conditions with our carts, while cleaning companies have American and European vehicles worth 200 million pesos. We can't be competitive like this. We have to learn to develop projects" (cited in Rodriguez 2002).

For its part, the MST is mired in controversy, mainly stemming from its syncretism. In this movement, enthusiasm for agrarian reform and the "classless society"—inspired by liberation theology and Castro's revolution—coexists with an attachment to the traditional values of land, family, and religion. It provokes both fascination and mistrust vis-à-vis its ideological "rapture" and "canonization" of collective action. The indisputable mobilization that it produces—which it amplifies through its driving role in Via Campesina—is thrown into question. Because of the centralized control of its internal debates and funding, Navarro refers to "mobilization without emancipation" and a disdain for democracy, to which Martins de Carvalho replies that the MST is a movement under construction, saying it has not so much the characteristics of a mass social organization as those of a network of marginalized Latin American peasant classes. For de Carvalho, the MST's current vagaries are explained by the discovery of new cultural codes through flows of information as well as symbols that—despite their problems—forge an autonomous social identity.[18] He says that emancipation is real for many peasants who were previously illiterate but are now involved in a process of popular education.

As can be seen, the new wave of popular economy has attracted its share of controversy. One point of reference is the work of Razeto, who emphasizes the consolidation and democratization of these economic practices that are rooted in a community fabric that they are nonetheless reconstituting. Their transformative impact is also highlighted by Sousa Santos (2002). Quijano (1998) is less optimistic, believing that individualism is prevalent in popular economic organizations and that necessity determines action more than solidarity. Within these organizations we can certainly find a logic of reciprocity, which is undeniably specific to them, but this is not enough. In Quijano's view their dependence is too marked to speak, as Coraggio does, of a labor economy set against the capitalist economy.

New Alliances

In any event, the diversity of interpretations proves that the popular economy is no longer perceived as a phenomenon doomed to fail in accordance with the "iron law" of capitalist growth. This solely negative vision is replaced by questions about the present and future role of this economy. It may be that its initiatives have not fully emerged from the margins, but they are no longer simply consigned to the management of scarcity. Nevertheless, questions remain about how to move from the level of survival and subsistence to certain forms of accumulation; how to move beyond the level of the simple reproduction of life's necessities to that of expanded reproduction, to use the Marxist terminology of many South American authors. The popular economy is caught between technical efficiency and the dynamics of solidarity, between educating participants and respect for the original values that were the reason they got involved in the first place.

It is clear, however, that there has been a shift in perspective among observers, and that attention is now being paid to the foundations of the popular economy. This attention is evidence of the popular economy's legitimization and puts pressure on public policy to accord it its rightful place. Academic networks have been established in several countries to provide support, and nongovernmental organizations are now both more aware of the subject and actively involved. Changes have occurred in Peru, Mexico, Argentina, Colombia, and Uruguay— but Brazil is undoubtedly the best example of the progress that has been made. Since 1980 Caritas has financed thousands of "alternative community projects," and in 1999 the Central Única dos Trabalhadores (Unified Workers' Central), commonly known as CUT, became deeply involved through its Solidarity Development Agency (ADS). Providing training and information for trade unionists and cooperatives, it was set up in partnership with Unitrabalho, which brings together more than eighty universities. This foundation is also one of the originators of the Incubadora Tecnológica de Cooperativas Populares (ITCP), which helps to start up cooperatives and associated production groups (see Cunha Dubeux 2004).

In recent decades, the popular economy has thus attained unprecedented visibility. Even if the links remain tenuous between "self-managed" companies that result from industrial collapse and new service cooperatives (in areas such as cleaning, recycling, artistic production, and training), a range of groups emanating from churches, trade unions, and universities are now promoting the popular economy in conjunction with both emancipation and rights movements and environmental organizations.

This recognition stands in sharp contrast to the usual analyses of the informal sector, which, starting from different premises, are unanimous in denigrating it and considering it outdated.[19] As for the conventional economy, apart from the microcredit movement as represented by de Soto, there is a dualist approach that pits the urban, industrial world against the rural, agricultural world. The hierarchy between these two worlds also exists in the structuralist movement, in which marginalist theory assimilates the informal sector to survival, and functionalist theory insists on the superiority of the capitalist logic. In all these movements, the informal sector is considered to be harmful, behind the times, passive; if it is to be allowed, then it can only play a transitory role en route to "real" development, which equates to industrial accumulation.

On the other hand, the term *popular economy* introduces "another perspective on the informal sector";[20] thus for Zaoual (1996), the popular economy is based on a symbolic site from which it draws meaning and energy, while for Latouche (1991) it obeys a logic that cannot be separated from forms of sociability.

Fighting for Recognition

Admittedly, previous hierarchies have not disappeared,[21] but the popular economy is gaining recognition and attracting some dedicated research. This research highlights the diversity of issues—which are obvious to both individual and collective actors—in rural regions such as Totonicapán in Guatemala and Uniapas in Mexico (Yépez del Castillo and Charlier 1999). A study conducted in Bolivia on women members of peasant economic organizations attests to this diversity: "The family's survival strategy, the network's sociability, market integration, and the quest for autonomy and self-affirmation are thus closely intertwined with the logic of solidarity" (Sarria Icaza 2005, 155).

The importance accorded to the popular economy in fact means that its public dimension is accentuated. According to Hirschman (1971b), in Latin America's popular economic initiatives, the struggle to improve members' living standards is intrinsically linked to the fight for citizenship rights. It oscillates between making general demands and dealing with personal problems, and does not separate material issues from those of living standards and fellowship. There is an obvious parallel with what Thompson referred to as the moral economy. As Scholnik says: "It is another way of doing politics" (1984, 28), put forward by women's groups protesting against the scandal of establishing an opposition between public and private. According to these groups, imposing a division between production and reproduction assigns them to unpaid activities for two-thirds of their working hours, while men are paid for two-thirds of their working hours. In the past, women's confinement to an unrecognized domestic economy explained their physical and symbolic underrepresentation in the public sphere. The fact that they constitute a majority in popular initiatives is due to their belief that these collective approaches are able to identify and contextualize their needs, express them, and bring them into the public sphere. Faced with the limitations of standardized and universalist measures, these initiatives are a means of enforcing rights and translating them into the capacity to act; they bring together a collective that is a resource for developing self-confidence, for relieving the burden of responsibilities assumed in the family sphere, and for reconciling these responsibilities with a commitment to social justice. First and foremost, these collective actions are intended to be pragmatic responses to everyday problems. But they also formulate social and environmental demands, creating a link with ecological feminism, which is rising up against a materialistic and economistic concept of wealth that assimilates domestic knowledge to "innate" qualities, to "altruism" and female "duties."[22]

{ 5 }

Local and International Initiatives

THE GLOBAL SOUTH'S POPULAR ECONOMIC INITIATIVES are not solely income-generating activities. To varying degrees, the many women who participate in the popular economy combine the necessary pragmatism of the unemployed with the pride that comes from a political desire to change social relations. They advocate a change of perspective toward domestic activities that involve giving care and attention to others, with a view to sharing these tasks more fairly and raising awareness of the wealth they generate. In this respect, there are significant similarities with some of the aspirations expressed in the North regarding domestic and caregiving roles. It therefore makes sense to take a look at a range of new approaches. This is the subject of chapter 5. Community-based services,[1] but also fair trade, solidarity finance, and complementary currencies can, of course, all be studied separately, but these social phenomena may also raise questions about what they have in common—that is, their significance for society. From this point of view, they bear the traces of the first and second crises.

Contrary to what is often claimed, the second crisis did not cancel out the effects of the first. The succession of the two crises resulted in a shaken-up associative landscape that combined aspirations for participatory democracy with a concern for social cohesion and employment. Associations did not restrict themselves to narrowly limited responses. To varying degrees, local and international initiatives combined the desire to contribute to a different kind of economy more focused on the common good with the desire to defend threatened ways of life. They were also supported by the structural change in productive activities connected to the rise in service relationships.[2] Alongside other changes, the development of a service sector gave rise to a multitude of grassroots initiatives that rejected the subordination of the social to the economic. They prioritized direct demands that criticized the welfare state's modes of intervention while supporting it in principle.

These initiatives, which argued for new local regulations within the same country, were supported by social mobilizations that went beyond national borders in an attempt to respond to rights violations and environmental destruction. They constituted a form of self-organization that, due to its international scale, claimed to be a kind of globalization from the bottom up—one that sought, according to Falk (1999), to minimize violence, maximize economic well-being, achieve social and political justice, and safeguard the quality of the environment. Solidarity finance and complementary currencies provide examples of how this approach is present in both the South and the North. The integration of these initiatives into fair trade networks gives them a role in a "globalization of solidarity," according to Ortiz and Munoz (1998), or what Rodriguez calls a "counterhegemonic globalization" (2002, 364).

With the two successive crises, associations thus found they had a new way of moving into politics and the economy. As Prouteau says, "one of the main features of the changes that have affected the associative world over the last quarter of a century is undoubtedly the increased power of its economic activities" (2003, 8; see also Demoustier, Rousselière, Clerc, and Cassier 2003). The other striking feature is the emergence of a global civil society defined as the "sphere of cross-border relationships and activities carried out by collective actors—social movements, networks, and civil society organizations—that are independent from governments and private firms and operate outside the international reach of states and markets" (Marchetti and Pianta, 2006). The different forms this multidimensional process takes can be identified more clearly by describing initiatives that are seeking new bridges between politics and the economy—initiatives where both associative and cooperative forms are being reshaped. We should avoid only seeing in associations the impact of an economic crisis so brutal that it swept away vague desires for social change. Yet in many cases the desire for change has indeed been combined with more restorative actions, which renders the majority of practices highly ambiguous.[3] All the fields of activity examined below gave rise to disagreements about what to prioritize, and it is important not to deny or neglect this fact.

Community-Based Services

In the countries of the North, a new form of activism emerged around services. People who had unresolved problems (local residents, social workers, parents) decided to set up their own services in order to improve their everyday lives. Critical of a welfare state that reduced users to passive recipients, their goal became collective services that depended on dialogue with service beneficiaries, along with good jobs. When it came to caregiving tasks, they also took action to promote a fairer division of labor within households so that women shouldered less of the burden. These services might be called "solidarity-based services." They are usually provided within a particular local area and respond quickly to the needs of their users. However, the focus is not merely on the fact that they are local. The services provided are individual and personal; they are felt, experienced, and internalized by those involved. The services are also created jointly with the support of a community. Instead of everyone trying to solve their everyday problems on their own in the private sphere, community-based services aim to resolve them by opening up the private sphere to the public sphere. Supply and demand can be reconciled by taking multiple realities into account in collective discussions. However, acceptance of these participatory approaches has been made more difficult by the fact that welfare states are facing a crisis. Their implementation has, therefore, depended on the welfare state systems mentioned in chapter 3.

A Citizen-Centered Approach to Services

In the Scandinavian countries, some organizations have been operating in a way different from previous associations since the 1980s. Instead of lobbying political authorities, they have directly implemented "new organisational forms and types of problem-solving with regard to social problems at the local level" (Klausen, P. Selle 1996, 99–122). In Denmark these have included organizations called "project developers," which are supported by public authorities in order to encourage volunteers to take responsibility in areas of social policy. In Sweden, women's organizations set up shelters and advice centers for women escaping domestic violence, which led more than half of the country's municipalities to establish public initiatives to help women. In the same decade, parents established new forms of childcare because they felt public services were not meeting their needs due to their standardized approach to running childcare facilities. The social-democratic government granted childcare cooperatives the right to be 85 percent publicly funded, and in 1991 all restrictions were lifted on the legal status of childcare facilities. Fifteen percent of preschool children are cared for in nonpublic daycare centers. The majority are parent cooperatives, but some are worker cooperatives or have the legal status of associations (Pestoff 1998; 2004). In this context, cooperatives and associations have been just as involved in restructuring existing services as they have in the creation of new services. The "cooperatization" (Lorendahl 1997) of social services was primarily aimed at expanding the role of users, such as parents, in organizing their children's care. It was permitted because of financial pressures on the public sector.

In disadvantaged areas of the United Kingdom and North America, "community" approaches are based on people getting involved in improving their lives in their local area. This understanding of community is grounded in a desire for social change on a cultural basis, because—it is thought—a sense of belonging is what provides the resources for an emancipatory struggle. According to Alinsky (see also Quinqueton 1989), the first form of conditioning that has to be combatted is resignation; local action is a means of overcoming the feeling of powerlessness and becoming aware of the power of collective action. This approach is less workerist than that of the socialist movement in Europe. It is rooted in the grassroots democracy that is widespread in America, which was reactivated not just by the civil rights movement but also by the environmental and feminist movements. In the United States in 1980, 8,000 national organizations and more than 500,000 mutual aid groups were listed as being part of this community movement (Boyte 1981), which took an economic turn when it set up community development corporations—organizations that aimed to revitalize neighborhoods and rural areas by mobilizing their residents. In the United Kingdom, community approaches included the development of the Community Transport Association, recognized at national level as the representative body of groups that had formed to address the transport deficit; community enterprises, particularly in Scotland; community foundations; and community development trusts. All these initiatives emerged in rural and urban areas where the market economy was in decline. In the 1990s, a grassroots initiative was set up to counter the marginalization of disadvantaged communities. On the environmental front, Groundwork Trusts have involved local people in designing and running more than 3,000 projects, in partnership with environmental associations, local communities, and businesses. Playgroups for young children were set up by parents in response to the shortage of childcare facilities. In 1998 there were 18,000 such playgroups, accounting for 19 percent of available childcare places for children under five years of age (see Taylor 2004). And associations representing cultural minorities and people with disabilities formed, developing approaches that—with a view to combating what their spokespeople described as the paternalism of the authorities and the blindness of the market—encouraged users to get involved in developing the services they needed.

In Germany and Austria, similar initiatives are referred to as "mutual aid," reflecting their desire to give responsibility to those they support. They can be divided into three subgroups: semi-informal groups; "self-help" groups, i.e., groups that bring together people affected by the same problem; and groups that advocate on behalf of people who have been marginalized. They are set up on a voluntary basis and paid professional work is only ever complementary to voluntary work. By the end of the twentieth century, there were 70,000 such initiatives in Germany, involving around 2.65 million people (Evers, Bode, Gronbach, and Graf, 1999). They began to proliferate in the 1980s, especially in the areas of health and social action, with between 5,000 and 10,000 groups in healthcare alone. In the 1990s, they took root in the midst of criticism that public services and large charities were becoming too bureaucratic. This led to the emergence of new local organizations. In Vienna, for example, 65,000 children are cared for, half in the public system and half in traditional associations and others that have emerged from these grassroots initiatives (Leichsenring 1997). As in France and Belgium, the aim is to change the services offered by associations by recognizing that the absence of a profit-making objective does not in itself guarantee respect for users. Whether these innovations involve revamping old associations or creating new ones, they all see the original associational ways of working as central to their activity. According to their proponents, the legitimacy of associations' provision of services depends on their ability to encourage users' voices (Pestoff 1998) and to mobilize a wide range of voluntary commitments, while finding new financial equilibria suited to a context where there is less protection from the welfare state.

Work Integration

Like other activities, community-based services that arose as a result of the redesign of social services were unable to escape the economic crisis. From the 1980s onward, one of the main causes of increasing inequality was the rise in unemployment and exclusion. This led to the development of services that sought to reintegrate people through access to work, the primary objective of which was to secure salaried jobs for people experiencing hardship. The main challenge for these work-integration services was that of promoting economic activity without thereby multiplying exceptional work schemes, which further deteriorates the regular workforce's conditions by establishing a secondary labor market. As pioneers in active labor-market policies, work integration initiatives combined social support with the quest for economic efficiency. In doing so, they oscillated between merely functioning as "sluice gates" to the market economy, on the one hand, changing the rules by getting people involved to increase the supply of jobs by getting people involved in managing the productive entity, on the other. Their aim was either to help people enter the labor market, in which case they restricted themselves to offering work-based training to the future employees of private companies, or they had the broader aim of incorporating these workers as legal subjects and economic actors.[4] In the first case, work integration initiatives are limited to a desire to reintegrate disadvantaged people into the market economy without questioning why it is exclusionary. In this way, integration is turned into an individual responsibility by improving employability. In the second case, the integration process is linked to the possibility of creating relevant jobs in fields of activity corresponding to social and environmental needs, in line with a civil society–based approach to service provision.

These initiatives are similar to those mentioned earlier because they propose a new way of thinking about services. Their initiators argue that the creation of a market cannot be considered the sole solution to providing services—even that it would be less a solution than a problem where services involve caring for others and intergenerational relations. By advocating associative and cooperative forms, they are calling for a conception of services that does not turn them into yet another object of consumption, but rather a means of strengthening "*le vivre ensemble*" ("living together"). Despite their differences, some of the constitutive elements of the popular economy described above for countries of the South also exist in solidarity-based services in the North. In both contexts, initiatives do not have the sole aim of creating employment; rather, this is just part of the quest for what they see as a sustainable social model.

The Politics of Everyday Life or the Prioritization of Employment

The strong convergence between the contemporary popular economy in the South and solidarity-based services in the North lies in the value they place on everyday activities. While their demands are not limited to material needs alone, they do deal with fundamental aspects of the process of creating and reproducing human society. In both cases, improving everyday life is inextricably linked to respect for human rights and providing access to services. Fundamentally, solidarity-based services and the popular economy are disruptive because they challenge the separation of the private and public sectors. Their proponents are well aware that they are taking on a taboo, but they believe it is right to tackle this separation. This is, first, because it does not correspond to people's everyday experiences, and second, because it neglects the educational and mediation skills needed to successfully do the emotional work of caring for children, dependents, and the sick.[5] In both North and South, these initiatives are determined to remind us that care has traditionally been undertaken by the family, and within the family by women. They claim that, contrary to the way that the economic, political, and domestic spheres have been separated from each other and placed in a hierarchy—with men installed at the center of the first two and women confined to the third—concern for decent, humane life leads us to conclude that "it is impossible to choose not to care or not to work" (Giullari and Lewis 2005, 97–98). Care cannot be totally outsourced to the state or the market without taking into account intergenerational transmission; it cannot be instrumentalized in the name of the kind of job creation that neglects its human dimension and status as a public good. The responsibility for providing care should be shared by families, public authorities, the market and civil society, and family responsibilities should be shared by men and women, ensuring that they have equal opportunities in the labor market. This sharing should be discussed openly in a society with an actively engaged citizenry, where questions of policy are also issues that affect everyday life and gender relations.[6] In this way, the ethics of care (Brugère 2011) refuses to treat the issue of employment in isolation and situates care services within an approach to human vulnerability, considering social policies as "a critical resource in an alternative vision" and not as "a key element of the economic market" (Le Blanc 2011, 194–95).

However, these issues elude many officials who are obsessed with cost-cutting, which they see as the only way to create large-scale employment. In this way, a service society can mutate into a society of servants.[7] When public policymaking is driven by media hype about the number of new jobs created while neglecting the quality of employment, it can lead to the multiplication of demeaning jobs and the weakening of social ties. There is a prevailing obsession with cutting the cost of creating new jobs, whether by lowering taxes or giving out service vouchers to households. Supported by the spread of a discourse focused on the economy, the reform of welfare states has resulted in a consumerist approach in which priority is given to the client's individual freedom. The private sector has provided an alternative in the more profitable niches, particularly in the area of elderly care. In addition, organizations that mix together private and public, private for-profit and private nonprofit, have emerged to meet the new demands of a society in which, according to the European Commission (2010), competition, solidarity and public interest are all in play. The desire to promote rational choice also affects the beneficiaries of integration via the use of the notion of workfare or quid pro quo. Recipients must be held responsible and have to prove they are trying to find work if they want to continue receiving benefits in a welfare state that is now described as "active." The objective is to reduce the budgetary burden of expenditure and introduce market incentives into welfare systems. On the one hand, private-sector management methods are imported into the public or parapublic sector through what is commonly referred to as the "new public management," a logical extension of the neoliberal project. This increases control over results and budgets and develops performance indicators. On the other hand, services are further commodified as the outsourcing of the domestic sphere is equated with the construction of a market,[8] which has been achieved in France through the shift from solidarity-based services to personal care services.[9]

As a result, associations have had to deal with the opportunities and constraints of the market. Their innovative contribution is dwindling under the pressure of managerial and professional rationalization. By promoting individual well-being in the home, personal care services exclude many other solidarity-based services from their scope, such as intercultural women's restaurants, self-production, and art initiatives (Devettre, Jany-Catrice, and Ribault 2009). It is against this threat to their existence that grassroots organizations committed to a solidarity-based approach to service provision have continued to mobilize.

Fair Trade

Solidarity-based services can therefore be understood as an element of the popular economy that is specific to the service society; they are part of the already long history of local initiatives. The emergence of initiatives that bring together North and South, meanwhile, is more recent.

As we saw in the first chapter, the countries of the South dominated by oligarchies linked to the elites of the North have, for centuries, opted for a mode of development that relies on exporting raw materials and agricultural products. In the 1990s, the price of these commodities increased at a slower rate than those of industrial products in the North. Opening up trade without binding social and environmental standards being incorporated into international legislation—along with the austerity policies in force in the majority of countries—had an impact on hundreds of millions of small farmers worldwide. Roughly 795 million people suffered from hunger and malnutrition and more than 3 million children died every year. This phenomenon was amplified by a selective reduction in public interventions. Maintaining high subsidies allowed rich countries to export at such low prices that they led to the disappearance of local production,[10] while in the North technical requirements were erected as customs barriers against imports from the South. Indeed, countries' negotiating powers were unequal and multinationals interfered in international agreements by controlling half of world production and two-thirds of world trade. According to the United Nations Development Program, 82 percent of international trade is controlled by countries that are home to one fifth of the global population, while the countries that are home to the poorest fifth control just over 1 percent. The countries of the South account for 30 percent of international trade in goods, and the figures are lower still for financial transactions and services. Fair trade was set up to fight these injustices endorsed by international institutions. It seeks to place trade relations within a framework that protects both producers and the environment. The definition given by activists is the following: fair trade organizations, backed by consumers, are engaged actively in supporting producers, awareness raising, and in campaigning for changes in the rules and practice of conventional international trade.[11]

Fair trade emerged from an encounter between representatives of the South—who were calling for development aid to be converted into "fair" trade practices; environmental associations from the North; and human rights nongovernmental organizations. To continue with the definition given by the activists themselves: trading partnerships based on dialogue, transparency, and respect, that seek greater equity in international trade. It contributes to sustainable development by offering better trading conditions to and securing the rights of marginalized producers and workers, especially in the South.[12]

Fair trade amounted to more than €5.5 billion in 2012, up from €1 billion in 2003. It has helped improve the lives of 5 million people, of which 2 million are producers. It is also experiencing a boom. In France in 2014, total sales were estimated at €499 million, an increase of 29 percent compared to 2012. The concept is familiar to 97 percent of French people, 94 percent of whom have a positive view of it. However, their average spending on fair trade products is a mere €7.50 a year. Of this, 80 percent goes to food products, 13 percent to cosmetics, and 4 percent to textiles.[13]

From Producer to Consumer

The first form free trade took was the direct sale of artisanal and agricultural products from the South through worldshops. These were started in the Netherlands in 1969 by associations and cooperatives, mainly in the international solidarity sphere. There are now more than 3,500 worldshops in eighteen European countries, managed by 60,000 volunteers and 4,000 employees. Since 2000, they have grown at a rate of 20 percent per year, but national disparities remain high—for example, turnover in Holland is 500 times higher than in France. Products are imported by alternative trading organizations. The first of these purchasing groups was created by Oxfam in 1964, and there are now more than 100 of them, eleven of which—based in nine different countries—are members of the European Fair Trade Association (EFTA), created in 1990. EFTA imports fair trade products into Europe from 370 producer groups in the South, with sales of €184 million in 2015. Its role is to ensure compliance with criteria in purchasing and relations with producers. EFTA achieves this by establishing sustainable relationships and prefinancing production; limiting speculative intermediaries; monitoring production conditions; supporting local development projects; providing information on how the global market works; and paying a "fair price" that takes into account costs and guarantees a "reasonable" standard of living. Fifteen federations of worldshops from thirteen countries have been part of the Network of European Worldshops (NEWS!) since 1994. Their aim is to harmonize and help coordinate progress across the thirteen countries, as well as to organize European awareness-raising campaigns targeted at consumers and public bodies alike. Since 2008, this network has been the European branch of the World Fair Trade Organization (WFTO).

Certification Processes

In 1988, once again in the Netherlands, the Max Havelaar movement was born as a way of expanding the market for fair trade goods. Its objective, which spread to a number of countries including France, was to set up a labeling system to guarantee that products complied with fair trade standards. This system is in fact a form of certification: under French law the label means that each product has been validated by an independent monitoring body and officially approved by the public authorities. There are sixteen national associations in Europe, North America, and Japan. In 1997, they set up Fair Trade Labelling Organizations International (FLO International), with the aim of harmonizing standards by product type, helping to strengthen producer organizations, and facilitating market access for their products. FLO International covered nine sectors: coffee, tea, cocoa, sugar, rice, honey, fresh fruit, fruit juices, and footballs. Involving 357 producer organizations, these products were sold in 70,000 sales outlets, including 50 of the main supermarket chains and 33,000 smaller supermarkets. In 2004, it was split into Fairtrade International, which sets standards and supports producers, and FLO-CERT, which carries out audits for certification.

The approaches thus vary depending on whether the producers go down the route of direct sales or certification. They reflect different strategies for engaging consumers. Importer-distributors, including the worldshops, are primarily a response to trading practices in which the producer and consumer know nothing about each other. The focus is on restoring the human, cultural dimension of the exchange by enabling buyers to understand more about the conditions involved in making the product that they are purchasing. Anonymity should, according to this strategy, be replaced by a personalization that allows the reality of people's lives in the South to be understood by consumers in the North. For certification bodies, the priority is to avoid limiting themselves to activist shoppers, raising wider public awareness of fair trade by making such goods available in as many sales outlets as possible, which entails negotiating with supermarkets. The key aim is to increase sales so that more and more producers are able to reap the financial benefits.

Strains and Diversification

These approaches are coming under increasing strain, with several stakeholders rejecting the move to large retailers because they believe their attitudes to suppliers and employees go against the values that underpin fair trade. This is reflected in the words of the head of Minga, who believes "fair trade in large retailers" is a "trick." According to him, "the criteria of solidarity, political and economic sovereignty (particularly in terms of food), democratic means of knowledge, production and distribution, and respect for our environment are essential. Price is just one of many criteria, including transparency, which is vital to build trust, and, above all, a democratic and permanent fundamental debate, genuine popular self-education, but also discussions on how to improve our approaches and practices, and self-regulation by citizens" (Besson 2008; 2014, 17–35). Alongside the Confederation Paysanne and some forty other organizations in France, Minga opposed a 2006 bill that seeks to limit fair trade to the exchange of goods and services between developed countries and disadvantaged producers located in developing countries. They saw this as reeking of paternalism and as focusing on volume at the expense of building a true social movement. These organizations refuse to work with large retailers, in agreement with networks like Artisans du Monde and the Association de Solidarité avec les Peuples d'Amerique Latine.

On the one hand there are international networks such as the International Federation for Alternative Trade, founded in 1989, which brought together 370 organizations from 70 countries (including FLO, IFAT, NEWS !, and EFTA), and later became the WFTO. They tackle what they consider to be the common concerns of all the fair trade organizations that they represent. They challenge the unequal weighting of countries in the World Trade Organization as it currently operates, as well as the subordination of social and environmental rights to economic rights. They also oppose the systematic opening up of markets at the expense of food sovereignty. Alliances have been formed with trade unions and consumer associations[14] to challenge companies about their social practices as well as those of their subcontractors, focusing on respect for "decent" working conditions in accordance with the International Labor Organization's standards. There are also campaigns to influence national and international legislation. The creation of platforms bringing together nongovernmental organizations, international solidarity collectives, and trade unions is a means of amplifying awareness campaigns and promoting broader reform movements. An example of this in France is the Plate-Forme pour le Commerce Equitable, established in 1997.

On the other hand, in order to avoid reproducing the conventional trade pattern in which the countries of the South are merely suppliers for the North, there are networks where farmers can help to define criteria and set prices, and networks that analyze marketing channels to help implement forms of public regulation under the control of both public authorities and local civil society organizations (see Auroi and Yépez del Castillo 2006). From this point of view, fair trade—which was designed on the basis of a critique of North–South relations—is expanding to include South–South and North–North networks. Activists' main concern is to reduce the environmental costs associated with long-distance transport and to move toward a more self-sufficient economy at regional or subregional level. A model such as that of the Associations pour le Maintien d'une Agriculture Paysanne (AMAP) in France illustrates the emergence of North–North networks: a group of consumers enters into a contract with a farmer, purchasing their produce at a mutually agreed price sufficiently far in advance to ensure that risks (e.g. of crop failure) are shared. Consumers regularly meet with the producer to collect fresh, natural food, and a committee of volunteers ensures the association runs smoothly. This new model, which is like a form of local fair trade, is also being adopted in Latin America, as evidenced by the Latin American conference on fair trade and ethical consumption held in Lima in 2001, whose focus was global solidarity. Among the successes highlighted at this meeting was the Latin American Network of Community-Based Marketing (RELACC), which includes twelve countries. Its objective is to promote increased national trade while cutting out intermediaries so that the mainly indigenous, rural producers receive a better price for their goods, and consumers have access to essential products at a controlled price. In Peru, more than 3,000 cooperative restaurants are supplied in this way. The label *Comercio Justo Mexico* is another example of how South–South trading is promoted through commercialization in national markets.

As this diversification shows, fair trade has been spectacularly successful since the 1990s, almost to the point of implosion. For some, the growth in sales reflects consumers' increasing awareness of their power. Others insist that international campaigns to defend workers' rights in both the South and North are more important than the volume of transactions. Campaigns to raise awareness are just as important as fair trade itself, which must reach a threshold that is sufficient to question the realities of global trade without losing its distinctiveness.[15] Despite these differences, fair trade's impact is undeniable and is not limited to its original spheres of activity. The questions it asks are multiplied by those raised from the perspective of responsible, solidarity-based consumption.[16] They are transposed into other areas by solidarity and fair-trade tourism networks (see Collombson, Barlet, and Ribier 2004). In France, members of the fair trade platforms Tourisme et Développement Solidaires, Route des Sens, Croq'Nature, and Djembé have drawn up a charter based on the principles of agreeing to joint, long-term contracts with host communities, transparency of transactions, concern for local development, and remaining attentive to the risks of disrupting social, cultural, and ecological equilibria.

This example of tourism shows how a movement that began with trade is now expanding to other areas. In conjunction with other movements, fair trade helps challenge what has become free-trade dogma, and the same applies to microfinance and complementary currencies.

Microfinance and Complementary Currencies

While the fair trade movement is protesting against the growing marginalization of small producers, alternative financing methods are seeking to remedy the exclusion of many entrepreneurs from the banking system. This is no coincidence but rather a response to the same process of deregulation.

Access to Credit

Microfinance aims to "offer financial services that respond to the needs of the large number of people who live on the fringes of 'formal' finance, or who have only very limited access to it," and "it has grown exponentially since the 1990s across almost the entire planet; a 36% annual increase in the number of clients or members of the organizations involved is cited for the period 1997–2004."[17] In the South, solidarity microfinance is characterized by the type of entities supported, activities carried out, and resources mobilized. It is available to collective businesses as well as to initiatives with a social or environmental goal. Along with loans, it provides other services (guarantees, venture capital, insurance) and invests time in following up on projects. It arranges a savings scheme with input from public funds in which subscribers can voluntarily waive a portion of their remuneration. In short, it embeds financial interventions in a socialization process that distinguishes them from private banks caught in the spiral of virtual exchanges. On this basis, solidarity microfinance has spread to the countries of the North. In Europe, for example, the European Federation of Ethical and Alternative Banks (FEBEA) has brought together institutions from eleven European countries since 2001. It promotes savings and investment by negotiating favorable tax arrangements. One of its members is the

Banca Popolare Etica in Italy, which provides an opportunity for savers who are looking for "more responsible and conscious management of their money" to finance social and economic initiatives that subscribe to the principles of a sustainable human and social development model. When depositing their money, savers can choose the areas that they would like to invest in: social and health services and education; combating social exclusion; preserving the environment and cultural goods; development cooperation and international aid; fair trade; and well-being, sport for all, and cultural initiatives. The International Association of Investors in the Social Economy (INAISE) is a network of organizations in twenty-nine countries whose objective is to finance social and environmental projects.

The current movement is reviving the idea of popular credit (see Richez-Battesti, Gianfaldoni, Gloukoviezoff, Alacaras 2006), which was introduced to France in the mid-nineteenth century with Proudhon's proposed Bank of Exchange; in Germany with the Raffeisen mutual agricultural credit union and the Schulze-Delitzsch popular bank; and then in the United Kingdom with the credit unions. It is doing so through a return to the original objectives of former cooperative and mutual banks,[18] and through new operators. An example of the first type of case is the Cooperative Bank in the United Kingdom. Founded in 1872, it seemed doomed to inevitable decline in 1990 when, to the surprise of the cooperative movement itself, it renamed itself an "ethical bank" and drew on this new assumed status to overcome an attempt at demutualization (Taylor 2004, 134, citing Yeo 2001). Examples of the second type of case are those institutions in France that intervene through equity participation and loans (Alcolea-Bureth 2004, 245–92). At regional level these include Femu Qui in Corsica and Herrikoa in the French Basque Country, and at national level there is the Nouvelle Economie Fraternelle (NEF) and the Clubs d'Investisseurs pour une Gestion Alternative et Locale de l'Epargne (CIGALES). In 2014, CIGALES comprised 251 active clubs with a total of 3,133 members. It supported 120 enterprises, creating and financing 200 jobs with ongoing investment of €2.2 million. When it comes to local and solidarity venture capital, it brings together 7,000 shareholders providing around €6 million and is involved with a total of 650 companies. Since 1995, the Finansol association—whose focus is "solidarity-based finance"—has brought lesser-known initiatives to the attention of a wider public. Despite their heterogeneity, Finansol's initiatives mainly see themselves as entities that, in order to combat polarization between rich and poor, cannot be confined to individual aid and need to support the social networks that protect the weakest members of society and their collective activities.

An Economy without Money

This idea that money can serve to build community networks[19] extends to the exchange of goods, services, and knowledge organized on the basis of complementary currencies. According to Blanc, these exchanges have the characteristic of being civic—either in the sense that they are community oriented, when they are guided by reciprocity without being exchangeable into the national currency, or commercially oriented, when they are exchange-oriented and convertible.[20] The objective here is no longer the democratization of access to the official currency but rather the creation of a unit of account among members of the same association. Complementary currencies are issued by a group of citizens who choose a name for them. The aim is to build interpersonal relationships by creating spaces of trust where the rules governing them are debated, thus enhancing local capacities. The general idea is to replace contractual exchange based on individual independence with a community network that brings people together and provides a space for multilateral exchanges. These exchanges build ties between members that continue after the transaction, encouraging collaborations to be renewed.[21] Complementary currencies do not preexist trade itself. They are drawing rights, and their circulation is encouraged in order to prevent hoarding, for example when they take the form of "melting" currencies—that is, currencies whose accumulation and retention is penalized because their value regularly depreciates.

Complementary currencies have had predecessors. One of the most famous was set up in Austria in the 1930s, when a local currency was established to combat the economic depression. It was quickly outlawed by the Central Bank. Local currencies also existed in the 1950s in France and Brazil, but today their expansion is more striking. Data is sparse but suggests that Local Exchange Trading Systems (LETS), first established in 1983, have in excess of 1.5 million members in more than 2,500 associations across 30 countries, mainly in Europe, Latin America, and Japan.

In some systems, such as Italy's time banks, France's Systèmes d'Echanges Locaux (SEL), and Germany's Tauschringe, the unit has no equivalence with the national currency, as the aim is to promote a system based on voluntary contributions. Returning to a key idea from the first half of the nineteenth century that was implemented via Owen's fair labor markets, they transfer all value created straight back to workers with no deductions of any kind. In this system of time-based banking, the relevant unit of measurement is the length of time spent on the activity. For the system to keep functioning, people must regularly take part in its activities. In order to encourage these egalitarian and participatory relationships, the encounters and sense of fun that they engender are maintained through the evocative names given to the currency units and attendance at exchange markets. The LETS systems used in English-speaking countries such as Australia, Canada, New Zealand, and the United Kingdom have a somewhat different purpose. Like solidarity finance, their main aim is tackling the exclusion induced by traditional financial systems, and they focus on promoting payment methods that counter the restrictions of the money supply. It thus makes sense to ensure that the complementary currency is partially convertible into national currency, and to provide opportunities for inter-LETS exchanges. These systems are less about promoting fundamentally different practices than about reintegrating certain sections of the population into the economic mainstream.[22]

Self-production and Reciprocal Exchanges

The rapid expansion of all the LETS schemes fueled optimism that they would bring about a spontaneous mutual assistance economy. In 2002, Argentina's schemes had more than 5 million members, but the boom was short-lived and finally collapsed. However, apart from this particular example, the typical cycle is less irregular. After an initial boom it usually plateaus, as was the case in France, where the number of SELs stopped growing in 1998 and fell slightly to around 315 per 30,000 members in 2000. Reality has replaced the dream of a new model of trade that will transform society with a more modest capacity for intervention[23] that helps legitimize initiatives in the economy without reference to their ownership of capital. In this respect, LETS are similar to other schemes that free themselves from using the official currency in the exchanges they encourage. Two examples can be cited in French-speaking countries. The first is that of the supported self-production networks that are beginning to group together: neighborhood workshops, community kitchens, allotment gardens, self-renovation and self-construction of housing, leisure activities, repairs, etc.[24] The forms of support they involve can be quite diverse and so the connections between them do not form immediately, but they are all instances of self-production in the sense that the people involved are carrying out activities intended to produce goods and services for their own and their immediate circle's consumption.[25] The second example is that of longer-established networks that have formed a social movement over several years: networks for the reciprocal exchange of knowledge. Each network aims to connect people who are seeking all kinds of knowledge with those who can provide it, through nonhierarchical relations. These forms of knowledge might include: "functional knowledge (knowing how to fill out forms), classical knowledge (literature, musical instruments), and know-how (using computer software, cooking, gardening)" (Héber-Suffrin 1992, 417). In these two examples, as in the LETS schemes, the associative framework is conceived as an "attempt to constantly restore balance, to align economic activity with equality in a constructive cognitive tension" (Héber-Suffrin 1998, 214).

The popular economy, solidarity-based services, fair trade, microfinance, and complementary currencies—the kinship between all these examples is confirmed by the existence of multidimensional initiatives that draw on these different forms. For example, Villa el Salvador in Peru—a slum of 350,000 inhabitants near Lima—is a self-managed community that in 1987 worked with the national government to create an industrial park. This development center for the popular economy provides financing, training, help with marketing, and technical assistance, and has generated 30,000 jobs in 8,000 small businesses. In Brazil, the inhabitants of the Palmeiras housing complex—which lies in a favela on the outskirts of Fortaleza—set up an association that has become famous under the name of its popular bank, Palmas. It supports crafts, tailoring, and the manufacture of leather goods and cleaning equipment, along with a tourism agency. This large neighborhood makes use of solidarity finance, a complementary currency, and fair trade, in the form of a store where local producers can display and sell their wares. This success has spread through a federation of community banks representing complementary currencies that, when combined with other tools such as microfinance, have an impact on local development—an impact strengthened by the fact that the scope of these currencies is decided locally through discussions in the neighborhood or village.[26] In the United States and Canada, community economic development can involve a diverse range of activities. Eighty percent of local initiatives combine advocacy activities with forms of mediation, as well as the creation of social services and businesses.[27] Despite unfavorable conditions under conservative federal administrations, these efforts have continued with the support of local and state authorities. Thus, in the United States, since the 1983 election of a mayor supported by a popular coalition, the city of Chicago has supported some famous examples of collective action such as Chicago Works Together and the Greater Southwest Development Corporation. In all these cases, in both the South and the North, economic rules are established with the participation of people who have no voice when the economy is dominated by the power plays and maneuverings of large multinationals.

Although they operate in different fields, the examples just mentioned have many common characteristics. These have emerged gradually during two crises—the crisis of values and the economic crisis—whose combined effects have been discussed.

The first wave of solidarity introduced demands for direct participation, whether by workers or service users; their voice thus became an important supplement to that of their representatives. From the 1960s onward, huge changes in people's lifestyles resulted in collective action focused on a politics of everyday life—a politics concerned with protecting the environment, criticizing users' lack of involvement in designing the services that affected them, and critically reflecting on gender and intergenerational relations. The way in which people engaged in the public sphere also changed. While volunteering in the most institutionalized associations saw a downturn, another type of associative activity flourished—one that that combined social cooperation, mutual aid, and protest.

The second wave of solidarity was more pragmatic. Although the pressures exerted by the welfare state's budgetary constraints were partly responsible for the initiation of new activities, the involvement of civil society actors was also linked to the promotion of forms of active citizenship.

The initiatives born by these two waves thus combine the aspiration for a more humane society with a response to everyday problems. Their search for meaning attests to the crisis of values expressed at the end of the 1960s, and their empirical approach reflects the way they internalized the austerity that resulted from the subsequent economic crisis. This dual ancestry is reflected in their reference to general values that are connected to the desire to solve concrete problems in a given field.

{ 6 }

In the Face of Crises

Initiatives that raise political questions about the economy are reminiscent of those from the pioneering period mentioned in part 1. And it is notions of democratic and economic solidarity that are re-emerging at the heart of a renewed associationalism. Here we will examine this largely ignored phenomenon. Once we have done this, we will be able to return to the surprising gap between the vitality of the various associationalist initiatives we have discussed and the widely held view, highlighted at the start of chapter 4, that associationalism is in decline.

In reality, the associationalism mentioned above finds itself caught between two traps. On the one hand, it has come to be seen in ways that accentuate its role in transforming public action,[1] and on the other it collides with an institutional framework that is largely unfavorable because it fails to acknowledge civil society. For example, associations trying to reduce inequalities, which have their roots in the two crises mentioned earlier, one of values and the other of the economy, have thus been confronted with repeated attempts to bring them into conformity with existing norms. The situation is disrupted by a further, third crisis: a systemic crisis of the new capitalism, which is based on maximizing shareholder value. This form of capitalism has benefited from both the liberalization and deregulation of capital markets and reforms to accounting and corporate governance. It has drawn its strength of conviction from an ideological offensive that turned these developments into an inevitable trend, a forced adaptation to a rational and hence indisputable economic order. This strategy of the inevitable—already weakened by the "antiglobalization movements" (Wieviorka 2003; Pleyers 2010)—becomes untenable when its proponents appeal for state aid. It is no longer possible to downplay the social fragmentation it has caused. The one-sided contractual vision of business, as well as the alignment of executives' interests with those of shareholders through their remuneration and management methods, have led to a more marked separation between these privileged groups and others who, quite literally, no longer belong to the same world. Barriers have also been created between a core group of workers in protected jobs—even if they are subject to wage flexibility—and precarious or unemployed workers.[2]

There is thus a growing and increasingly obvious dissociation between the objectives set by economic decision makers and social and environmental demands. This is the source of a discourse seeking to reduce this gap and mitigate the economy's excesses (Aglietta and Rébérioux 2004) by calling for capitalism to be reconstituted or moralized. It is a discourse that has an impact on associations, which are now being asked to act as auxiliaries to companies seeking to regain their legitimacy. With this comes a new phase of associations' cooptation, which leads to the following question: Are we seeing an associationalist invention or associative instrumentalization? It all depends on whether we focus on the most innovative associative initiatives or whether we look at the trajectory of the most institutionalized associations. Is there renewed autonomy or increased dependency? In fact, these two scenarios exist side-by-side. The internal divisions within associations thus shed more light on the current situation than any overall judgment about associations as a whole. Associations' contemporary ambiguities are due to this contrast between a reaffirmation of democratic associationalism, on the one hand, and a cooptation of associations that is even more extensive than in previous periods, on the other. That is why this chapter ends by considering a paradox specific to associations, stressing both their fragility and their importance for the future.

Associations and Public Action

The associationalism described in the first chapter showed that not all economic activities were subject to the authority of capital, and that they could be based on a collective construction by the actors affected—whether as producers or consumers. But since the end of the nineteenth century, the footprint of this type of associationalism has become fainter. At a time when it seemed almost to have been erased, however, a new wave of associationalism is reviving this desire to democratize society translated into economic terms. In particular, this wave introduces greater attention to the nature of its protagonists' activity. While the initiatives described in part 1 were more structured around meeting the needs of a particular group, many of the more recent ones have focused on selecting projects with broader solidarity-based objectives. Work collectives dedicated to renewable energy and organic agriculture; fair trade networks that address the marginalization of small producers in the South; solidarity finance organizations that provide loans to people excluded from conventional banking; and users of complementary currencies who trade "without money"—all of these initiatives are looking beyond their individual concerns to society as a whole. This even applies to some cooperative actors who have taken over companies, such as arms manufacturers, and diverted them to other uses.[3]

The idea of an alternative system may have faded, but the desire to contribute to the common good has thus been maintained and affirmed. It is expressed in collective services that benefit everyone, such as those concerned with protecting the environment. It is also found in services that can be described as quasi-collective in the sense that they have the deliberate aim of reducing inequality. Although they are individual to the extent that they are directed at people, these services—which range from the global (fair trade) to the local (solidarity finance)—nonetheless have benefits for the community in terms of strengthening social cohesion. They are trying to incorporate the qualitative dimensions of well-being, which are ignored in the quantitative approach to growth. Some initiatives that have retained traces of their alternative roots advocate degrowth; others are less intransigent and invoke sustainable development to mean an improvement in quality of life rather than simply an increase in standard of living. But the differences between degrowth and development should not be overestimated. Whichever way they lean, the associations mentioned in the previous chapter are united by the objective of horizontal solidarity—fighting injustice—and vertical solidarity—protecting future generations. They are thus reconnecting with their initial impulse toward solidarity. And they are expanding on it by aligning themselves with the sustainable development priorities set out in the Brundtland report, which emphasized a dual solidarity—both within the same generation and between generations.

Notwithstanding the differences between degrowth and sustainable development,[4] local and global initiatives agree on how to combine means and ends. Their solidarity-based goals result from the public engagement of those involved. Production not only serves the collective interests of a group, it is determined by interaction between people who are voluntarily involved in what may be defined as a micro–public sphere (see Eme and Laville 1994; Gardin and Laville 2007, 77–104). In this respect, the initiatives are not merely businesses; they are involved in a form of public action that provides a place for civil society initiatives.

From the Alternative Movement to a Desire for Institutional Change

The trajectory of local, community-based initiatives is a good example of this. Participants occupying different positions (users, employees, volunteers) come together to devise the service, thus jointly constructing supply and demand. French childcare initiatives in particular exemplify this approach while at the same time illustrating the shift from alternativism toward public policy. The first projects were part of an alternativist imaginary. After 1968, the *crèches sauvages* movement that began in Paris spread across France and to other countries such as Germany, leading to the establishment of Berlin's kindergartens. The *crèches sauvages,* nurseries set up and run by parents, took a countercultural, antiestablishment stance, rejecting public childcare centers and the grip of institutions that they considered conduits for the dominant ideology. "The longing for independence and the desire to be able to freely develop the search for a new pedagogical and relational expression kept existing groups away from public institutions that, it was felt, were necessarily exercising a power of control and normalization." In these parent-run childcare centers, the dark side of alternativism was unexpectedly revealed: a lack of resources, isolation, the precariousness of actions, a fast turnover of volunteers, and a high ratio of responsibility with respect to the rewards garnered from the experience. Exhaustion led many initiatives to disappear, but their power lay beyond these abandonments, in their ability to constrain and contextualize their initial utopia without renouncing it. Since their objective was only to launch services in a limited area, experiments in community living—some of which had resulted in interpersonal clashes as the planned transformations failed to materialize—found it easier to reorient themselves in this way. In short, utopia was the catalyst for a movement that each project strongly tempered with realism as it evolved. This development was then amplified by the economic crisis, which foregrounded issues such as how to create jobs and maintain collective services accessible to all.[5]

The vision of commitment that accompanied alternativism was so demanding that it restricted action to a very militant minority. Reducing this demand has not just been an act of renunciation; it has also been an opportunity to broaden the scope of the groups behind the initiatives. The evolution of childcare facilities has been characterized by two main trends. The first is an increase in the diversity of those initiating projects. Users have been joined by professionals who want to create their own jobs, and even local authorities and institutions. The second is an increase in the number of people concerned. The parental movement has diversified from its urban roots. By opening itself up to professionals, it has become more adaptable. Doing so has enabled it to offer part-time childcare services and to establish itself in rural areas and disadvantaged neighborhoods. With these expansions, the alternativist ambition is gradually making way for intervention by public bodies. In Europe, forms of multilateral local governance combining public and associative dimensions are multiplying. From this point of view, alternativist innovations have done a great deal to promote a debate about different childcare options (see Fraisse, Lhuillier, and Petrella 2007). They were the first to raise the issue of inequality between social groups and genders.

The way in which childcare is organized is closely connected to how society views gender roles. Services have an impact on people's lifestyles, and the community has an influence on the way that seemingly very personal choices are made. That is why the protagonists in these initiatives, who initially claimed to be rooted in a counterculture, have gradually put pressure on the public authorities to intervene in funding for early childhood care. This is for reasons of social justice—including the desire to make this service accessible to as many people as possible and monitor service quality—and for externality related reasons, linked specifically to the benefits derived by the community as a whole—such as an increase in the number of women in the labor market, or the educational and preventive role played by childcare facilities (see Fraisse, Gardin, and Laville 2000).

In this respect, childcare illustrates the journey taken by these services, which began by criticizing institutions but then sought to join forces with them. The challenge faced by initiatives and their representatives is learning how to develop institutional formats that take into account the collective benefits generated by certain services while respecting the criteria of social justice and equality in the workplace. Caught between general and individual interests, the challenge is to define the criteria of social utility that would both confer a right to public funding, on the one hand, and be the subject of civic negotiation, on the other—extending collective bargaining to associative partners and local authorities. However, instigating such negotiation about social utility depends on two basic conditions: favorable legislation and the establishment of criteria for allocating public funds.

Social Cooperatives and Social Enterprises

Different types of status have been enshrined in legislation. In 1991, the status of social cooperative was given legal foundation in Italy. Two types of social cooperative were identified: service cooperatives (whether social, health, or education cooperatives) and integration cooperatives (which sought to reintegrate disabled or disadvantaged workers). This Italian model has produced some spectacular results, generating 300,000 new jobs in the 1990s, and has been emulated by other countries. In Spain, three regional laws provide for social cooperatives: in 1983 Catalonia adopted a law on mixed social integration cooperatives, followed in 1985 by the Valencia region, and in 1993 the Basque Country. At the national level, a 1999 law introduced social cooperatives that could manage public-interest services and public social services. In Portugal, social solidarity cooperatives were recognized by a law passed in 1996 and fleshed out in 1998. Their aim is to support "vulnerable" groups (children, the elderly, and the disabled), families, and disadvantaged communities. Full members who are beneficiaries of the services are distinguished from voluntary members who contribute unpaid goods or services. In 1999, a status of social cooperative with limited liability was developed; the status of multiservice cooperative was also created and deployed in local development. In France, a law on collective-interest cooperative societies was adopted in 2001.

Along with these additions to the cooperative status, the notion of social enterprise made an astonishing breakthrough on both sides of the Atlantic.[6] To begin with, it had an entrepreneurial slant in the United States, since the intention among large universities (first of all the Harvard Business School, which launched the Social Enterprise Initiative in 1993, followed by Columbia and Yale), was to show that initiative and risk-taking are not the sole preserve of for-profit enterprises. It was then taken up in the United Kingdom, where the government launched a Coalition for Social Enterprise and a Social Enterprise Unit to support these companies, estimated to number 5,300 (ECOTEC 2003), before creating the status of community interest company in 2005.

The Persistent Inadequacy of the Institutional Framework

But these legal advances can have little effect if the state provides no resources. These have begun to flow in—for example for local development and employment initiatives, which have been recognized at national level in experimental social and economic policies. At European level, the Commission's White Paper on the challenges of the twenty-first century is the first to refer to these services, announcing that "some three million new jobs could be created, covering local services, improvements in the quality of life, and environmental protection" (European Commission 1993, 13). The surveys carried out by the Commission then clarified the scope of these "local services"—known as *services de proximité* in French-speaking countries, translated as "community-based services" in this book—using more consensual terminology to refer to them as "local development and employment initiatives" throughout the European Union (see Jouen 1995). Four main areas are identified (European Commission 1995): everyday services, including home-help services, child care, and new information and communication technologies; services for improving quality of life, including improved housing, security, local public transport, the redevelopment of public urban areas, local shops, and energy management; cultural and leisure services, including tourism and the broadcast media, enhancement of cultural heritage, local cultural development, and sport; and environmental services, including waste management, water management, protection and maintenance of natural areas, regulation, pollution monitoring and related facilities.[7]

After these studies, local development and employment initiatives were financed by European pilot programs on innovation and rural development (Leader Community Initiative Program); on the "third system" (Directorate-General for Employment and Social Affairs); on regional and local strategies to support local job creation; and on integrated and innovative urban regeneration and planning strategies (Article 10 of the European Regional Development Fund). In total, at least 6,000 initiatives have been supported, demonstrating how approaches were identified that had previously gone unrecognized. But this support has not led to the establishment of stable budget lines. Initiatives are often told to self-finance in order to demonstrate their efficiency. But they cannot be self-financing because they internalize social and environmental constraints that their competitors externalize. Their public funding is therefore not the result of incompetence but a recognition of their solidarity objectives.

The notion of social utility seeks to draw conclusions from this. It is a way of taking into account both desired outcomes and collective benefits through a new form of public regulation that is agreement based, that is, based on objectives agreed though negotiation between associations and public authorities. This agreement-based regulation has sometimes materialized at the subnational level amid favorable policy conditions, thanks to the strong political will of local authorities who have facilitated the co-construction of public policies (see Vaillancourt 2008). Nevertheless, despite these few advances, associations are largely limited to implementing policies in which they have had no say. Agreement-based regulation has not achieved full acceptance at national and international level. The methodological obstacles are legion. As studies of social utility have shown, what is needed are new wealth indicators that allow for appropriate modes of evaluation.[8]

The initiatives studied recompose the relationship between the social and the economic through microcollective actions. Meanwhile, the dominant macroinstitutional regulations continue to juxtapose economic policies that justify deregulation by citing international competition, on the one hand, and social policies that attempt to reduce the social fragmentation exacerbated by these economic policies, on the other. Despite the importance of sustainable development, public authorities still address the majority of economic and social issues—but also newer concerns such as the environment and participatory democracy—through specialized services. This segmentation puts the initiatives in an awkward position.

It is time to replace this old view of associations as merely the Trojan horse of state disengagement with a view grounded in the political sociology of public action (see Lascoumes and Le Galès 2007)—one that addresses the relationship between collective action and public authorities. Contrary to popular belief, the associationalist projects presented in chapter 5 are implemented by officials who insist that public policy is indispensable, but they add that its modes of intervention must be rethought when faced with initiatives that aim to democratize society. The challenge is to develop policies that support these initiatives not just at the level of their economic and social contributions but also at the political level, since they stimulate learning about public life and encourage people to speak out on everyday issues.[9] When it comes to public action, it is entirely legitimate for associationalism to join forces with public authorities to achieve its aims. It is impossible for it to succeed without positive interdependence with public authorities.

The Grip of the Past

This account of the relationship between associations and public authorities is still far from being accepted, as evidenced by the recurring accusations of unfair competition leveled at associations.[10] The fact that these suspicions lack an empirical basis does not prevent them from being raised and peddled on a regular basis. The institutional structure of associations should, conversely, encourage further reflection on their relationship with public authorities. While massive economic problems have been generated by the constraint of maximizing shareholders' return on investment, associations escape such a requirement. Admittedly, this distinctive feature is not an absolute guarantee; its impact depends on the extent to which associations' internal functioning is genuinely democratic. But it should at least lead to a thorough examination of their strengths and weaknesses.

The reason why associations continue to suffer from a poor reputation in economic terms, as well as from being constantly confined to the social domain, is not just conjunctural. Relations between public authorities and associations are very much in the grip of the past, so it is only by looking back through history that we will fully understand the current obstacles. Due to "path dependency,"[11] associations follow the modes of integration carved out by the initiatives examined in chapter 3. Observations made in different national contexts highlight the persistence of associations' involvement in public policies over which they have little influence. Rediscovering some of its historical characteristics, contemporary associationalism considers stakeholders' voice as the mechanism for settling on a common good. Yet its impact does not match its ambitions. It is confronted with a statist culture that gives public authorities a monopoly over the common good. It also faces the institutional segmentation that has separated economic and social policies, with the first focused on businesses and the second on associations.

But this institutional reticence is not the only reason for the difficulty of rehabilitating associationalism. The initiatives themselves have been preoccupied with their economic sustainability and gradually abandoned their political dimension. Lemaître's (2009) comparison between the integration initiatives in Wallonia and the popular cooperatives in the State of Rio de Janeiro illustrates this tendency. The Belgian social enterprises that now implement policies for tackling unemployment are no longer able to challenge public authorities. Meanwhile the Brazilian entities may be economically fragile, but they remain spaces for public engagement that improves the lives of their members. In Europe, this frequent "ideological anorexia" (Mothé 1982) among actors—even though some have their roots in the alternative movement—has become a sign of the resignation that has followed in the wake of what were sometimes exaggerated hopes. It is the main reason for the advance of managerial ideology in many initiatives. This advance is also noticeable in cooperatives resulting from takeovers in Europe, but less so in South America, where the prospect of self-management has retained its appeal. The question that arises from these initiatives in South America relates more to the way in which their initial objectives, which are often anticapitalist, can be measured up against their practices. If the political is at risk of becoming overdeveloped in South America, in Europe the concern is more that the political may be forgotten. Despite these potential wayward drifts, some progress can be discerned on both sides of the Atlantic.

In South America, the popular economy is providing the basis for a new generation of socioeconomic policies. Faced with the limits of assistance intended only to curb poverty, these social development policies operate by investing in domestic units. Their aim is to strengthen households' capacity for action and to integrate them into a more inclusive economic system, increasing their resources and encouraging their participation (Coraggio 1998, 131–39).

In North America, Quebec's aptitude for experimentation—acquired through its mix of cultures and its welfare state inspired by continental Europe—has led it to introduce a new generation of public service in childcare based on associative networks. This development emerged after a long journey of more than three decades, which resulted in public funding for "a universal service controlled by citizens, in this case parents in liaison with staff" (Levesque 2015, 294)—although it remains at the mercy of political changes. Many associative practices arise outside the ambit of any public directive and even reveal public problems by constituting public arenas (Cefaï 2007, 711–16). But this particular example goes further, toward public action developed by hybrid state–civil-society initiatives. The models of agreement-based regulation (Laville and Sainsaulieu 2013, 81–83)—i.e., regulation based on the negotiation of shared objectives—and the co-construction of public policies (Vaillancourt 2015)—i.e., the participation of civil-society stakeholders in shaping policies—have been proposed as ways to understand how this dialogue, which is reorientating public policy, is being conducted.

This has happened in Europe with policies to improve early childhood care in Vienna (Leuchsenring 1997) and Sweden (Pestoff 1998), with social development policies in Denmark,[12] and with policies to promote solidarity-based services in the Nord-Pas-de-Calais region in France (Gardin, Laville, and Roussel 2005, 259–83).

These "prototype" policies are more prevalent at the sectoral, local, and regional level, as mesoeconomic spaces are better suited to changing macroeconomic institutional forms. At these levels, elements of civil society can, according to Mendell, promote "'hybrid' institutional subsystems, thereby constituting instituted processes of economic democratization" (2013, 165).

Associationalism's main challenge is to avoid being absorbed into forms of associative cooptation, as described in chapter 3, especially as these have produced effects that are still being felt today. Despite mesoinstitutional innovations, associations remain largely victims of the belief that they only deal in compensatory social benefits. This devaluation has increased since the 1980s with the drive toward a society in which the predilection for the market organizes the whole economy and requires social services to be restructured. In short, despite the existence of prototype policies, associations are still largely confined to merely complying with specifications or being subcontracted by public authorities. With the third crisis, which reached the heart of the economic system, we even find a conflict similar to that described in chapter 2 in the transition from the creation to the differentiation of associations: the rise of associations based on democratic solidarity is met by a capitalist adaptation coupled with an appeal to solidarity in its philanthropic sense. In other words, as in the nineteenth century, we cannot leave the capitalist response out of the equation. A new phase of associative cooptation—one whose characteristics still need to be defined—coexists alongside the revival of associationalism as described above.

Associations and the New Capitalism

The first part of this book showed how two worldviews came into conflict: on the one hand, a desire to infuse both society itself and its economic practices with social relations governed by the principle of democratic equality; and on the other, a tendency to consider the human subject as a "calculating machine," according to Mauss (2001, 272), i.e. a rational and opportunistic individual with an innate propensity for exchange. In the first view, the political order prevails and regulates the economy; conflicts over legitimacy take place in public spheres that are autonomous from financial and commercial powers. In the second view, the economic order subordinates the political; optimal production is achieved in enterprises, which according to their capitalist definition are economic units for generating profit. Meanwhile collective well-being is achieved thanks to equilibria between supply and demand on the market.

This conflict softened during the twentieth century, particularly between 1945 and 1975, but it regained strength at the turn of the twenty-first century. We are now far from the congruence between market capitalism and democracy that was so roundly celebrated at the end of the twentieth century. Democracy has not definitively triumphed; it remains under threat from the project of a "market society," to use Polanyi's evocative term (2008, 485–564). Neoliberalism is one episode in this tense relationship and, as an ideological project, provides a place for associations. Like in the second nineteenth century, efforts to justify capitalism rest on the connection between the market and philanthropy. It is the reconfiguration of this connection that needs to be understood in order to better identify the limits that today's associationalism is encountering.

Priority to the Competition

As seen above, neoliberalism is not so much a clear economic doctrine as a political project to limit democracy. It rests on developments in the neoclassical tradition of economics—often referred to as "monetarism"—which have taken advantage of the movement to formalize the discipline of economics and lay out its axioms.[13] We can get a better sense of neoliberalism's impact by looking at its genesis. Back in 1947, economists such as Buchanan, Becker, and Stigler—in addition to Hayek and Friedman, as mentioned earlier—took the forward-looking step of founding the Mont Pelerin Society to propagate their ideas. For many years they devoted themselves to disseminating their theories, which reaffirmed the primacy of the utility-maximizing individual and denounced state intervention. They provided a theoretical framework designed to guide the actions of governments, proposing concepts that went as far as altering the relationship between economics and politics; this was true, for example, of Hayek's economic constitution, which recommended "withdrawing the control of economic policy from political power, especially if it is democratic" (cited by Maréchal 2006, 110). Under the guise of rationalization and better management, the aim was to entrust the economy to experts by making their political opinions seem like scientific truths.

This expertism led to recommendations whose main thrust was summarized in the Washington consensus: to restore and generalize mechanisms of competition at both national and international levels; to restrict public intervention to sovereign functions; to privatize public services; and to make greater use of the market in public regulations, and private management techniques in public services. These suggestions did not go unheeded; they were widely adopted by governments. The policies emblematic of the late twentieth century placed their faith in the market to replace Fordist regulations, which were considered rigid and restrictive to growth. Under the influence of these precepts, a movement of radical derestriction and deregulation began in the 1980s.[14] International financial institutions condemned industrial and social policies as ineffective and prioritized the liberalization of trade, fiscal consolidation, and the privatization of health services. The World Bank and the International Monetary Fund gained importance, making their assistance conditional on structural adjustment programs. The resultant increase in social division, unemployment, and poverty within each country was accompanied by an increase in social inequality at the global level.

The link between growth and the reduction of inequality was broken. Just because growth increases overall incomes and improves the average standard of living in monetary terms, this does not mean that it reduces wealth gaps. As the World Commission on the Social Dimension of Globalization concluded back in 2004, wealth is being created, but too many countries and people are not sharing in its benefits. The resulting global imbalances were described by the same Commission as "morally unacceptable and politically unsustainable." For example, in the United States in 2005, 1 percent of the highest income earners accounted for more than 21 percent of national income; the situation has deteriorated significantly since 1992, when J. K. Galbraith was already denouncing the fact that 5 percent of the richest Americans possessed 18 percent of national income after taxes. Between 2000 and 2005, more than 96 percent of American workers experienced a decrease in their purchasing power. In France, where the minimum wage and collective agreements place more constraints on rising inequality than exist in the United States, there was still a noticeable explosion in high incomes between 1998 and 2005. The richest 0.01 percent of households saw their incomes increase by 42.6 percent, the richest 10 percent by 8.7 percent and the remaining 90 percent by only 4.6 percent.[15] The increase in the number of working poor is also a cause for concern (see Clerc 2008).

Moreover, the accumulation process is hampered by the fact that households in the North are already well equipped with durable consumer goods, so there is a pressing need to sell services. This leads to the commodification of new areas—a trend that is now affecting knowledge (Azam 2007, 110–26), the patenting of living things, and the human body and its reproduction. It is a trend that is making widespread advances in many other activities that were previously "uncommodified": culture, sports and leisure, health, social work, and personal services. The socioeconomic balance of the 1945–1975 boom years was based on market growth being optimized so that social policies could be financed by public redistribution. When the market invades previously "uncommodified" activities, the complementarity between market economy and public services that previously made social democracies successful is called into question. In these societies, democratic solidarity based on rights was dependent on the performance of the market economy, but it also benefited from its own exclusive domains such as health, education, social services, and so on. This is no longer the case.

The Reorientation of Public Regulation

Commodification results not just from the privatization of previously public activities but also from the spread of a market framework within public regulation. As noted in chapter 5, associations implement local development and employment initiatives with a public dimension. In order to achieve their objectives and realize their project for institutional change, their proponents call for agreement-based regulation, in the sense explained above. Yet competition-based regulation has become commonplace in several national contexts. In the period of economic expansion following the Second World War, the state exercised close control over associations through tutelary regulation. But the decline of this norm does not mean that more equitable relationships are being established. Instead, we are moving from tutelary regulation to regulation based on competition between services. This does not involve the state's disengagement, as the public funds allocated to associations are still massive, but it does require the adoption of "quasi-market" (Le Grand and Bartlett 1993) rules for their allocation: competitive tendering by different partners, calls for tenders, opening up to private companies, exemption from social and fiscal charges, and vouchers being given out to consumers. In the case of personal services, this has meant creating a market to deal with the exponential growth in needs caused by both longer life expectancy as well as increases in the number of working women and single-parent families. While association-based initiatives are still waiting for a new mode of public intervention that is less specialized and more transversal—one that integrates the issues of employment, social cohesion, and public participation—neocapitalism is benefiting from public regulations that encourage its extension into fields of activity that were previously shielded from the market.

In this context, the associationalism mentioned above can assert a different logic. But it is still not very visible, especially since many associations are subject to "managerialism" (Avare and Sponem 2008)—modeling their operation on that of companies—and to competitive regulation, which ignores their specificity. They are also weakened by being given a substantive yet subordinate role in a form of neophilanthropy that has become the auxiliary of a neoliberalism concerned about its influence on society as a whole. This linking of the economic vision of the world to an increasingly assertive moralization of those most disadvantaged in society evokes memories of the nineteenth century. But its current form deserves further explanation.

The Resurgence of Philanthropy

Market capitalism cannot dispense with legitimacy in society today any more than it could in previous incarnations. This is why it appeals to an ethic that is not transcendent—as the protestant ethic might have been—but rather immanent to the economic system (see Salmon 2009). More specifically, the ethical discourse of large multinational groups is not, contrary to widespread belief, a reaction to the protests of civil society. The plea for corporate self-regulation with respect to social and environmental issues is inseparable from a critique of public action. In response to this critique, "the company appears as a universal form of action" (Laval 2007, 333) capable of solving society's problems through its intrinsic efficiency.

The call for the removal of government regulations, which are considered too restrictive, is coupled with a call for businesses to voluntarily adopt a code of ethics. It is in this context that the new wave of philanthropy begins to make sense. Swept along by this wave, associations can now act as nothing more than cut-price providers of services and assistance reserved for the most disadvantaged who have "dropped out" of the market economy because of their inability to compete. They can become enclaves for the poor where fine humanitarian sentiments exist cheek-by-jowl with the subsidies of multinationals. This model of associations—in which private donations of time and money are manifestations of domination under the guise of caring for victims—is no figment of the imagination at a time when some foundations have more resources than many governments.[16] This reconfigured philanthropy aims to apply the methods of the most modern form of capitalism[17] to the nonprofit sector, with managerial rationalization guaranteeing improved results. According to a view that recalls that of nineteenth-century French Liberal economist Bastiat, if it is to be effective, solidarity cannot be legally mandated. Ethical investments mean there is no need for the political, and private initiative relieves the different levels of government of their responsibility for integration and social work, which are now addressed through venture capital. Behind the apparent consensus on partnership and good governance, we see both disenfranchisement and conditions being placed on social assistance, with aid being distributed on the basis of merit—returning to the relentless focus on the poor's moralization. As Servet has shown, the problem with the new philanthropy—which is connected to corporate social responsibility—is neither that of the corporation's performance nor of its shareholders' intentions, but that of the plutocracy replacing the law (Servet 2010, 212).

As with its predecessor, this updated philanthropy effectively nullifies democratic solidarity in the economy. This process is part of a historical pattern in which the rise in inequality itself is ignored as the focus is drawn to the fight against poverty. An example of this trend is provided by the Millennium Development Goals adopted in September 2000 by the United Nations General Assembly. Admittedly, these objectives show that, after two decades of domination, neoliberal precepts are being amended as the fight against poverty is prioritized, but this fight continues to overshadow the need to reduce inequality. Once the problem of inequality is limited in this way, public services are confined to assistance. For their part, associations are identified with humanitarian and charitable purposes. As mentioned above, their attempt to intervene in the economy could only be considered unfair competition.

The only exception granted to them is that of reintegration, i.e. a temporary intervention in which associations act as "gates" through which disadvantaged social groups can pass in order to become "employable" again in the "regular" economy, which is the market economy[18]. This new function of associations is an original form of cooptation specific to the "cultural triumph of the market" (Roustang 2002).

The Associative Paradox

Given this development, the serious concerns about the future of the public sphere, highlighted at the beginning of this book, appear to be well founded. The decline of totalitarian regimes does not signal that democracy's victory is irreversible (Fukuyama 1992). So it is now the fragility of democracy that needs to be examined. Many authors rightly point out that negative individualism encourages withdrawal, a refusal to engage, a decline in the sense of belonging, and a forgetting of mutual recognition and solidarity (Gauchet 1998; Castel 1995). This individualism—this detachment and disengagement—involves a retreat into the private sphere and indifference toward politics. It sees democracy as a simple institutional framework that provides negative freedom, even though it cannot subsist without either positive freedom or a concern for the common good and "togetherness" ("*le vivre ensemble*"). There therefore exists some uncertainty about democracy's future, but this uncertainty cannot be understood by looking only at trends within the political sphere. The changes in market neocapitalism have had such a significant impact that we must reconnect questions about the future of democracy to economic choices. The diagnosis of a new age of individualism thus pushes us to question the relationship between democracy and the economy once again.

Monetization without End?

From this perspective, it is important not to underestimate what makes consumer society attractive both to people who are immersed in it and to those who have no access to it. Daily life is largely structured around adherence to the market—an anthropological fact that cannot be overlooked. If the market is able to become one with social life, this is because it is conflated with a certain idea of individual freedom. Consumption encouraged by advertising can appear to produce emancipation much more than involvement in the life of the polity. Participation in collective decisions—with all that it entails in terms of mediation, deliberation and conflict—suffers from comparison with the immediate expansion of personal freedoms that consumption seems to offer.

Commodification thus partly explains why the appetite for democracy has declined, but it is also the manifestation of a more general and less obvious trend affecting contemporary societies. This trend can be described as monetization.

Simmel's work helps us understand this process. Many commentators only remember Simmel's notion that the monetary economy has emancipatory potential, but his analysis is more complex than this. In his view, the monetization of social relations has made it possible to objectify economic value; this has given economic value a justification that enables it to mediate interpersonal relationships. The value on which the economic is founded results firstly from the practical relationship that binds us to objects—and in particular from the resistance they exert on our desire—and secondly from the recognition of their value due to the desire of another (Simmel 1978, 47). The substance of the economic is therefore connected to productive work and the exchange of objects. In work, the resistance of the physical world is exerted in productive cooperation, while in exchange, the relation of opposition gives way to an agreement mediated by money. It is these two distinct and complementary moments of socialization that allow us to escape the arbitrariness of interpersonal relationships. However, Simmel adds, the liberating power of monetization has not been definitively established but is historically situated. More precisely, it is conditional upon the dignity of paid work and the delimitation of the economy as the sphere of the material. It is because these two characteristics are now being challenged that the contemporary economy is experiencing such profound disruptions.

Firstly, the connection between the development of the monetary economy and the achievement of personal autonomy is weakened by the attrition of the wage-earning system. The balance between work and exchange presupposes two conditions: that work should always be remunerated in accordance with its quantity and quality, and that this method of determining the social hierarchy should be recognized as legitimate by the parties concerned (Perret and Roustang 1993, 251).

These two conditions are now being threatened by mass unemployment and by the differentiation, or even atomization, of work.

Secondly, monetization takes on a new meaning when the economy's autonomy is challenged. "The expansion of monetary exchanges outside the scope of the acquisition of material objects weakens economics' claim to be the positive science of utility" (Perret 1999, 253). This claim was justified by the fact that the economy governed material life and livelihoods, but it is no longer justified when economic growth advances by taking over the worlds of information, communication, and culture (Roustang 2002, 11).

Monetization can no longer be considered emancipatory, yet it remains a powerful trend that encompasses associations. Previously bolstered by the welfare state, associations are now subject on the one hand to the influence of monetization, and on the other to the favoring of the market as a mechanism for allocating resources and the company as a productive organization. In the next chapter we will look at the relation between this trend and the conceptualization of associations as belonging to a "third sector." But for now it is enough to observe that this situation results in many associations aligning themselves with market standards. While providing services for the welfare state, they unreflectively adopt managerial techniques imported from large private companies in a process of managerial professionalization motivated by generalized competition—and do so without taking care to maintain associative projects.[19] Adding to the negation of democratic solidarity and the restoration of philanthropic solidarity described above, this managerialism leads to associations becoming increasingly watered down. This is reminiscent of what happened in the nineteenth century, but what is new is that—as mentioned earlier—these associations are no longer anything more than avatars of the company, which has become the model for all initiatives. Neocapitalism proposes to coopt association. It limits its political scope in order to turn it into a "capitalism without profit-making aims."[20] This incorporation of association into the new capitalism is not happening by chance; a strategy of appropriating innovations has been apparent all the way from self-management's diversion toward participatory management, right through to solidarity finance's conversion first into microcredit and then into social business.

The Risk of Political Neutralization

Theories of self-management were put at the service of the private company with the adoption of participatory management, which was supposed to correspond to work that called for both individual and collective intelligence as well as communication. Then the ode to the radical alternative became an elegy to microenterprise.[21] Fair trade, too, has been unable to escape reappropriation by supermarkets, which have launched their own labels using concepts such as ethical trade. But it is surely the confusion between microfinance and microcredit that is the most striking and therefore worthy of further examination. In the discourse of international organizations at the end of the twentieth century, microcredit became a panacea for poverty, and global summits set a target of 100 million clients. Two major features characterize the discourse that reduces microfinance to microcredit: the reduction of a plurality of initiatives to a single model, and the use of microfinance to challenge the wage-earning system.

First, all initiatives are reduced solely to the model of the individual entrepreneur. Any capacity for initiative that is emerging in society is reduced to a "barefoot capitalism" (de Soto 1987) that does not reflect the diversity of real practices. Indeed, as research on the countries of the global South has shown, the popular economy cannot be interpreted in these terms. Women's initiatives are good examples (Guérin 2003): they cannot be understood via the individual enterprise model, as they are usually part of a collective approach to improving everyday life. The women who participate transform their traditional skills into professional skills. In the North there are similar approaches, such as neighborhood restaurants, catering services, and mediation services. Their challenges are both economic and civic, and they reflect the desire to play an active role both in one's own life and in social transformation. Recognizing the innovative capacity of women's initiatives, among others, thus requires us to take account of their forms of collective organization (Berger, Fraisse, and Hersent 2000). Otherwise, they are looked down on because they are confused with simple initiatives aimed at market integration.

Another striking feature of the discourse about microcredit is its suggestion that multiplying the number of independent microenterprises is an alternative to the protective rules of the wage-earning system. According to this view, state intervention—which is supposed to have created harmful rigidities—should be replaced by the activity of a private sector driven by concern for social well-being. The discourse about microcredit is thus often supported by a plea for the state to disengage. As in the nineteenth century, the fiction of individuals' contractual equality is used to mask the power relationships that exist between contractors with dissymmetric positions. But this ideological interpretation is also invalidated by the facts. The types of support for initiatives that have emerged require relationships of trust and locally embedded action. Associative mediation therefore seems essential. Moreover, this mediation cannot be self-financed at present. Public finance is essential, either directly or through guarantee funds.[22] It provides a bulwark against overindebtedness.

Yet the idea that poverty can be a profitable market is spreading. Those responsible for establishing a new regime of capitalism since the 1980s have been adapting their discourse based on a number of theories, including that of Yunus (2008). A new argument is emerging: until now, capitalism has been "a half-developed structure"; it required the addition of social business, i.e. a "company that is cause-driven rather than profit-driven." When social business becomes more familiar, "the flood of creativity that this new business channel will unleash has the potential to transform our world" via two distinct mechanisms: investors maximizing social benefits and disadvantaged people seeking to maximize their profits. In this framework, the association converts itself into a social enterprise and is then treated as a company "in every sense" because it functions "in accordance with management principles just like a traditional [profit-maximizing business]" and aims at "full cost recovery." Importing its management methods from private enterprise, the social business "brings the advantages of free-market competition into the world of social improvement."[23] The media success of such a promise—although rarely held up against reality[24]—results from its being strongly promoted by governments, lobbyists, and business leaders, and its influence amplified by institutions such as the G8 and the European Commission. A whole stack of reports now mix together social business, neophilanthropy, and corporate responsibility, spreading the word that there is a system that can solve the problems it generates. When we connect this up with mechanisms such as "bottom of the pyramid" marketing techniques and social-impact investment in social initiatives, culture, or international solidarity, we see that a modified form of neoliberalism has emerged in the wake of the antiglobalization demonstrations and the uprisings of the Arab Spring. Neoliberalism no longer simply advocates the generalization of competition but internalizes responses to social inequality in order to defuse any sweeping opposition. Faith in entrepreneurship, partnership with major companies, and a paternalist approach to the people of the South have all become established at the international level, reinforced by the market being lauded as a social achievement[25]—praise that is enthusiastically echoed by liberal think tanks.

It is not surprising that this vision is gaining an audience at a time when capitalism is seeking to restore its image. It essentially proposes to eliminate any political dimension, as the solicitude of the wealthy and "barefoot capitalism" (Prahalad 2004) are supposedly sufficient to eradicate poverty.

It is therefore undeniable that new associational forms are being drained of their political dimension—and that this process is inseparable from their cooptation as a functional subset of an unchanged system, as advocated by Hayek (1973, 59–60). This new type of associational cooptation has not, however, invaded the entire social sphere. It collides with another imaginary, that of democratic solidarity in the economy, revived by the recent upsurge in associationalism. It would therefore be an exaggeration to conclude that a new spirit of capitalism is now reigning supreme. The "artistic critique"—which emerged in France in 1968 among creatives and focused on freedom, autonomy, and authenticity—has not been completely separated from the "social critique"—which emerged in parallel principally among workers and focused on inequality, solidarity, and security—and utilized by capitalism, which is endlessly drawing new energy from its contradictions. Our discussion in this section leads us to a nuanced observation: there are new threats of associations being instrumentalized in order to moralize capitalism; nonetheless, the theory that critique has been reinternalized by neocapitalism is too one-sided.[26]

The new spirit of capitalism has not eliminated the "new spirit of solidarity" (Frère 2009), and it is precisely because of the dangers inherent in current monetization processes that the associationalist renewal is also able to repersonalize direct relationships that had previously become standardized. It does so by producing a shift: personalized social relations are once again becoming relevant, even though these relations' abstraction and formalization seemed characteristic of advanced modernity. This shift is not, however, a return to traditional dependencies because—to use Simmel's words again—engagement is limited to the service itself and does not reintroduce an engagement of the whole person that would negate the benefits of individuation. These are personalized forms of involvement (see Ion 1989, 486) that allow for the differences sought by associationalist intervention in the economic sphere. The establishment of lasting relationships so that everyone can identify the actors behind economic activities makes it easier to include criteria of fairness within these activities. For example, in fair trade, knowledge of production conditions—or even meeting producers—helps people to rediscover the human exchange behind the exchange of things. While many activists have run out of steam, the associationalist revival is asserting itself through forms of public engagement in which concrete links and common projects are seeking to strengthen themselves through interpersonal respect.

Ambiguities to Analyze

The ambiguities of the contemporary associational landscape were highlighted at the beginning of chapter 4. They are very real, and—now that we have identified the various forms they take—we can encapsulate them in a single opposition: on the one hand, there is a tendency to negate democratic solidarity, which has been the hallmark of the market society project since the nineteenth century; on the other, there is a vitality of this form of democratic solidarity evidenced by many civil society groups. All in all, despite the force of monetization, the existence of associationalism reminds us that the story of democracy has not yet been written. Indeed, even as negative individualism spreads, public engagement is not waning but changing. It is reactivating that capacity to question the organization of the political and economic spheres which has historically been the hallmark of associationalism—but in a very different context. We must therefore be careful not to make hasty judgments about the phenomenon of association, and in this respect reclaiming the past can only help us better describe and understand the present situation—hence the reference to the history of the present in the introduction, which has guided us though the first and second parts of this book.

Finally, discussion about the pathologies of democracy leads to truncated observations if we do not take the trouble to study the dilemmas and tensions that plague associations. Reflections on democracy cannot neglect associational dynamics. Admittedly, democracy today seems at risk of receding, but it also contains the potential for becoming deeper. It is these ambivalences that must be grasped. They are summarized by the associational paradox: in many associations, the renewal of associationalism—evidenced by the emergences mentioned in this part of the book—collides with an increasingly forceful erasure of its distinctiveness. We must explore this paradox in greater detail rather than denouncing today's democracy outright. Democracy's future is not settled, and it will be largely affected by the place that associations take in the social contract. Will they be dominated by the role assigned to them by neocapitalism, or will they be able to avoid instrumentalization and influence society's choices?

This question requires us to take an analytical detour. Given the paradox that has just been outlined, we cannot answer it without comparing in detail the different paradigms used to study associations' empirical realities. The coherence and autonomy of associational possibilities is strongly dependent on these paradigms. While the "science of association" that Tocqueville called for has long been out of the limelight, it is gradually recovering the centrality that Durkheim, Mauss, and Dewey (1939a) also attached to it. Association is once again attracting attention, and there are several theories that attempt to define it. But the various conceptualizations of association that dominate contemporary debate are far from being equivalent in terms of the history and the present reality reconstructed in the first and second parts of this book. Through their epistemological choices, they help format and shape associational initiatives, and this is why it is important to examine these conceptualizations in detail from an associationalist perspective. Identifying an alternative vision requires us to make theoretical choices that partially reconfigure the initiatives we are studying. These choices have performative effects that are all the more noticeable because they concern phenomena whose legitimacy has not been secured. The wide range of descriptions of these phenomena reflects both the disparity of their components as well as the variety of prisms through which they are seen. Part III will summarize the distinguishing features of the three main theories at international level—those of the third sector, the social economy, and the solidarity economy.

The Contemporary Debate

{ 7 }

The Third Sector

AS PREVIOUSLY MENTIONED, political debates still largely focus on the respective roles of the market and the state. In this respect, they converge with most economic and social-scientific studies that distinguish between two sectors, private and public. The idea of the third sector has developed as a response to the inadequacy of this division. It refers to a negatively defined sector of activity: neither capitalist nor part of the state, it is a sector composed of nonprofit organizations, which are distinguished from both "for-profit companies" and "public services" (see Archambault 1996, 1).

A Nonprofit Sector

Attempts in the international literature to define the third sector start from the growing role of nonprofits in the provision of jobs and services. This expansion of nonprofits' economic role is connected to changes in the structure of production. As the previous chapter shows, in today's economy more than three quarters of jobs are in services. But not all services are following the same trajectory. It is interpersonal services that are creating jobs, that is, services with a high degree of direct contact (in education, health, and social services). Indeed, these services combine a technical aspect that is focused on delivery and a civic aspect that involves attending to the presence of the other. Exchanges of information can only be codified and automated to a very limited extent. Interaction between service providers and recipients remains essential, and this need for face-to-face contact makes it possible to create a large number of jobs as long as the mechanisms for funding them exist.

The existence of for-profit companies and public services cannot hide the fact that there is also a significant number of nonprofits involved in all these interpersonal services. Given this empirical evidence, and the extent to which the economy is now tertiarized, we cannot focus on the respective roles of the market and the state while ignoring associations. Alongside the private and public sectors that have already been studied, nonprofits are now becoming worthy of attention.

An International Survey

The interest in the third sector is thus inextricably connected to the growing role played by nonprofits in the provision of services and employment. The rise in service activities largely explains the desire to remedy the lack of knowledge about nonprofits. This is why international research in the last decades of the twentieth century focused on identifying the extent of the associative phenomenon, designated as the third sector. The Johns Hopkins University comparison project undertaken in 1990 was a benchmark in this respect, measuring the third sector in seven countries (Germany, the United States, France, Italy, Japan, the United Kingdom, and Sweden). Five countries in the global South (Brazil, Egypt, Ghana, India, and Thailand) and one country in transition (Hungary) were subsequently added, and by 2005 the study had expanded to include thirty-seven countries following the addition of national studies in North and South America, Asia, Africa, and Europe.

In this research project, which provided the first systematic database on the size and content of this previously statistically overlooked phenomenon, the nonprofits constituting the third sector were defined according to four main criteria:

> They are formal organizations, meaning that they are registered, which differentiates them from mere temporary gatherings and many informal groups, for example those involved in neighborhood activities.

> They are also private and independent, that is, separate from governments (so para-public associations are excluded); they have their own decision-making structures and cannot be controlled by either public authorities or companies, even if these entities can contribute to their financing.

They do not distribute profits to their members or managers. This nonprofit constraint does not mean that they are prohibited from making a surplus, but they are not primarily commercial, and any surplus must be reinvested in the service of their social purpose.

Finally, they are distinguished by a significant degree of voluntary participation through either volunteering, or gifts of time or money.

Religious organizations and political parties were considered external to the sector in order to enable unbiased comparison, even if they met these criteria. The Johns Hopkins study has had a profound influence on the demarcation of associations. In particular, as Prouteau notes, the "nondistributions constraint that characterizes these organizations throughout the world" (2004, 42) is considered their essential feature, and the third sector is treated as the sector in which they can be found.

Data gathered at the end of the twentieth century from thirty-seven countries showed that the third sector accounted for 47.6 million full-time equivalent jobs, or 4.5 percent of the working population and 7.7 percent of nonagricultural employment.[1] Of these, salaried jobs accounted for only 56 percent of the workforce, since 44 percent of it was made up of volunteers performing unpaid voluntary work. The highest percentage of the working population involved in associative work was found in the Netherlands, where the figure was 14.4 percent—9.2 percent of whom were paid and 5.1 percent volunteers; the figures were 8.4 percent and 2.7 percent respectively for Canada, 6.3 percent and 3.5 percent for the United States, 4.8 percent and 3.6 percent for the United Kingdom, 3.7 percent and 3.7 percent for France, and 1.7 percent and 5.1 percent respectively for Sweden. This quantification is important because "what isn't counted doesn't count," to quote Anheier (1995).

But the uncovering of this reality did not just lead to the quantitative description of its size. It also increased curiosity about the phenomenon. Hypotheses about the reasons for nonprofits' existence were first formulated in the 1970s and 1980s, long before the Johns Hopkins project began. Nevertheless, researchers' interest was revived by this demonstration of what had become an important empirical reality. The theory of the third sector was established in the 1990s, mainly among English-speaking authors working within the paradigm of orthodox economics.

Since its emergence, neoclassical economics has focused on "objective" issues, eliminating any historical, normative, or political consideration in order to base its scientificity on the methods of the natural sciences. The aim was to set aside questions of justice and ethics in order to focus exclusively on the search for efficiency. Thus Pareto demonstrated the market's ability to guarantee the optimal use of resources when there is pure and perfect competition. To do this, five conditions must be met: atomicity, i.e. the presence of a large number of actors independent of each other; the homogeneity of products, in other words the identicalness of different goods meeting the same need; free access to the market; the mobility of production factors; and finally the transparency necessary for actors to be perfectly informed.

Once these conditions had been established, the issue became the difficulty of fulfilling them in the functioning of real markets. Neoclassical economics then set out to find appropriate solutions to deal with the discrepancies between theoretical and real situations, which were seen as imperfections. Instead of limiting themselves to the state as the only alternative to the market, various advances gradually made it possible to consider other institutional solutions. Coase and later Williamson in particular contributed to the recognition that organizations can take the place of the market. When the functioning of a market has costs related, for example, to opportunistic behavior, the creation of an organization can help to avoid or reduce them. If we accept this first point, we can move on to a second point: that the type of organization performing this role may vary. Private for-profit businesses are not the only possible type of organization. Orthodox theory argues that in some cases, described below, it may be better to turn to the third sector rather than private for-profit enterprise.

As early as the 1970s, economists began to address this apparent contradiction: even though it is the pursuit of profit that is supposed to encourage efficiency, nonprofit organizations exist in certain fields of activity. They explained this by highlighting the particular characteristics of services with a strong interpersonal dimension. Since services are not products whose characteristics are known before the transaction, problems of trust and quality are especially acute, as exemplified in the area of home-help for the elderly and childcare. The market therefore fails in these areas—areas where public services are not always able to provide solutions, either. According to orthodox economics, the fact that nonprofits are involved in these services is due to noncompliance with the Pareto principles.

Market Failures

The reason for this noncompliance—from an orthodox point of view—is that when some agents have more information than others, the former may use it in transactions to the detriment of the latter. This means that producers, who have the advantage of possessing information over which they have a monopoly, can take advantage of this to mislead consumers. The desired market transparency is replaced by an opacity that is detrimental to trade because it favors some players and unbalances their relations with others. This risk spreads in a service economy, since it is more difficult to assess services' quality in advance; unlike with goods, their quality only exists during their consumption, as a result of a coproduction between the service provider and the user. The more personalized the service is, the more pronounced this characteristic becomes, as in personal care services. Services such as home help for the elderly and early childhood care are emblematic of multidimensional services in which the information required to assess quality is particularly difficult to assimilate. In the patriarchal system these services have traditionally been provided by women within the family sphere, but they are increasingly being outsourced. This is mainly done through the provision of services by nonprofits. There are very few for-profit companies in these areas.[2] If nonprofits are more numerous, then this is because their legal structure makes it possible to reduce the information asymmetries that disadvantage users. At least this is the argument put forward by the theory of the third sector: the comparative advantage of nonprofits lies in the fact that the nonprofit constraint constitutes a guarantee for consumers, which is useful for services that involve entering into their personal sphere. The absence of profit as a goal provides protection against two negative phenomena: adverse selection and moral hazard.

Let us first examine the issue of adverse selection. For the consumer, the exclusive possession of information by the service provider makes it difficult to distinguish between providers on the basis of price. Faced with the difficulty of objectifying criteria of quality, users are deprived of reliable information to help them to make a choice. When many dual-earner couples are forced to rely on external services to care for their elderly parents, they feel guilty about using "strangers," as if this means they are somehow abandoning them. In the face of this sense of discomfort, they may be reassured when the services are expensive, confusing a high price with a guarantee of quality. They feel that if they spend a lot of money it is clear that they have done their best for their loved ones and have no reason to reproach themselves. As with other services for families, bad providers may take advantage of the situation in order to overcharge, selling a poor-quality service for the price of a high-quality one (Enjolras 1995b). But the situation is hardly any better if the price is too low, because bad providers can end up driving good providers out of the market. Expenses incurred for staff training or to monitor services may result in a higher cost when compared with less rigorous competitors. Such situations come under the general heading of adverse selection, where bad services drive out good ones.

To counteract this tendency, providers make the quality of their services clear through signals accessible to consumers. As Hansmann (1980; 1987) points out, the criterion of the nondistribution constraint may be one of those signals that reassures consumers that they are not in danger of being manipulated by producers. According to the ortho-dox approach, this is the main reason for the existence of nonprofits in today's economies.

Let us now consider the issue of moral hazard. This occurs when one party to the transaction is required to take action while the other party is not in a position to observe, monitor, or constrain the execution of the service requested. In childcare, for example, it is not possible to monitor the services provided when the parents are absent. The less-informed party can only observe the result of the action and not the effort deployed during the action. This may result in service providers delivering a service that is inferior to the one they have undertaken to provide under the terms of the contract. But even when the parties to the contract are present, opportunistic behavior may occur when the user is in a state of dependency, or when circumstances arise that were not anticipated in the original contract. A home-help provider can easily take advantage of service users' weakness, for example if an elderly person's health deteriorates.

Moral hazard can also develop when a transaction requires significant investment, for example when the user has had to spend a lot of time finding the right service. Once again, service providers may take advantage of this situation to not completely fulfil their commitments, something that has been called the "hold-up" problem (Milgrom and Roberts, 1992). Since the user has made a "sunk investment," they may hesitate to change service providers even if they are no longer satisfied with the service. The structure of this environment also leads to quasi-rent situations. Many of the areas that have been mentioned, such as childcare and home help, are characterized by a rationing of providers because demand outstrips supply. This gives an extortionate amount of power to existing entities. They are able to choose the solutions and formats that best serve their own interests because competition is restricted. This rationing discourages users from changing providers because they are not sure that they will find better services elsewhere. Information asymmetries are converted into market power that prevents transparency and atomicity in the system of supply and demand, and hampers the freedom and perfect mobility of buyers and sellers.

Finally, moral hazard may concern a third party: the funder of the service. In personal care services, it is difficult for the people or institutions that fund these services' expansion to protect themselves against their funds being misappropriated, or against the cream-skimming of users. Providers have an interest in taking care of the "easiest" users and disregarding clients for whom the unit cost of intervention is too high, either because their health condition is too "serious" or because their geographical location requires too much traveling. Krashinski (1986) emphasizes this problem in an approach focused on transaction costs, i.e. the costs related to preparing and monitoring economic transactions, which can be broken down into coordination costs (relating to information, decision making, and monitoring) and motivation costs (relating to incentives for individuals to perform their tasks).

The literature on the nonprofit sector thus belongs to a branch of neoclassical research that explains the presence of organizations in a market economy. While remaining faithful to rational choice theory—for which any economic fact can be understood in terms of the aggregation of individual behaviors resulting from a constrained optimization based on complete and transitive preferences—it nevertheless admits that the market is not the right mechanism for resource allocation in all circumstances. It thus recognizes the existence of organizations that are more suitable than the market. But not all organizations are identical, either—and they are not all for-profit companies. The peculiarity of not redistributing profits can therefore be an asset for nonprofits in services where information, trust, and personalization are essential. As Badelt (1990) argues, it is this nonprofit constraint that is considered key to overcoming information asymmetries. Whether the issue is adverse selection or moral hazard, nonprofits are supposed to provide particular security for consumers because the surplus generated by their activities cannot be used to remunerate shareholders.

State Failures

The theory of the third sector—which explains nonprofits' prevalence in interpersonal services by their ability to remedy market failures—also highlights how they complement state intervention. To examine how nonprofits do this, we should first note that some interpersonal services may not affect the protagonists of the exchange alone. These services can have an impact on other actors or even the community as a whole, triggering what are known in economics as positive or negative "externalities." For example, childcare services generate positive externalities by facilitating women's access to employment and training. They also reduce gender inequalities—which are particularly pronounced in domestic care tasks—thus creating externalities by reducing undeclared work and expenditure on unemployment benefits. Meanwhile home help can have a positive impact outside the home by, for instance, creating jobs for women who now have fewer family responsibilities, or reducing public spending if looking after elderly people at home is less costly than housing them in communal facilities. In this respect, childcare and home-help services are both individual and quasi-collective services. They are aimed personally at consumers while having a wider impact on the community through positive externalities—externalities that are both complex and multilateral because they affect various actors (Petrella 1996).

To restore the balance sought in exchange, the solution usually adopted consists of internalizing externalities, because otherwise, as Pigou has shown, services with positive externalities are seen as under-productive compared to the collective optimum (see Généreux 2001, 87). To achieve this, it may be possible to hold bilateral negotiations that result in the beneficiaries of positive externalities paying some monetary compensation. However, such a solution is difficult in the case of multilateral collective externalities. An alternative is to subsidize the producer of the externality in accordance with the social benefit that it creates. It is therefore justified for funding to be tax-based for services that are both individual and quasi-collective—services characterized by the scale and complexity of their externalities. The same kind of state involvement is recommended for strictly collective goods and services. These are defined as goods and services that are nonrival (consumption by one person does not prevent them being consumed by another, and the same applies to protecting the environment) and nonexclusive (the producer cannot hinder the consumption of those who have not helped finance the good or service, like the use of a road without tolls). Thus neoclassical economics accepts the merits of public funding for all quasi-collective and collective services. But while such funding may prove necessary, it is not sufficient to respond to all demands. This is what Weisbrod (1975; 1977) establishes using the framework of public choice theory, which approaches political decisions from the perspective of rational choice. He emphasizes the state's propensity to satisfy the median voter, concluding from this that there is "excess demand" corresponding to other voters. The more heterogeneous the population, the more "differentiated" the excess demand (see James 1987). It is because there are minority groups that are not taken into account by the state that associative responses have arisen to meet their needs. Needs that are not directly addressed by the state lead voters to feel there is a lack of resources. This encourages them to come together to set up nonprofit organizations dedicated to providing the services they want.

A Theory of Institutional Choice

In general, nonprofit organizations respond to market and state failures, or more accurately to the inadequacies of private for-profit enterprises and public services. But they are not a third solution without drawbacks. Salamon (1987) identifies three major deficiencies of the nonprofit third sector: philanthropic inadequacy stems from a lack of resources, with volunteerism suffering from "free rider" behavior; philanthropic particularism consists of the selection of certain groups and problems, tipping into philanthropic paternalism, where the selection of needs is the prerogative of those who finance them; and philanthropic amateurism can take hold through a lack of incentives for efficiency in the absence of profit distribution.

A Subsidiary Sector

Alongside the two main arteries of the private for-profit and public sectors, the third sector provides a subsidiary route. It is deployed in services with a strong interpersonal dimension, where complex provision cannot be fully gauged before it is undertaken. Studies on the third sector show that in those services that coproduce a "relational good" (Gui 2000) and that enter into the personal sphere of users, with emotional and communicational implications, lowering the price is far from enough to boost provision. This is evidenced by the disillusionment that followed after hopes were placed in jobs being created in interpersonal services.[3] The question of trust is vital when the "exposure" (Duriez 1996) of intimacy—entry into the private sphere—is inherent in these services. For demand to form and grow, resistance to the outsourcing seen in personal care[4] must therefore be taken into account. Doing so requires the mediation of funders and third parties, of information intermediaries other than the beneficiaries. In contexts where information becomes essential for economic exchange and requires investment by beneficiaries, nonprofit organizations are better placed than private companies to reassure users, funders, and other stakeholders. Additionally, within collective or quasi-collective services, the state's failure to cover people's needs leaves room for them to deal with the excess demand.

The theory of the third sector thus suggests that standard economics does not see private enterprise as superior in personal care services. Similarly, orthodox economic theory in no way supports the practice that is prevalent in many countries of assimilating the development of services to building a market. On the contrary, it highlights the diversity of the organizations involved in this field of activity, whose struc-

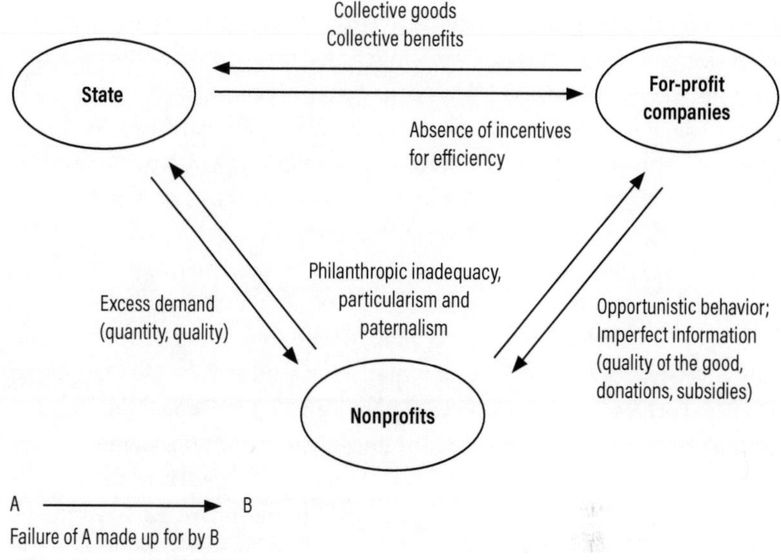

FIGURE 1. The third sector and the triangle of institutional choice

ture calls for due reflection on these organizations' respective roles and limitations. In other words, neoliberal discourse and neoclassical analysis do not agree. On the contrary, the latter emphasizes the comparative advantages of nonprofits in interpersonal services. This conclusion is not insignificant, as it tends to be ignored in political debate by representatives of for-profit enterprise who presume the superiority of the organizations they defend.

Going beyond the Nonprofit Constraint

The economic approach to the third sector thus departs from market dogmatism. It offers a nuanced view that seeks to explain the reasons behind the use of different sectors. As such, it is referred to as the theory of institutional choice. In this framework, the main asset attributed to associations is their nonprofit nature, which generates particular trust in the area of interpersonal services. But this foundational observation of the third sector approach has been qualified as more detailed research has been done. Various avenues have been explored with a view to moving beyond the overly mechanical depiction of the relationship between trust and the nonprofit constraint.

As the previous paragraphs show, the theory of institutional choice initially sets up the criterion of nonprofit-making as independent, considering it to be the principal factor behind users' confidence in the services offered by nonprofits. Yet this criterion does not appear to be the only one likely to inspire confidence. It may face competition from standards adopted by for-profit providers. Other mechanisms can be employed by any organization (such as ethical codes, certification, and labeling schemes), as various studies have confirmed—this is true in the legal profession, for instance, where Karpik (1996) speaks of "market judgment," and in business consultancy, where opinion-formers intervene to vouch for quality (see Sauviat 1994). It is therefore difficult to see when and why the nonprofit motive should prove decisive in the decisions taken by the individuals concerned. Adverse selection and moral hazard are found in many services and point to the problems of the "market," understood in the standard sense of the term. These characteristics have not prevented markets from developing in many service activities, such as legal and business advice; but the market is a "market-network" (Bressand 1994) characteristic of a contemporary economy very much concerned with service quality, in which customers do not choose particular products or services but rather particular companies because they are reputed, familiar, established, and "make" the quality of their members. The limitations of the classical market model can be overcome by markets with quality rules and institutions that guarantee ethical standards.

The nondistribution constraint is, therefore, not sufficient to build trust in personalized services (Ortmann and Schlesinger 1997; Steinberg and Gray 1993). This is both because it is just one among many indicators of reputation and also because it can be abused. The awarding of salary supplements to managers (James 1990) is just one illustration of the propensity for managers' interests to take precedence over those of consumers. In the absence of financial incentives to maximize profit, cost and quality control may be neglected. Looking after managers and professionals may become a key priority around which an unspoken consensus forms.

Social Entrepreneurs and Stakeholders

The simplistic nature of the reference to nonprofit-making also results in a focus on demand at the expense of supply. The first conceptualizations of the third sector outlined above are demand theories, describing the reasons why users or donors select nonprofit organizations. They assume nonprofits' prior existence, making it possible to see how they are chosen—but these theories provide little detail about how the supply side is constructed in the first place. To remedy this weakness in understanding processes of creation, work is being done to reduce the asymmetry between demand and supply-side explanations. This work focuses on the motivations of entrepreneurs and the involvement of stakeholders in nonprofits.

Those studying entrepreneurs' behavior try to understand why someone would set up a nonprofit when this kind of entity risks being appropriated by its managers. They respond to this question by including nonmonetary variables in social entrepreneurs' utility functions. Young (1981) treats them as actors who are not so much seeking financial benefits as seeking autonomy or spaces for creativity. The motivation to set up nonprofits lies in these objectives, to which James (1990) adds the religious motivations of groups keen to increase their beliefs' influence, swell their numbers, and expand their public audience. Rose-Ackerman (1986) establishes a typology of the motivations of social entrepreneurs who are involved in nonprofits organized by ideology. Reference to social aims is claimed in the very notions of social entrepreneur and social enterprise, and it is this reference that becomes the key criterion used to account for economic commitment, replacing the nondistribution constraint.

Other studies are more oriented toward stakeholder theory. They hold that the aims of a company depend on the configuration of property rights—that is, on the stakeholders who hold these rights, since they determine the objectives. Nonprofits do not allow investors to dominate among stakeholders. Unlike capitalist companies, they are not owned by investors but by other types of stakeholders, and they therefore have objectives other than accumulating capital. As Hansmann (1996) and Gui (1991) point out, there are as many potential forms of ownership as there are types of stakeholder: apart from investors, these include workers and consumers. However, the associative status does not in itself guarantee that stakeholders will produce a high-quality service. In order for them to be able to do so, the legal equality between the stakeholders that the associative status ensures must be enhanced by real involvement in their association's operation. According to Ben-Ner and Van Hoomissen (1991), the best way to overcome information asymmetry is through stakeholders involved in the demand controlling the supply. The least informed stakeholders—the users and funders—can become members of the organization in order to counteract their information deficit. For them to make such an effort, they need to expect a net benefit (Gui 1992a), which requires the transaction to be valuable in their eyes, as well as both regular and lasting. As it is not possible for everyone to be a member of the organization, their representatives tend to be more effective for all where the organization provides a nonrival service; in other words, where the quality of the service cannot easily be varied according to the beneficiaries—for example in a daycare center where it is difficult to differentiate between the way different children are treated. Either stakeholders themselves recruit professionals for the service, or professionals aware of the information problems faced by stakeholders support them by designing a service that meets their needs. This is illustrated in France by the Association des collectifs enfants-parents-professionnels (ACEPP), a network formed by parents critical of previous forms of childcare. ACEPP has been strengthened by the actions of professionals committed to setting up organizations in which they can find jobs while respecting their work ethics and bringing together families who support their project.

Critical Perspectives

Starting from the empirical observation of the part nonprofits play in creating highly interpersonal services, the theoretical approaches that we have just examined explain the role of a third sector defined as the totality of nonprofits. They help to explain how organizations that have neither the financial incentives of profit-making companies, nor the stability or resources of public services, are nevertheless far from being insignificant in an economy where their role in employment and the provision of highly personalized services is growing.

Let us briefly summarize the achievements of these theoretical approaches. The first approach, initiated by Hansmann, is premised on contractual failures due to imperfect information. The second, begun by Weisbrod, focuses on the action of consumers of collective and quasi-collective goods whose demands are not met by the state and who organize to deliver themselves the services. Salamon's contribution, on the other hand, shows that the third sector is not immune to philanthropic failures. In short, no single sector offers a solution that is valid in all circumstances, so it makes sense to look at the advantages and disadvantages of each of the three sectors. The theory of the third sector is often referred to as a "theory of institutional choice" because it specifically aims to define the circumstances that lead actors to opt for nonprofits. This perspective is refined by supply-side approaches to social entrepreneurs' motivations, as well as the synthesis between supply and demand proposed by Ben-Ner and Van Hoomissen around the notion of the "stakeholder."

Despite these achievements, several objections can be made to the theory of the third sector. The first critique is internal: the theory's reasoning about the sources of trust could be further developed in order to more precisely identify the types of service in which these sources play a different role. This first internal critique leads to an external critique, which is that the paradigm of rational choice leads to aporias with respect to the relationship between selflessness and self-interest. Two more external critiques can be added to this. One is that the sectoral conceptualization contains a hierarchy reflected in the term "third sector." Finally, beneath the guise of universality we can see the preeminence of the North American context, which leads us to argue for an approach that takes other sociohistorical realities into account.

Types of Trust and Services

The arguments developed so far suggest that nonprofits benefit from a distinct domain of activity to which they are better suited than other providers. But the reality is different. In several countries, for-profit companies are fighting against nonprofits' precedence in personal care services by placing emphasis on specific mechanisms for labeling and applying standards. For-profit companies claim they are at a competitive disadvantage as nonprofits are allowed to obtain tax relief, as was the case in France when they were subject to a lower rate of value-added tax. In fact, competition is growing between different providers. Rather than assuming nonprofits' superiority in interpersonal services, it is better to study the mechanisms that generate trust and how they are mobilized by various organizations. Giddens's distinction between trust in expert systems and trust in people may be useful in this respect. It helps us to see how impersonal mechanisms (the nonprofit constraint, but also labeling, standardization, and professionalization) may either compete with or be reinforced by more personal mechanisms.

More generally, the diversification of service providers accentuates lobbying practices concealed within calls for neutrality in public intervention (Cette, Héritier, Taddéi, and Théry 1998). Consequently, increased competition may lead nonprofits to adopt more impersonal methods of building trust, such as certification schemes, in order to protect themselves against companies that use more standardized quality criteria. Conversely, nonprofits can accentuate their local roots and personal proximity to users by expanding their means of communication. Word of mouth can convey a reputation more effectively than abstract standards. In other words, recent developments raise questions about the coherence of the associative sector, which is increasingly torn between adopting new, imported management techniques and building upon its specific features. But they also raise questions about the homogeneity of the private sector: in the area of elderly care, subsidiaries of large groups are very different from small companies owned by professionals who have come from the public sector and who only run one or two institutions (Hansmann 1981; Goodspeed and Kenyon 1993). The latter are not driven by the desire for high returns on investment. They are ultimately motivated by three objectives: a desire to be more independent, a linked desire to have more control over their work, and a desire to develop high-quality services based on their knowledge of elderly people's daily lives (see Laville and Nyssens 2001b, 243). The demarcation between organizations may be based less on status than on size, as Hansmann suggests, and as confirmed by the study of residential services for the elderly in the United Kingdom, as "small companies—most of which are owned by people initially trained and employed in the public sector—are developing dramatically" (Kendall 2001, 97) while operating in a way similar to nonprofits. This analysis, which locates the third sector in the space left vacant by the market and the state, sidesteps the issue of increased competition with for-profit companies. To understand how this competition happens, we must take into account the full variety of providers, which does not necessarily correspond to the simple demarcation between statuses. But it is also important to note the full diversity of services and the importance of local rules governing their operation, which affect nonprofits and for-profit companies alike.

Furthermore, the balance between for-profit and nonprofit providers is not the same from service to service. At least this is the view of several experts who agree that there is a distinction within services. Borzaga stresses that social services are specific types of service characterized by "multidimensionality, strong relational intensity, and incompleteness of the employment contract" (2004, 34), which, he believes, make hierarchical control ineffective. Meanwhile Pestoff, extending Hirschman's discussion on exit and voice, distinguishes between two categories of service: short-term services, which are minor services in the sense that they do not involve strong relations between producers and consumers (hairdressing, housekeeping, gardening, meal delivery); and long-term services, which are major services for users because they involve greater intimacy and close contact (childcare, home-help). The costs of exiting long-term services are considerable for both consumers and providers, which leads them to see developing a collective voice as a better way of improving them (Pestoff 1998, chapter 4: "Economic Aspects of Civil Democracy"). It is this classification that is used to contrast household services with personal care services (Laville and Nyssens 2001b). For-profit companies are growing more rapidly in the former because here services have a strong technical component linked to clearly discernible tasks, while the latter result from a difficult process of socially constructing the service situation.

As a consequence, personal care services are not merely subject to information asymmetry. Here we can also speak of informational uncertainty (Dewey 1929) that causes a feeling of fear or even threat for the users and professionals concerned. As Nyssens puts it, apart from information asymmetries, "more fundamentally, it is necessary to take into account the radically incomplete nature of the information that guides the thought and practice of the protagonists in the service relationship . . . In this context, the construction of trust between agents cannot be reduced to a contractual arrangement . . . We cannot avoid the debate on standards and their foundations" (2000, 564). And as Gadrey adds: "These standards often integrate social considerations into the obligations of trading partners" (2000, 602). The theories of nomenclature and probability that, according to Orléan, characterize the traditional approach in economics are called into question. The first postulates the possibility of choosing between goods of homogeneous quality. The second assumes there are exogenous events or states of the world that provide an exhaustive description of everything that could happen tomorrow. Yet the people who are considering whether to get involved in interpersonal services do not have this information. Their ability to engage in exchange hangs on the construction of common reference points (Orléan 2002, 202–29).

We are reaching the limits of the axiom of rational choice here. The contradiction it contains is obvious when it considers the nonprofit constraint to be what allows consumers or funders to be sure that their interests will be respected. The analysis is schizoid: the selflessness of those who run nonprofits is supposed to explain other actors' individual economic interest in nonprofits. Because they are not driven by personal gain, those who run nonprofits inspire the confidence of partners, who then use these organizations to maximize their own interest. This aporia is pushed to the limit by the economic theory of altruism, which shows how selflessness itself is economically rational and constitutes a way of realizing individual interests. The satisfaction that comes from helping others is introduced into the utility function of the consumer (Orlean 2002, 202–29). Philanthropy is thus reintegrated into a broad conception of utility.

Another weakness of this theory is that it assumes that the individuals receiving the services are considered only as consumers. The role of organizations is therefore only seen through their function of producing goods and services, leaving other dimensions in the shadows. Social integration and democratic participation are ignored. The theory of the third sector may even go so far as to interpret rich and complex cultural legacies as obstacles to logical decisions or as insignificant data. It reduces all human decisions to choices based on behavior that is oriented toward the result of action—which ends up, in Etzioni's (1988) words, denying society's existence.

So while neoclassical analyses of the nonprofit sector have made advances, they also have their limitations. It is true that they move away from the belief in the generalized benefits of the market and capitalist enterprise. Nevertheless, by remaining within a framework that refers back to agents' optimizing rationality, they see nonprofits through a lens that brings everything back to utility maximization. As Favereau (1989) points out, this is the ambivalence of an expanded standard theory that takes into account norms and organizations while subjecting them to an economicist perspective, losing in coherence what it gains in extension, as Nyssens also notes (2000, 563). Because it is so focused on the organizational dimension—that of rational behavior—it cannot consider the institutional dimension, which opens up a line of inquiry about the foundations of legitimacy and the quality of modes of coordination (Rizza 2004). It is this extension to the institutional dimension that economic sociology allows for when it considers the genesis of a field of economic activity as an institutionalized process, to use Polanyi's words. From this perspective, we should note that personal care services were established in the orbit of the welfare state before they experienced a succession of different forms of regulation that profoundly affected their trajectories (Laville 2009).

A Separate Sector or an Intermediate Sphere

Hence the apparently high degree of formalism in approaches to the third sector that focus on identifying the universal laws it obeys. We remain in the frozen waters of selfish calculation, to use Marx's evocative words. Even the theories of supply that focus on social entrepreneurs and stakeholders fail to establish the motivations for associative engagement. This is because they conceal what gives warmth and depth to subjects and social relations, the traditions in which they are immersed, the groups to which they belong, the socialization processes that shape them and the forms of mutual recognition that give them dignity. By limiting itself to considerations of utility maximization, the sectoral conceptualization produces a functional and pacified view of the relations between market, state, and the nonprofit sector, because it promotes discourse that seeks to be free of any allusion to democracy or social justice.

An approach that starts from market and state failures does not stop at considering the market, state, and nonprofits as—by definition—separate entities and "compartmentalizing them" (Lewis 1997, 166). It goes further, proposing an analytical grid in which the market and the state are seen as the pillars of society and nonprofits as a complement.

According to this approach, as Godbout points out, "the market and the state represent the normal way of circulating goods and services" (2000, 98), and if the state can be replaced by nonprofits, then this will be in order to succeed it, because it has failed in its task of providing protection by sliding into bureaucracy.

As we can see, the theory of the third sector—adorned with the virtues of axiomatic neutrality claimed by neoclassical economics—still lends itself to a clear ideological use. Summoning up the nonprofit sector to justify the state's withdrawal echoes both the introduction of the concept of governance itself and an approach defended in the International Monetary Fund and the World Bank, in which the aim of "good governance" is a minimal state.[5] In a context where the state is invited to strengthen the role of the private sector, civil society—through international nonprofits such as nongovernmental organizations set up as civil society's representatives—is becoming a tool at the service of financial institutions: in 1988, they were involved in 5 percent of World Bank projects; by 1997 in 47 percent (see Azoulay 2002, 300–308).

The shift toward promoting civil society as an alternative to state intervention can, therefore, be seen as an extension of a rational choice theory where agents choose between market, state, and nonprofit solutions. In this respect, the shift from the notion of the nonprofit sector to that of the "civil society sector"—a shift made by those who lead the Johns Hopkins program (Salamon and Anheier 1997)—is marked by ambivalence. It introduces an interesting way of accounting for associations' embeddedness in civil society while moving beyond the nonprofit constraint; but the corollary of this is that it too quickly equates associations with the whole of civil society, and it also fails to properly examine their interactions with public authorities.

A strictly sectoral view neglects the intermediary role of associations, which can be understood as conduits between the private and the public spheres. Associative action, which results from encounters between people, opens the door to the public sphere, i.e. it offers these people an opportunity to help build a common world that is essential to democracy, through voluntary engagement that accommodates a plurality of opinions, conflicting interests, and different perspectives. Mediation between private and public spheres takes place in many different ways. The combinations of resources and logics of action that this mediation draws on are poorly reflected in accounts that assume a clear delimitation between sectors with well-established borders.

If, like Cohen and Arato (1994), we characterize civil society as being a sphere different from the state and the market, then associations are part of organized civil society. This is because they influence the configuration of the public sphere through innovations and through disagreements that they manage to express—including through the very nature of their socioeconomic production. However, they are not only rooted in civil society. As Barthélémy rightly states, "the activities of civil society cannot be separated from political society" (2000, 15–17), and associations affect both dimensions of the political: on the one hand, noninstitutional politics based on citizens' potential for action, which depends on them practically seizing the positive freedom that they formally possess; and on the other hand, institutional policies based on the exercise of state power. Indeed, it is this dual political aspect of associations that is hidden in the notion of the third sector.

From Ethnocentrism to a Contextualized and Historicized Approach

The hypothetical-deductive approaches of neoclassical economics are supposed to identify laws with universal scope, but from this promise emerge accounts that in fact reflect the North American configuration of associations. When Salamon talks about associations, he brings up their philanthropic inadequacies, consequently eliminating any reference to initiatives guided by democratic solidarity. When Anheier takes up James's arguments to highlight the fact that, internationally, nonprofit organizations are frequently religious organizations, he recommends that we take into account religious values "as a guide for the organization, its founders, and its employees," and leaves other ideological reasons with more political connotations in the background (Anheier 1995, 63–64). The French Mouvement Populaire des Familles shows that even within Christian movements a logic of mutual aid and self-organization can be a reaction against charity, which points to the plurality of ideological frames of reference even within religious movements (Duriez and Nizey 1990).

In short, what is erased in this approach—which is intended to be free of normativity—is the historical process that has led to the primacy of philanthropy among associations. The display of neutrality actually obscures the naturalization of philanthropy and religious engagement as complements to the market and state. It leads to a modification of the existing system, but this is only a marginal amendment that leaves intact the processes of exclusion and denial of justice at the heart of the dominant model of development.

It is not surprising that South American authors are particularly sensitive to this ideological enrollment of associations into a model where they become both agents for implementing social-assistance policies as well as supports for structural adjustment and debt repayment programs. Coraggio points out that "the growth of the third sector and volunteerism in Argentina does not necessarily mean an increase in social solidarity, but it may reflect the decline in the recognition of social rights and in the security guarantees provided by the state, since both the national productive and public sectors have suffered systematic destruction" (2002, 2). Razeto shows how questionable the label "third sector" really is, affirming as it does the subordinate status of the forms of social and economic organization that belong to it. He accurately summarizes the concept's strengths and weaknesses; in his view it lacks clear reference to its proponents' motives. But he does not see any danger in it because it does not fit into a "determined," "rigid" project predefined by "enlightened avant-gardes." Presenting it in this way can only serve to make it broadly acceptable to leaders on all sides, particularly in a cultural and political atmosphere characterized by the end of great ideologies. But this broad acceptability has a counterpart: few actors claim to belong to the third sector. It is difficult to attract people to join such a composite group. In Razeto's view, the concept's future thus hangs on its appropriation "in a participatory process of seeking alternatives, of defining and constructing a shared identity, of developing a new project" (2000, 4).

It has gradually dawned on those who initiated research into the third sector that, because they are embedded in the English-speaking cultural universe, their lines of investigation—which initially had pretensions toward universality—are not without presuppositions. In an effort to contextualize their results, various researchers have attempted to demonstrate correlations between the significance of association and national macrovariables such as population diversity (Weisbrod 1977. 3; James, 1990), religious competition (James 1990), trust in private enterprise (Hansmann 1980, 839–901; 1987, 27–42), and per capita income (Titmuss 1974). For its part, the Johns Hopkins project focused on the relationship between the nonprofit sector and democracy, drawing on the distinction Weaver and Rockman (1993, 10–16) make between different national contexts on three institutional levels: their system of government (presidential or parliamentary), their party system (e.g., multiparty, single party), and their degree of economic development. But an accumulation of correlations should not be considered a causal link, and these various explorations appear less heuristically useful than an approach that emphasizes the interdependencies between associative action and public action. The experience of the last two centuries shows that the voluntary sector does not promote the state's disengagement any more than associations provide residual services in the gaps left by the market and the state. By drawing clear boundaries between nonprofit organizations and public action, the notion of the nonprofit sector therefore becomes problematic in light of historical realities. In practice, association both preceded state action and made it conceivable; as Enjolras points out, the two complement rather than replace each other: "The state is in a position to generate stable and sufficient resources through taxation, to set priorities on the basis of the democratic process, to provide equal access to public services for all and to standardize the quality of services. The nonprofit sector is able to customize services, operate on a smaller scale than bureaucracies, adjust services to needs and generate competition between providers" (1995, 47).

Moreover, associations' role in the welfare state's genesis should not lead us to forget the extent to which public regulation has influenced their evolution. Enjolras cites the development of legislation in the United States allowing the government to enter into contracts with profit-making organizations. As a result of this change, their share in providing social services for the elderly increased from 1.9 percent in 1972 to 17 percent in 1982 and 31 percent in 1986, while associations had to lower their quality standards to compete (Bergthold, Estes, and Villanueva 1998).

Finally, when we look more closely at these third sector theories in conjunction with the practices they claim to shed light on, the notion of the third sector gives rise to some strong reservations. The reasons why associations are able to compensate for market and state failures have been identified based on neoclassical economics. A link is established between the growth of interpersonal services and the expansion of the nonprofit sector's role in employment. This approach thus sheds particular light on the relationship between the rise of associations and the service economy.

That said, it raises a major concern by explaining associations' existence solely in terms of their economic functions. Since members' motivations are seen through the prism of rational choice, the result is a consumerist perspective on demand and a deficit when it comes to understanding the motivations of those providing the supply. These shortcomings have led to the nonprofit constraint being relegated in recent iterations of the economic approach to the third sector, in favor of a focus on social entrepreneurs and all stakeholders. However, by remaining within the framework of a universalist analysis, these theoretical adaptations make it difficult to historicize and contextualize associations and ignores their sociopolitical aspects.

While the different variants of third sector theories consider associations as organizations that intervene in the event of market or state failure, this view is undermined by reality. A more historical approach—one less focused on searching for variables that are supposed to explain associations' significance—leads to the conclusion that associations "are not only producers of goods and services but important factors of political and social coordination" (Seibel 1990, 46). The expansion of the market has led to reactions from civil society, including the formation of associations and the development of a protective welfare state. What will decide the future of democracy is neither the liberal mythification of a civil society driven by mere compassion but ignoring rights, nor a welfare-statism that has proved unable by itself to realize the desire for recognition (Honneth 1995), but rather how associations are connected to the public domain.

Some analysts aligned with the third sector approach have begun to study this historical process, this mutual engendering, admitting that associations were indeed the "first line of defense" (Lewis 1997, 166) developed by society, but that their weaknesses then forced them to cooperate with the state. Thus, after the first Johns Hopkins study, Salamon and Anheier (1996; 1997) turned toward "a social origins approach" aimed at better understanding different national situations by analyzing their historical genesis. This revitalization of the problematic is connected to the creation of a broader research community that promotes both international and interdisciplinary debate—debate that is less dominated by Anglo-American economic approaches and more open to a variety of contributions. It is in this context that we see a confrontation with conceptualizations of associations in terms of the social economy and solidarity economy. Unlike theories of the third sector, these conceptualizations are based on theoretical frameworks other than rational choice.

The Social Economy

IT IS IN EUROPE THAT THE CONCEPT of the social economy has been developed. It is broader than that of the third sector because it encompasses cooperatives and mutuals. It reflects the reality described in the book's first section better than studies that refer only to the nonprofit sector. Rather than a nonprofit sector, we can speak of a not-for-profit sector. Cooperatives and mutuals emerge from the same melting pot as nonprofit organizations—that is, they are forged from a perspective that is not focused on return on investment. Undeniably, the history of the last two centuries justifies bringing these organizations together under the same label.

The Originality of the Approach

The notion of the social economy thus underlines the extent to which the definition of the nonprofit sector suffers from an anglophone bias. The concept of the third sector is influenced by this sector's configuration in America, where there is positive discrimination in favor of philanthropy, a predominance of the nondistribution constraint, and a marked role for foundations benefiting from strong tax incentives. Having arisen from other contexts, the idea of the social economy, by contrast, emphasizes the coherent group formed by organizations for which it is not the nondistribution constraint that is key but rather the fact that the distribution of profits to capital providers is restricted. From this perspective, the differentiating criterion is the fact that there are limits on the private appropriation of the profits generated by the activity. It thus distinguishes between organizations in the social economy and other organizations involved in production. Moreover, by adding mutuals and cooperatives, the concept of the social economy makes it easier to include forms of collective action based on mutual aid and the participation of citizens affected by social problems. This is another point of divergence from the third sector approach, which focuses on nonprofit organizations and views volunteering from a more economic perspective as an individual behavior connected to the provision of services.

Criteria for Defining Organizations

Social Economy

> Criterion of limiting the distribution of profits and power of the capital providers

> Cooperatives and mutuals are included along with "nonprofit organizations"

Third Sector

> Priority to nondistribution constraint

> Subsector composed by nonprofit organizations

> Cooperatives and mutuals are excluded

The Various Components

The fundamental components of the social economy are cooperatives, mutuals, and nonprofit organizations. Their legal status is reflected in a particular form of capitalization that offers no advantage to particular individuals in terms of either decision making or the redistribution of surpluses. In addition, in the event that the organization's activity is terminated, no member may individually appropriate the accumulated reserves (Lévesque and Ninacs 1997). Desroche identifies these organizations as:

> cooperative enterprises, which are either worker cooperatives or service cooperatives, and also combinations between these two types of cooperative, whose members are, in the case of the former, its workers, and in the case of the latter, its users,

> mutualist enterprises, which share many characteristics with cooperatives but also have specific features (in cooperatives, the

principle is to each according to their transactions; in mutuals,
it is to each according to their needs),

nonprofits which are associations focused on services, even
if they are also concerned by advocacy and/or sociability.
(1983, 204)

To these three central components, Desroche adds four peripheral components, which are respectively located at the borders of the private sector (participatory enterprise), of the public sector (municipal enterprise), of the trade union sector (joint enterprise), and of the community sector (community or popular enterprise). This definition based on statuses makes it easier to gather statistics, so it represents a considerable contribution. While the conception of the nonprofit sector links this sector to the emergence of a service society, by looking in detail at consumer and producer behavior over the long run, the social economy approach is rediscovering these organizations' historical depth. More descriptive than hypothetical-deductive, this approach makes it possible to explain these organizations' legal and normative specificities by retracing their trajectory—yet it leaves open the question of their relationship to the economy and politics.

Taking the Historical Perspective into Account

The nineteenth-century collective actions mentioned at the beginning of the book led to compromises that legalized organizations in which agents other than investors were granted property rights. In light of this genesis, we can see that the real line of demarcation does not pass between profit-making and nonprofit organizations but between capitalist companies and social economy entities. The latter favor the creation of collective property over the return on individual investment. The social economy approach therefore emphasizes all statuses that restrict the private appropriation of profits and promote the creation of collective property.

The common origin of associations, cooperatives and mutuals is undeniable, as highlighted in the first part of this book. Thus cooperatives in many European countries are extensions of associative projects. This is the case in France, where the associative reform projects of the first half of the nineteenth century are continued in cooperatives (Ferraton 2007). But cases in other countries also highlight contiguities between associations and cooperatives over the long term. In Italy, in 1942, the Civil Code specified that associations could not engage in economic activities. In parallel, the fascist regime attacked the part of the cooperative movement that was closely connected to workers' movements, establishing a single authority controlled by the state and the party to oversee it (see Borzaga 2004, 45–62). Sweden illustrates the fact that associations do not have a monopoly over the nondistribution of profits, as some cooperatives—such as construction cooperatives—have never distributed their surpluses. In addition, two categories of association exist in Sweden: voluntary associations and economic associations,[1] and cooperatives have adopted the latter status. This is clear evidence that the two legal statuses are intertwined around entities that limit the distribution of surpluses, have significant economic activity, and have a substantial paid workforce. In both the United Kingdom and Germany, there are two types of collective action—the first dominated by philanthropy, with middle-class groups involved, the second more organized by working-class groups—and the divisions between these two types are more significant than those between associations and cooperatives: in the United Kingdom, charities are distinguished from friendly societies, which involve egalitarian self-organization; while in Germany, church-related charitable associations are moving away from other associations grouped in the social-democratic "pillar," which are closer to cooperatives and mutuals.[2]

The contemporary understanding of the term *social economy* took a long time to emerge, however. In the first half of the nineteenth century,[3] "social economy" was defined as a scientific approach that extended and modified the project of political economy.[4] As Gide pointed out: "Political economy, which, from its origin until the middle of the last century, presented itself as a 'natural science,' has taken two divergent paths. Along one, it has sought to constitute itself as pure Economics, the mathematical science of exchange, or the hedonistic science of utility. In the other, it has sought to reconcile justice with utility. This insight—some would even say this contamination—of political economy by Morality has been criticized" (2000, vi). To clarify what was at stake, Walras distinguished between pure economy or the "domain of the true," applied economy or the "domain of the useful," and social economy or the "domain of the just" (1990, 4–5); in so doing, he represents this first understanding of social economy as a discipline that aims to react against the separation between economy and morality. However, Gide and Walras's common desire to reconcile interest and justice diverges when it comes to the means employed. Gide assigns a primary role to cooperatives whose function is productive, while Walras excludes them from a social economy dedicated to the redistribution of wealth. This difference is due to the fact that, for the former, morality consists in the union of personal interest and the general interest (to which justice refers), and so it is in the economy itself that ethical considerations arise; while for the latter, these considerations emerge after the natural laws of production have taken their course. While Walras's social economy is about redistribution and relies on state intervention, for Gide the "institutions of social progress" that it deals with include associations, public authorities, and patronage, which tend to provide better working conditions and comfort in all its forms, to ensure the security of the future against all social risks, or to safeguard economic independence (1890). Without being stabilized, the term "social economy" was then used—by Weber among others[5]—to encompass "economic theory" (the study of "economic phenomena" obeying the strict logic of interest), economic sociology (the analysis of observed facts' "cultural significance"), and economic history (the observation of "concrete historical facts").

This scientific project was not sustained, however, and in the twentieth century "the expression narrowed somewhat in relation to its original meaning and scope" (Parodi 1984, 100). It now no longer refers to a science, but to a sector of activity. Fauquet distances himself from the divisions between consumer and worker cooperatives to focus on identifying the "relatively invariant relationships" that constitute cooperatives as a sector[6]—namely the combination of an enterprise and an association of individuals.

This observation of cooperatives' dual nature—that they are both economic and cultural—is extended by Defourny and Develtère, who identify two conditions for development: "necessity" and "belonging to a social group united by a collective identity or a common destiny" (Defourny, Develtère, and Fonteneau 1999, 23–29 and 38).

An Organizational Approach

Beyond identifying the conditions for its creation, the social economy can be characterized through a legal approach; doing so makes it easier to gather statistics about the organizations concerned, since they take three legal forms: cooperatives, mutuals, and associations. But while the adoption of one of these legal forms "is an important indicator . . . [it] does not in itself guarantee that an organization belongs to the social economy. In some countries, there may be many companies that are only cooperative in name . . . Similarly, their associative or mutualist status may sometimes serve as a legal front for profit-making activities or para-public structures" (Defourny, Develtère, and Fonteneau 1999, 38).

It is therefore suggested that a normative approach be combined with a legal approach in order to separate organizations that have the same legal configuration but differ in behavior. According to this hybrid approach, "the social economy includes the economic activities carried out by companies, mainly cooperatives, mutual societies, and associations, whose ethics are reflected in the following principles: the aim of providing a service to members or the community rather than seeking profit; self-management; democratic decision-making processes; [and] the primacy of people and work over capital in the distribution of income" (Defourny, Develtère, and Fonteneau 1999, 38). This list of principles may set out the values claimed by the organizations themselves, but it calls into question the simplicity of the classification that results from the legal approach. This is the source of an ambiguity in the social economy literature, which wavers between including all entities corresponding to these legal forms when it wants to emphasize their significance in the economy, and excluding certain entities on the grounds that there is a gap between their observable reality and the principles affirmed.

So as not to restrict ourselves to defining social economy entities by their status and their affirmation of general ethical principles, it has been proposed that we approach the social economy via its system of rules. This approach aims to go beyond debates about which values are specific to the social economy and clarify the distinct properties of the organizations that are part of it. Desroche and Vienney have identified specific features that stem from the voluntary combination of a group of people, on the one hand, and an enterprise, on the other—which are linked together by a relationship of association and activity (Vienney 1994). The resulting system of rules can be traced back to the two poles of this combination and the relations between them: members have equal rights in those management bodies that have general jurisdiction; the share of operating surpluses reinvested in the enterprise remains common property on a permanent basis; if operating profit is shared between the associated persons, then it is shared on a basis proportional to their activities with the enterprise. Fauquet's sectoral approach is thus extended to all social economy entities, which are defined not only by their combination of an enterprise and an association but also by the socioeconomic relationships they maintain (Draperi 1998, 12). According to Vienney, the social economy is therefore the work of actors who have limited economic power but who nonetheless hold resources, for example small-scale farmers or skilled workers. They rely on their own assets to take on activities that are necessary to them, but which are neglected by capitalism because they are not profitable enough.

These approaches make it possible to illustrate graphically what distinguishes organizations in the social economy. As Noguès (2004) says, the capitalist enterprise is under the control of people who have invested in it and expect a substantial return. The requirements differ depending on the number and profile of shareholders (sole proprietorship or limited company, listed or not), but control by capital is exercised even if the form this takes varies. In the social economy, this dependence on financing that is external to the actors involved in the economic activity being carried out is replaced by a capital contribution from voluntarily associated members who get involved because they expect the activity to provide a service and possibly a limited share of the surplus generated. This characteristic makes social economy governance more complex. As it is not guided by a unifying objective; it is subject, according to Desroche, to the risk of rupturing the "cooperative quadrilateral" in cases where tensions emerge between shareholders, directors, managers, and employees (Demoustier, Rousselière, Clerc, and Cassier 2003, 149–53). Despite these dangers, compromises between actors can allow the social economy to occupy a place in the productive landscape that capitalist enterprises have now vacated. As the latter comply with performance criteria that—in line

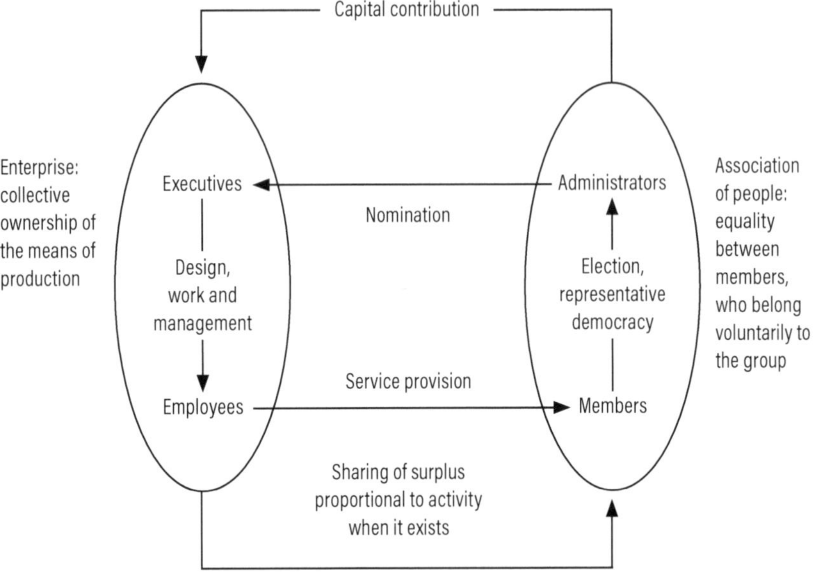

FIGURE 2. The social economy organization. Based on Desroche 1983 and Vienney 1994.

with international financial market standards—have become more demanding, they can abandon profitable activities that do not perform as required, select production factors, and engage in market segmentation that is not conducive to social cohesion (Noguès 2004). They define their activities around demands from which they can make a profit, ignoring those from which they cannot. Business takeovers and work-integration social enterprises are evidence of this growing gap between activities that are attractive to international investors, on the one hand, and those that may be both profitable and conducive to local development without generating prospective profit considered sufficient by financial investors, on the other.

The contribution of the notion of the social economy is indisputable: it points to a set of activities broader than the nonprofit sector in a context where collective entrepreneurship emerging from civil society makes use of both cooperative and associative statuses. It also helps to build bridges between these legal forms. Moreover, the role played by the social economy has the potential to grow in the current economic climate, because its organizations are partially resistant to financialization—precisely because they are partnerships, not capital enterprises. The social economy also demonstrates that, in the creation of trust relationships,[7] the nonprofit constraint can be replaced by other organizational characteristics: the definition of a shared objective, the participation of members on the basis of legal equality, the mobilization of a network. Yet all these advantages are accompanied by questions that cannot be ignored because they arise so regularly in studies on the subject. These concern the relationship with the economy but also with politics.

The Relationship with the Economy

The most recurrent observation is of these organizations' tendency to lose their distinctiveness. This was already apparent in the 1950s, in the obstacles encountered by workers cooperatives, which had wanted to revitalize the cooperative ideal after the war: "The ever-growing gap between managers and subordinates, the difficulty of selecting and replacing leaders capable of handling such heavy responsibilities, the problems of internal hierarchy between the different skill levels, and the distribution of social benefits between investment and direct or indirect remuneration" (Friedmann and Tréanton 1962, 486). Evidence of this gap widening has since become abundant.

Converging Findings

From the 1970s onward, competition increased as pressure for greater capital intensity grew, and some captive markets were challenged. These contingencies led to a growing emphasis on cooperatives' technostructure and an "empowerment of the management team" (Chiffoleau 1999, 32). Champagne notes that in agricultural cooperatives, annual general meetings "are often very poorly attended and serve merely to confirm the cooptation of new directors by the board of directors."[8] Bloch-Lainé (1996) acknowledges that the democratic functioning of associations that is guaranteed in theory has in fact been diluted, which has "given rise to some massive scandals." According to him, "when there are many contributors . . . the real influence of these potential voters is very weak. Only a small proportion of them attend meetings to appoint directors, so directors are coopted by a narrow circle of people who are the only ones who follow how things are progressing and who can be more-or-less easily steered by the board, generally in a less than transparent way" (cited in Bidet 1997, 196).

In addition, management practices are taking precedence over the ambitions of the original project and cause real ruptures between the economic and moral dimensions of mutualist practice (Gibaud 1986). In contradiction to their initial openness, agricultural cooperatives and health mutuals select their members. In the case of health mutuals, an official French report recommends that insurance methods be enshrined in law in order to maintain specific features that otherwise "vary widely by institution" (Rochard 1999): often "the undifferentiated tariff has been abandoned regardless of the age of the person insured" (Bode 2000), and policies with contributions that vary according to age, sex, region, and so on "are offered in contravention of the rules of mutual solidarity" (Dumont 1995).

These are not isolated examples of how the rules are gradually being aligned with those of other companies. Although the partnership status may, as mentioned earlier, be a safeguard against neocapitalism's excesses, it hardly plays this role when the competition is pushing it to search for financial partners. In these circumstances, we more often see the dilution of any particularity associated with this legal status. Cooperatives' membership is further disintegrated when they search for funding on the financial market and open up to noncooperative investors. This leads to the formation of complex groups that combine the cooperative and private sectors. Subsidiaries are jointly owned by several cooperatives, or even in conjunction with industrial capitalist companies, as a way of increasing their flexibility and coping with greater competition. "Additional compensation" is offered to nonmember investors—in addition to members with more limited financial means—in order to attract them (see Bidet 2001, 49). Measures "that have the effect, if not the aim, of bringing the status of [social economy entities] closer to the dominant model of the economy" are numerous (Espagne 2002; see also Marchand's 2009 chapter on the European Cooperative Society). They undermine the characteristic dual status of being both a shareholder and participant in the activity, which "can only put an end to the cooperative enterprise as it has existed up to now" (Lévesque and Côté 1995) and give rise to a new breed of enterprises which can no longer be defined according to classic cooperative principles (Koulytchizky and Mauget 2003). Leading experts on the social economy agree that "enterprise" has gradually taken precedence over "association" (Chomel 2000), to the point where there is "a kind of reversal of the relationship between people and the enterprise" (Vienney 1994, 114). The importance of resources linked to commercial relationships increases in relation to transfers corresponding to legal moral obligations or donations (Perroux 1960, cited by Vienney 1994, 114 and 8). This dilution of the solidarity process means that "large cooperative enterprises are almost conflated with large noncooperative enterprises" (Malo 2002), or that social economy enterprises adopt "economic behavior that is fairly close to that of companies in the traditional private sector" (CIRIEC 2000) in the areas where competition is fiercest, such as banking and insurance.

This gradual loss of specificity has thus become a constant refrain in case studies. The law of oligarchy also affects the social economy: democracy is not conceivable without organization, but organization contributes to a weakening of democracy. The thesis of inevitable degeneration maintained by Marxist theorists[9] has been defended more recently by sociologists such as Kirkham (1973) and especially Meister (1974) on the basis of studies of various associations. It suggests a four-phase life cycle that, after an initial stage characterized by idealism and commitment, ends in a phase where democracy is reduced to its representative form. The gap between management and workers, which grows with the rationalization of production, gives managers effective power because of their expertise and ability to control information. The logic of reaction against the effects of capitalism—which explains the birth of social economy entities—is fading in favor of a logic of functional adaptation to this mode of production.

This evolution in the life cycles of social economy entities is also evident in the history of national movements. This is what emerges, for example, from Singer's study of Brazil (Singer 2006, 290–302). As he points out, many cooperatives have disappeared in Latin America: consumer cooperatives have been supplanted by supermarkets, and production cooperatives overtaken by the integration of workers into the capitalist wage system. Those that remain have evolved in the same way as the Rochdale Pioneers cooperative in England, with the end of participation and the separation of members and elected officers. The status has even been instrumentalized by businesses to turn their employees into subcontractors, thereby cutting labor costs through "false" cooperatives. As for agricultural cooperatives, they have become gigantic agribusiness groups that promote a productivist conception of agriculture. In addition to this alignment with the possibility of competing in a global market, which has also occurred among cooperative banks, there was also a cooperative populism thanks to which the number of cooperatives in Latin America rose from 7,500 to 25,700 between 1950 and 1970, and the number of members from 2 million to almost 10 million. As in the communist regimes of the Eastern bloc and in African nations during the same period, cooperatives and other "popular" organizations were placed at the service of national governments' economic objectives, resulting in a sector that lacked its own dynamic (ee Defourny, Develtère, and Fonteneau 1999, 31).

The paths taken by the social economy in Europe echo these findings. Referring to the loss of savings capacity among the working class, the real turning point was not the state's assumption of responsibility in 1911, but rather a waning of the spirit of mutuality and member control, which was central to the first mutual aid societies (Harris 2018). While the latter were crucial for the emergence of the UK's Labour Party and its access to power, the party then applied the dynamism of mutualism to new causes, such as trade unionism, and adopted a more centralizing ideology, shedding its local traditions. When talking about collective ownership of the means of production, the architects of the Labour Party, the Webbs, spoke of nationalization rather than socialization. In 1948, Beveridge noted that mutuals were becoming "more official and less personal, more of insurance agencies and less of social agencies" (1948, 78–79). In the 1950s, according to Taylor, cooperatives and mutuals lost their identity as a common movement for social change (Taylor 2004, 130–31, citing Yeo 2001; see also Evers and Laville 2001). In Germany, from the end of the Second World War onward, the Social Democrats considered the reform of the economy and social protection to be a matter for the state. Without their former social and ethical foundation, most of the cooperatives that survived the Nazi regime—especially those in the housing sector—expanded and lost their legitimacy due to corruption and scandals. The most famous of these scandals was that of the union-owned company Neue Heimat, which marked the end of the *Gemeinwirtschaft,* the economy for the public good, which had been composed of municipal and cooperative enterprises (Bode and Evers 2004, 105–6). Meanwhile charities connected to the churches or the bourgeoisie "have often gradually transformed themselves into commercial or state organizations" (Evers 2000, 567–85). Moreover, during the Thirty Glorious years, the period of economic growth that lasted from 1945 to 1975, European conservative parties were in favor of expanding the market and socialists were in favor of state intervention. This obscured a social economy divided into two subsystems: the social market economy and the nonmarket social economy.

An Endorsement of the Market Economy

The decline's acceleration is sometimes spectacular, as with the demutualization of building societies and insurance associations in the United Kingdom or the "great decline of French consumer cooperatives."[10] The Nordic countries have not escaped this decline; as Pestoff notes, consumer cooperatives have become large bureaucratic organizations, impermeable to any influence by their members. In 1992, the Swedish consumer cooperative movement abandoned its legal status as an economic association in favor of that of a company, eliminating any trace of democratic control and becoming just one commercial chain among others. In 2001, it merged with its Danish and Norwegian counterparts to create Co-op Norden. The merger was designed to preserve all three organizations' market share. This strategy resembled that of the agricultural cooperative movement, which launched itself into international mergers; the commercial conglomerates that resulted no longer have anything to do with their origins in popular movements (Pestoff 2004, 73–74).

The facts are incontestable: social economy organizations are only partially protected by their legal status. Like any other organization, they are subject to institutional isomorphism—that is, "a constraining process that forces one unit in a population to resemble other units that face the same set of environmental conditions."[11] This could, according to Enjolras, be either normative isomorphism via professionalization, coercive isomorphism resulting from the influence of public authorities, or mimetic isomorphism via the importation of solutions tested elsewhere (1996, 63). This process of isomorphism is as obvious as it is multifaceted, ranging from a shift to "coopitalism," to mergers, integration into noncooperative groups, and the creation of subsidiaries over which members no longer have any control. These tendencies evidently call into question the original identity of the enterprises concerned, and prompt us to ask whether it is possible to maintain the specific characteristics of the social economy in a context of intense competition and the rapid concentration of capital (see Defourny, Develtère, and Fonteneau 1999). This line of inquiry is all the more pressing given that, as Dubois and Abhervé (2009) write, cooperative banks "have allowed themselves to be swept up in the global financial turmoil, and have taken foolish risks with several billion euros" (see also Frémeaux 2009, 30–33).

Observations on this theme are so widespread in the literature that they call for real reflection and not merely a rhetorical reply—though we should acknowledge that such reflection may not be generalizable to all social economy organizations. In fact, the problem lies in the way in which we understand their involvement in the economy. The conceptualization of the social economy that is based on microeconomic units' legal status has given rise to an "economicist" drift which only takes into account these organizations' performance on the market. The desire not to be confined to social issues and to be accepted as a constituent part of the economy explains the emphasis placed on the fact that "it has never been the social economy's goal to systematically leave the market; it was, moreover, principally born within the market" (Jeantet 2001, 24; also see Jeantet 1999). The counterpart of this legitimate concern to appear as a fully fledged economic entity is a propensity to equate the economy to the market. The representation the social economy promotes is that of noncapitalist enterprises in the market. Their indicator of success is that of growth in the volume of market activity, overshadowing any questioning about the economy's nonmarket spheres.

Within this perspective—which places the emphasis on market presence—it is logical that the cooperative should be central. With Fauquet (1965), and later Vienney (1980–82; 1994), the cooperative model became the reference for the entire social economy, which has led to the inclusion of only those associations that are highly economically significant. Thus associations—whose resources derive largely from taxation and volunteer work—cannot gain complete recognition under a French social economy charter that declares that its constituent organizations "live in the market economy" and develop "institutions that the traditional market economy does not give rise to." The discrepancy with reality is even more marked now that associations make up the largest part, in terms of employees, of a social economy that accounts for 6.6 percent of civilian employment in the European Union (see CIRIEC 2000). "The overly industrialist and cooperative perspective that downplayed the rise of services and associations" (Desmoustier 2001, 130) explains why the social economy was disrupted by the initiatives of the late twentieth century.

This discrepancy between empirical developments and conceptual framework merits further analysis. Isomorphism is only one of the consequences of the hostile environment. It is supported by the formatting of practices carried out by the theory of the social economy, which evaluates cooperatives, mutuals, and associations with regard to the development of relations between members, on the one hand, and economic outputs—assessed by the degree to which they are integrated into the market economy—on the other. The social economy perspective looks at the activities of mutuals and associations through the prism of cooperatives and forgets their broader societal role, including the development of collective action that can provide the matrix for public action. Yet their effects on public policy have been significant. To cite just one example of the institutional changes brought about in this way, mutual help initiatives prefigured social security systems and contributed to their construction. As such, they were a genuine innovation that overcame the limits of the market economy. But an approach centered on organizations and enterprises cannot account for this.

The Limits of an Organizational Approach

The creation of new public regulations cannot be captured within social economy microorganizations, because it involves these organizations' interaction with the existing rules, as well as their contribution to the development of macroeconomic regulations. To shed light on this creation, we need to introduce an institutional dimension into the evaluation of practices—one that goes beyond the framework of the organization. Put differently, the focus on the organizational dimension of the social economy does not allow us to see the institutional dimension of collective action—either in its genesis or its impact.

Social economy also evades questions about the definition of solidarity. By reducing solidarity to the collective interest, it "leaves to one side a vast world of nonconsumerist and noninstrumental motivations" (Evers 2000). In a sense, it stops at the threshold of a conception of solidarity as an independent principle; or else, when this principle is recognized, it has only a palliative role, one that is "derivative and secondary, fulfilling tasks wherever other principles are absent" (Salamon 1987; Herman 1984). In this analytic framework, solidarity is expressed through the sharing of surpluses among partners in proportion to their participation. The reference to rational choices guided by the mutual or general interest (see Gui 1992a; 1992b) reduces thought to discursive reason and discursive reason to strategic calculation. But the subjects concerned are also careful to take into account the experience and modalities of socialization in the dynamics they generate, so we should not neglect the symbolic aspect of their action. Because, as Ricoeur suggests, the symbol always provides more to think about than discursive reason can consider, precisely because it is not of a discursive order (Caillé 1993, 205; quoting Ricoeur 1986). Yet where the impulses behind solidarity are not made explicit, relations between people and enterprise are inevitably reversed: initially, people's belonging to a solidarity-based collective is a prerequisite for the formation of an enterprise, but once this enterprise "defines the field of their common interests," its operation "reclassifies the associated people according to the functions that link them to its own activity." The enterprise selects its partners according to criteria connected to its own development, "from which comes an obsolescence of relations of assistance, in favor of productive efficacy evaluated by each partner with reference to that of other enterprises."[12] The social economy becomes a Sisyphean boulder, as enterprises' operation erodes the very solidarities that gave birth to them, while new organizations appear seeking to reactivate them—organizations that evolve in a way that is identical to those that preceded them.

In a sense, the theory of the social economy is too quick to equate solidarity to shared interest. Through this implicit inclusion in a paradigm of interest that it does not question, it obscures—by definition—the intersubjective dimension of collective action. What is left in the shadows is the institutional logic, understood as a common higher principle on which participants agree. In setting up what becomes their initiative, these participants construct principles of legitimation, starting from the feeling of institutional inadequacy and ending up at the defense of common goods that they have elaborated together. As such, this is not merely a process of organization, but one of institutional creation. This creation corresponds to the principle of legitimacy claimed by the collective action and also to the compromises social actors have agreed to in order to develop the "rules of the game" that govern their relations.[13] It thus goes beyond the phenomenon of the organization managing the production process.

The Relationship to Politics

The reasons for the social economy's loss of distinctiveness do not have only to do with market isomorphism and an exclusively organization-centered vision; they also stem from the relationship to the political. On this issue, two problems can be identified in the social economy approach. The first appeared during its genesis, when—as the discipline of social economy—it stressed the moral dimension of activity. The second appears in the contemporary definition of the social economy as a sector composed of "different enterprises" that "prioritize the service provided over profit, and integrate the social dimension into economic life,"[14] without saying anything about the political dimension.

Contrary to the theory of the third sector, that of the social economy does not eliminate the political dimension by definition. But the conditions under which social economy emerged—at a point in history when philanthropy was preferred—has helped downplay any political project. If its moral connotation is then abandoned, then the social economy will only be conceptualized in terms of the enterprise's internal rules of operation, which lessens its political impact.

From Politics to Moralization

Classical political economy sought—through knowledge of mechanisms of growth—to reduce poverty via economic progress. The adoption of the laws of the market was justified by the eradication of destitution, relieving all of those who were previously condemned either to the gallows or to pity. But at the start of the nineteenth century, liberal optimism was contradicted by the facts and "the problem of the meaning of modernity and the fundamental threat it bore" was raised: "the risk that—unless it renounced industrialization—economic progress would lead to complete social disintegration" (Castel 1995, 230). The coincidence of private interest and collective interest asserted by classical thinkers was subsequently contested by theorists like Sismondi (1827), who stipulated that, in order to attenuate the harshness of transition periods, there was a need to study how wealth was redistributed in addition to production (see Azam 2001, 51). Yet these authors all rejected worker associationalism, considering social reform to be a remedy the worse evil. In particular, they intended to settle the question of redistribution without altering the organization of work. Understood by Say as synonymous with political economy, social economy broke away from its counterpart from the 1830s onward in order to critique it from the point of view of social inequality. The books dedicated to the topic came one after another: in 1830, a *Nouveau Traité d'économie sociale* [New treatise on social economy] by Dunoyer, in 1839 *L'Économie sociale* [The social economy] by Pecqueur, in 1844 *Études sur l'économie sociale* [Studies on the social economy] by Marbeau. The problem of destitution became central. The term "social economy" was employed to denote attempts to reconcile economy and morality in the context of a "nonjuridical conceptualization of social relations," as Procacci put it, or a "politics without the state," in Castel's words. To make "wealth into a means of social happiness" (Frégier 1840, 1:5; cited by Procacci 1993, 181), production should be regulated by demand. According to Sismondi, philanthropy had to be distinguished from charity because philanthropy has the ambition to become a science of morals[15] with a personalized relationship to those assisted, which creates a "mutual obligation." The link between increased wealth and the population's well-being was not a given, and studies emerged to investigate it. Thus in 1840, Buret published *De la misère des classes laborieuses en Angleterre et en France* [On the destitution of the laboring classes in England and France], and in 1855 Le Play published *Les Ouvriers européens* [European workers].[16] These accounts sought to paint a picture of destitution, and Le Play encouraged such observations by founding the Société internationale des études pratiques d'économie sociale [International society of practical social economy studies] in 1856. These observations resulted in Le Play's recommendation of a kind of science-based patronage in order to reforge social ties within the context of the enterprise. He was joined in this by economists like Chevalier, which led Levasseur to write: "Thus the entire social economy school, following the master, recommended patronage" (cited by Azam 2001, 58). Scholars made themselves into advisers to the ruling classes, who saw social economy as a means of developing forms of tutelage adapted to the liberal order.

Attacks against workers' organizations, the growing preeminence of charitable practices, and the affirmation by social economy's adherents of its moral role led it to be described as political economy "softened."[17] All these things provoked radical challenges in a worker's movement that distrusted this moralizing impulse. Marx himself spoke of social economy as "vulgar economy." In his view, it merely examined the conditions that would allow the economic mode of production to be reconciled with a reduction of the poverty that threatened the established order. Leaving to one side the search for fundamental laws, it thus limited itself to "proclaiming for everlasting truths, the trite ideas held by the self-complacent bourgeoisie with regard to their own world, to them the best of all possible worlds" (Marx 1986, 73).

Vienney mentions two doctrines on which social economy in the French tradition is founded; more specifically, four major schools of thought are generally listed: a liberal school, a socialist school, a Christian school, and a solidarist school (Gide 1890; Defourny 1983; Desroche 1983; Gueslin 1987). Their roles, however, were far from equivalent. "The fear of sacrificing the sacrosanct principles of liberalism on the altar of association doubtless explains why the liberal contribution, except on the topic of credit cooperation, is very weak" (Gueslin 1987, 144). For its part, the socialist tradition refused to rally behind social economy because it was allergic to patronage, which it fought against; it could not recognize itself in social economy's vocabulary of assistance, stigmatization, and dependency. In other words, it is only with some difficulty that the socialist school can be cited as an original strand of social economy. It was therefore the Christian tradition that played the dominant part in social economy's invention, itself divided into two Catholic tendencies: one reactionary in the sense that—with Le Play, La Tour du Pin, and de Mun—it turned toward tradition and the "family-line"; the other—represented by de Lamennais and Ott—opposed all restoration and was as attached to democracy as to Christian principles. In the first half of the nineteenth century, there still remained a clear distinction between the terms "social economy" and "socialism." The Christian tendency was not, of course, monolithic: the inflection of liberalism by moral concern attracted "hygienists, philanthropists, saint-simoniens, doctrinaires." Nonetheless, there were "no socialists" among social economy's champions. It "asserted itself to be far removed from socialism, even radically opposed to it," as Procacci (1993, 166) puts it.

Initially, the moral economy of association was confronted by social economy's moralization of the poor, in which philanthropy mixed "industry and morality," moving "from medical policing to social medicine" (Procacci 1993, 174–92). The rapprochements between the socialist and Christian schools came later. Under the impetus of solidarism and the Nîmes school, these rapprochements took place in the name of worker cooperation; at the cost of the stability that Gide sought to maintain, they made cooperation not the "work of individual salvation, but of social transformation," the fruit "not of force, but of love, not of revolution, but of conversion"; and they proclaimed this cooperation's "neutrality" while asserting that it was "socialist by definition" (cited by Gueslin 1987, 196–97). The debates around association and cooperation thus cannot be conflated with those around social economy. The ideological diversity of social economy—praised for its tolerance toward different schools—in fact obscures an ideological conformism that has long prevented its rapprochement with movements advocating social change.

A Tutelary Tendency

All in all, social economy cannot be considered the extension of solidarity-based associationalism since, in the latter, the quest for emancipation sharply contrasted with paternalist conceptions. What happened with the emergence of social economy was not the recognition of associationalism, but its reorganization in favor of new forms of tutelage. In France, the Empire sealed the shift from popular mutualism to supervised mutualism.[18] As Louis-Napoleon Bonaparte publicly declared in 1850: "Mutual assistance societies as I understand them have the valuable advantage of bringing together the different classes of society . . . We reconcile the classes and we improve the moral character of individuals" (cited by Gueslin 1987, 214). These approved societies had 665,000 members in 1869. As coalitions not under the control of elites, workers' associations were for their part perceived as a danger: they had, according to some parliamentarians, "the manifest effect of destroying or modifying the effects of competition," representing an "immense danger to public order."[19] Social economy was born from the anxiety engendered by pauperism, and succeeded associationalism following a violent repression described by Gueslin as "terror." Police violence and the arrest of those responsible dismantled the worker groups, which were considered an "act of hostility to power." In this context, social economy did not contribute to emancipation; instead, it introduced another interpretative lens by proposing personalized links capable of improving the moral character of the "dangerous classes."

This raises several questions about the change in direction reflected in the legal recognition of social economy statuses (cooperative, mutual, nonprofit, etc.): can associationalism be presented as a project that, when confronted with the facts, reoriented itself "in a pragmatic way toward models of social economy" (Gueslin 1987, 28)? Is it composed of "precooperative institutions" that are going to shed their "communitarian coating" (Gueslin 1987, 188)? We must not be misled by an urban associationalist movement that took place within a "quite narrow artisanal milieu" (Gueslin 1987, 185); but it is important nonetheless to avoid presenting what was in fact a bifurcation as a continuity. From this perspective, the Quebecoise experience converges with that of France. A purely adaptive interpretation would neglect the "desire for autonomy" and the "profound wish for democratization" that was "rooted in the popular experience of the world" (Petitclerc 2007, 230). Associationalism is not just an imaginary project, it is a putting-into-practice—one that is admittedly inspired by utopias but nevertheless anchored in real problems and distrustful of any flight beyond reality. It is "an accommodation of doctrine to workers' realities" (Gueslin 1987, 171), and the materiality of its demands is shown by Gossez (1967), who counts 612 worker petitions addressed to the Commission du travail (Labor commission) before June 1848, 472 of which made pay-related requests. Pioneer associationalism aspired to a political role, because it established egalitarian social relations and subjected economic activities to objectives of democratic solidarity. The adoption of the social economy's statuses was inseparable from a desire to see this role reduced.

The social economy approach oversimplifies things, viewing institutionalization as solely the result of pioneering associationalist approaches.[20] But the ambivalences of the institutionalization process require further study: the recognition of the social economy's legal frameworks goes hand-in-hand with associationalist initiatives' loss of distinctiveness. History shows as much. Throughout the second half of the nineteenth century, the various forms of self-organization were discriminated against in favor of philanthropic activity. Mutual aid societies were closely surveilled and subject to control by local members of the ruling classes, which had knock-on effects on their political impact.

The Limits of an Enterprise-Focused Approach

The social economy gradually freed itself from the tutelary designs that gave birth to it. But the resulting business realism has not allowed for a political renaissance. Proponents of the social economy are right to say that analyses that suggest an inevitable alignment with other businesses are too cursory. This is the position Develtère defends, for example, when he maintains that the law of oligarchy's application to the social economy is not inevitable.[21] Following Giddens, he suggests that the bureaucratization highlighted by Weber does not take sufficient account of zones of spontaneity and autonomy retained within organizations. According to Gouldner, the iron law of democracy could even be opposed to Michels's iron law of oligarchy. But while there may be no determinism here, the isomorphism described earlier is nonetheless significant enough to have consequences for our approach: if we are not going to merely confirm the social economy's loss of distinctiveness, then we must identify the repertories that can be mobilized to avoid oligarchic and bureaucratic processes. These clarifications are not common enough in studies of social economy. Democracy is too quickly assimilated to collective ownership, without any examination of the practices capable of propping up the legal arrangements. The question of *praxis*, that is, of collective acts of participation, is dodged.

The social economy is a concept that encourages analysis oriented toward the efficacy of the productive organization. The conflation of members' formal equality, on the one hand, and democracy in decision-making processes, on the other, has proved harmful. All sociological and socioeconomic studies emphasize that equality in law, no matter what capital is possessed, must not be equated to democracy in practice. Besides, the claim that legal statuses alone guarantee internal democracy can hamper recognition of the divergence of logics, the representation of different groups, the establishment of checks and balances, and the search for ways of organizing work and work-related social conditions more favorable to employees. The distinction between equality accorded to members by legal status and internal democracy opens up a new line of investigation. Rather than equating the legal equality of members to democratic functioning, we should ask under what conditions this legal equality translates into a democratization of internal functioning. As Bloch-Lainé notes, "where the rule is 'one member = one vote,' the imbalance is obvious from the manifest inequality of individuals"; association "should not only be a status" and it thus requires "constant revitalization" (1999, 160–62). He is absolutely right. Instead of assuming that social economy organizations have resolved the problem, we should ask about the mechanisms put in place so that a process of democratic decision making can be realized within them. This is starting to be done, for example, in problematizations that are not centered on market concerns but which instead situate cooperatives at the heart of a "cooperative trilemma"—or set of trade-offs—between market, society, and state institutions (see Gijselinckx, Develtère, and Raymackers 2005; 2007). "Cooperatives must not only respond to the demands set by the economic market . . . they must also take into account the interests and needs of civil society while positioning themselves in relation to public systems of regulations that were born in our welfare states" (Gijselinckx, Develtère, and Raymackers 2005, 79).

Consequently, to understand whether social economy organizations are truly democratic we cannot look only at how they function internally. What also matters is the variety of ways in which they contribute to institutional change. A number of associations formulate projects whose aim is institutional change; this makes them into intermediary institutions between the actors belonging to them and already-constituted institutional systems. As mentioned earlier, the historic role of mutual assistance societies lies just as much in their contribution to the genesis of the welfare state as—if not more so than—in the achievements of contemporary mutuals. Social economy entities are, in some cases, catalysts for society's democratization; they are able to extend and protect spaces of freedom and re-create forms of solidarity through activities that are necessary for certain social groups but neglected by the public and private sectors. Again, their political dimension must not be obscured or forgotten by the actors themselves.

In contrast to the third sector approach, the social economy perspective learns from history. It sees associative initiatives as having arisen from the dynamics of democracy before acquiring their distinctive legal statuses. In this respect, social economy set itself apart from political economy very early on by rejecting the separation between economy and morality. Initially a scientific discipline, social economy has redefined itself as the study of noncapitalist economic organizations. It takes account of a sociohistorical construction particularly salient in Europe and South America: not one single type of organization—the nonprofit, representing a specific sector—but rather different types of organization that share the characteristic of being both associations of individuals and enterprises. All adopt the indivisible collective property of their members and limit the remuneration of capital. This conception thus emphasizes that associative, cooperative, and mutualist statuses came out of the same associationalist crucible—an observation that conforms to the reality of the nineteenth century but has often been hidden by the different legal structures' subsequent trajectories. The social economy approach stresses this common identity so that the organizations concerned can more easily assert their significance in the economy by uniting together, and so that the diversity of forms of business might thus be restored. In these entities, solidarity is expressed through collective ownership and emphasis is placed on presence in the market economy via the reference model of the cooperative.

However, striving for this economic integration tends to weaken the original solidarity: on the one hand, formal equality in property rights does not prevent inequalities stemming from the division of labor; on the other hand, in a development model based on the pillars of market and state, the social economy does not escape their gravitational pull, as empirical research in various sectors and countries shows. The loss of the social economy's distinctiveness, as documented in numerous studies, is not accidental. It is a consequence of certain choices having been made about how to conceptualize the social economy. As a corollary of this, the social economy can only become an important societal issue once again if its actors deliberately re-embed it in a perspective that both questions how the economy is defined and promotes the political dimension of their practices. This is why it is important to move away from an overly vague reference to the various schools of social economy, returning to the acuity of Gide's analysis.[22] In 1890, Gide strongly differentiated himself from the liberal school—which he called the "old school"—on three points: while "it was concerned with what remains," the "new school" that he defended "is concerned with what changes"; it also replaced "the absolute demarcation between science and art" with "the intimate interpenetration of theory and practice"; and finally it no longer confused "individuality" with "individualism" (1890, 69–80). He distinguished himself equally forcefully from the Catholic school, whose program was too marked by "the restoration of a triple authority: the authority of the father of the family, the authority of the boss in the workshop, the authority of the church in the state" (1890, 81). Conversely, he moved closer to the socialist school. According to Gide, the new school had "numerous points of contact" with the socialist school: "we can even say that the left of the new school and the right of the socialist school merge into one another" (1890, 80). Conscious of the possible confusion perpetuated by the term "social economy," he defined his school as the "Solidarity school" (1890, 82), advocating what he "conceived of more topically, more specifically, and more precisely as a solidarity economy" (Desroche 1976, 10).

[9]

The Solidarity Economy

WE ARRIVE AT THE NOTION of the solidarity economy by starting with that of the social economy, conceptually filling out its economic dimension and reintroducing its political dimension. Fully reintegrating these two dimensions brings us back to associationalism, allowing us to take account of a multitude of initiatives that have emerged over several decades. The solidarity economy perspective does this by avoiding seeing initiatives only as organizations or collective enterprises, instead defining them as collective actions that are both socioeconomic and sociopolitical.

Empirical Realities and Theoretical Proposals

The desire to reinstate democratic solidarity at the very heart of the economy characterizes a new wave of initiatives that appeared in the last quarter of the twentieth century. They result from the search for new institutional regulations capable of combating intolerable levels of social inequality and environmental damage. They thus move beyond a palliative function, fueling reflection on the nature of social solidarity and the goals of economic exchange. These tendencies, which started to emerge in self-managed and alternative collectives, are reappearances rather than entirely new phenomena. Their reference to equality and to recognition achieved through gaining power in the economy echoes the associative enthusiasm of the first half of the nineteenth century, whether in solidarity-based services, fair trade, solidarity finance, or social currencies.

Practices on the Path to Recognition

These recent developments confirm the observation that associative and cooperative developments cannot be understood in isolation. They show that the boundaries between associations and cooperatives have become porous, and have given rise to new legislation that can be grouped around the notions of solidarity cooperatives and social enterprises. Under current conditions, international comparison helps us contextualize the choice of a cooperative or associative status—or alternatively those newer statuses that complement them. These statuses depend above all on the legal arrangements provided for by legislation in each country. In Italy, for example, social solidarity cooperatives emerged due to the fact that the economic activities that its founders wished to engage in were not admissible within the associative status. Project leaders chose the cooperative because it favored participation and came under enterprise status without being taxed on undistributed profits. At the outset these experiments came up against a contradiction: the 1948 law on cooperatives restricted their activity to that which benefited members, while the country's constitution allowed them to have broader social aims. The law passed in 1991 overcame this contradiction: it stipulated that "social" cooperatives intervene "in the community's general interest and to promote the social integration of citizens." While previously cooperatives had relied on the initiative of a single social group—workers or consumers, for example—founding groups now became more heterogenous. For the first time, cooperatives could have voluntary members, as long as their number did not exceed half of that of the other members: workers, users, and legal entities, among which might be public bodies. New cooperative statuses were inspired by the Italian experience of social-solidarity cooperation, extending cooperation beyond the collective interest of members to which it was previously confined and expanding its reach to "the community's general interest." After Italy in 1991, in the 1990s Spain, France, Portugal, Québec, and Sweden all ratified the possibility of constituting social or collective-interest cooperatives in which users, employees, and volunteers could all be included.

These social or collective-interest cooperatives are thus based on multimembership; that is, they have different categories of members, whose relations are governed by legal equality. In contrast to capital enterprises that mobilize a discourse about "stakeholders" while subjecting them to a strong hierarchy because they are not shareholders, stakeholders here are transformed into co–decision makers as they are promoted to the rank of members.[1]

None of these approaches—which have been legally enshrined in various national contexts—can be understood through the third sector approach. This is because it establishes a watertight separation between associations and cooperatives that is increasingly challenged by reality. Nor can these initiatives find a place within previously achieved social economy statuses, from which they are distinguished through their broader solidarity aims and through their status as multiple-membership enterprises. The explicit objective of serving the community, on the one hand, and sharing power among the various stakeholders, on the other, are the two most specific characteristics of these emergent realities.[2] We must therefore examine the connection between the two.

A New Problematic

Let us first come back to the aims. Once economic activities are put to work as means at the service of solidarity economy ends, the production of goods and services falls under a different logic: it is no longer determined by a quest for profit but rather by a desire to realize a common good. The driving force behind founding members' commitment is the pursuit of benefits for the collectivity, which are not effects brought about by economy activity but rather intentional goals. Thus in organic farming, in renewable energy, and in economic integration, environmental and social costs externalized by other enterprises are internalized; the ends chosen by the actors lead them to take on functions that are otherwise neglected, such as maintaining local heritage, environmental protection, or the integration of people experiencing hardship into employment. In fair trade, solidarity finance, and solidarity-based services, respect for the criteria of social justice and accessibility of services are considered essential priorities.

These initiatives' activity is not conceived based on a preexisting common identity but rather through collective reflection that helps define it. The appropriate means for achieving the desired ends consist in stakeholders coming together to clarify the details of a supply and a demand that previously were only latent or only vaguely alluded to. Thus, in solidarity-based services, there are not only information asymmetries, as the third sector approach identifies, but uncertainty about the very establishment of services in the first place. Founding members, who come together around the project, deal with this informational uncertainty in the context of an explicit search for social justice (equal access to services or to "dignified" work, for example [see Laville and Nyssens 2001b, 9–21]) or through the social construction of what the orthodox economic approach labels "positive externalities" (see Fraisse, Gardin, and Laville 2000, 192–207). Once these benefits are no longer something merely brought about by economic activity but rather something that founders explicitly adopt as goals, it is logical that these founders should be drawn from among users and professionals of the activity in question, who are joined—as volunteers—by partners who believe in the activity's merits.

Logically, the pursuit of collective benefits can hardly attract private investors; the stimulus for creation lies elsewhere, in the mobilization of social capital. It can thus be argued that the organizing factor—that is, the factor that determines the legal entity's objectives, according to Razeto (1993)—is, in this case, social capital. More precisely, this is civic capital[3] since it is formed around collective benefits that activate social-democratic ties (ee chapters by Evers, Laville, and Nyssens in Borzaga and Defourny 2001). While social capital is important in all productive processes, in the initiatives we are considering here it becomes the organizing factor of production and takes on a civic orientation.

This is what the solidarity economy perspective seeks to account for by emphasizing the project of democratizing the economy that unites all these approaches. To put it in Lipietz's terms, "the reason why we do it" takes primacy over "how, and under what status and which organizational norms we do it" (2001, 56). The solidarity economy approach has brought notions of social utility and collective interest into public debate. It has asked about the purpose of activities, which had been neglected in the social economy perspective, with its focus on rules and relations between activities and actors. In doing so, the solidarity economy approach goes beyond that of the social economy.

On the other hand, it agrees with the social economy approach about the need for formal, legally recognized equality between stakeholders. As collective endeavors, solidarity initiatives are an extension of the social economy, with the specific characteristic of diversifying membership. The purpose of the statuses mentioned above is to enable numerous types of actors who may be concerned in a given activity to coordinate with one another.

Two Dimensions

The presence of two dimensions—one political, one economic (see Figure 3)—in the solidarity economy approach underlines the need for associative, cooperative, and mutualist initiatives to influence institutional arrangements. By focusing on the organizational and economic aspects, the social economy approach has not been able to counteract the institutional isomorphism engendered by the division and the complementarity between market and welfare state. Indeed, it is in reaction to the perverse effects of focusing in this way on the economic dimension that initiatives in the last few decades have strengthened their political dimension. Nowadays they wish to be seen as just as much civic as entrepreneurial. They can only have an impact if they are able to promote democracy as much in how they function internally as in how they express themselves externally.

Once we admit that isolated initiatives' economic success is not decisive, we can begin to reflect on why their spread encounters so many obstacles. To do so we must come back to what emerged from the first

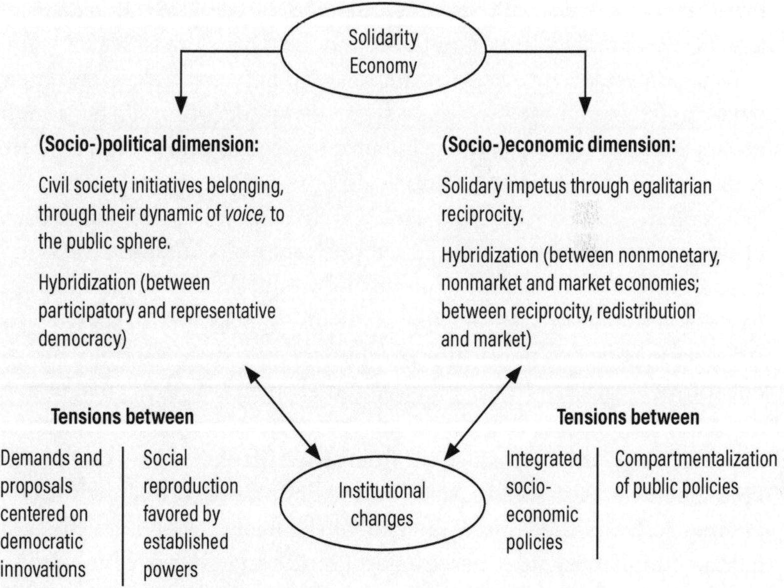

FIGURE 3. The two dimensions of the solidarity economy.

part of this book—that is, a dominant definition of the economy that fails to value these initiatives. If the solidarity economy has not yet been fully accepted, this is not explained by the inadequacies of its actors but rather by a deeper reason. The twofold nature of the solidarity economy challenges the categories of economics at both a conceptual and an empirical level; it does so by refusing to limit economic phenomena to those defined as such by economic orthodoxy. It questions this power of demarcation possessed by economic science and feeds a more general reflection about how the economy is defined and instituted.[4]

Challenging Economics

Polanyi[5] stresses the heuristic value of such a detour. In his view, the term "economic" that we commonly use to designate a certain kind of human activity oscillates between two poles of meaning. The first meaning—the formal one—stems from the relation between ends and means imposed by the problem of scarcity. The second meaning—the substantive one—emphasizes the relations and interdependencies between people and the natural environments in which they subsist, integrating these elements as constitutive of the economy. This distinction between one definition of the economic that refers to scarcity and another that takes into account the relation between people and their environment was noted in the posthumous publication of the principles of Menger (1923, 77), the originator of neoclassical economics. He thus suggested two complementary directions for economics: one was based on the need to economize in order to respond to an insufficiency of means; the other, which he called the "techno-economic direction," followed from the physical demands of production without reference to the abundance or insufficiency of means. In his view, these two possible orientations of political economy derive from "essentially different sources" and are "both primary and elementary."[6] This discussion has been forgotten and is not taken up in any existing presentation of neoclassical economics, since the findings of Menger's price theory encouraged his successors to focus on the first, more formal definition.[7] Polanyi suggests that this narrowing of the field of economic thought led to a complete rupture between economics and everyday life—a suggestion expanded on by economists anxious to reflect epistemologically on their science.[8]

The Two Definitions

By considering the economy as the set of all acts allocating scarce resources to alternative ends, the standard definition—that of Robbins—adopts the formal perspective. It does so in pursuit of an internal coherence that ends up postulating the universality of optimizing behavior. As a "positive" science, economics made itself autonomous by positing the existence of an isolable domain—that of tradable material wealth, which could be exempted from any pursuit of a common good via collective deliberation. As a "natural" science dedicated to shedding light on the laws of human societies, it thus worked toward practical changes while both obscuring how the economy had been instituted historically and naturalizing the choices that had been made regarding this institution. It owed its success to this pretension toward objectivity, which it boasted about and which contributed significantly to its influence.

It became possible to contest this equation of the economy to the formal economy—long validated by the fact that the improvement of production gave rise to an improvement in living conditions—when growth and increasing well-being no longer coincided. It was, however, precisely when its epistemological framework wavered that economics exhibited unprecedented disciplinary "imperialism." The corollary of the conception of the economy as a closed system had been the admission that there exist other spheres of different kinds. But this recognition of the difference between different types of activity is challenged. Activity that aims at allocating scarce resources—by calculating the costs and benefits of a given action or choice—is now extended to all domains of social life. According to rational choice theory—which operates with this generalization—because economics is distinguished from other social sciences by its formal rigor, it can become their universal grammar. All human behavior (cultural, aesthetic, amorous) can be brought back to calculation. This conception has a particular tendency to empty political activity of its meaning. Public action, as a form of intersubjectivity in the public sphere, is no longer conceivable when the economic model of analysis is applied both to individual choices and to collective action. Thus the school of public choice reduces every decision made by a citizen to the choice of a voter who is equated to a consumer, while the theory of resource mobilization interprets engagement through a comparative examination of the energy and resources invested. When it attempts to account for all human behavior, economics turns into an economism symbolized by the work of Becker.

Faced with this predicament, it is helpful to return to the other meaning of the economic that Polanyi highlighted. This substantive meaning is "derived from man's dependence on nature and his fellows, an interchange between his natural and social environment" (Polyani 1957; see also Maucourant 2005, chapter 2). Three different points can be distinguished in this definition: the reference to materiality, the interaction between people and with nature, and the instituted process through which the real economy takes shape.

On the first point, the substantive conception attaches too much importance to the materiality of production and to needs. This insistence, which is historically explicable, is no longer tenable in contemporary economies where immaterial production is continually expanding. The substantive definition can only be preserved if it frees itself from placing so much weight on materiality; this definition can be defended on condition that it does not equate subsistence and survival, and that it includes the pursuit of a "good life." It is thus possible to define economic activity as a human activity of producing and distributing wealth that helps realize individual but also collective objectives.

On the second point, interactions among humans and between humans and nature imply that the economy cannot be an isolable sphere. Economic activity involves an expenditure of energy that is difficult because it takes place under pressure, but social interdependence also gives it a horizon of meaning and understanding, while interdependence with nature compels it to care about environmental and energy-related matters.

This brings us to the third point: that the economy is embedded within an institutional framework. Contrary to the idea of the self-regulated market, it is important to acknowledge that its emergence and existence depend on social institutions.

In sum, despite its outdated focus on material production, the substantive approach makes clear that social interactions and interdependencies with nature are constitutive of economic activities that take shape through institutional construction. It allows us to identify what Polanyi called "disembedding,"[9] that is, an instituted process that privileges the economy in its formal sense[10] and is inseparable from a discourse that denies this process through reference to "economic neutrality" (Lebaron 2000). Using the term "disembedded" to describe the economy in modern societies may lead to confusion, but this can be dispelled if we understand disembedding as the privileging of the formal definition of the economy by political power. The "market system" analyzed by Polanyi corresponds to a particular form of political disembedding that privileges practices that come under a formal definition of the economy. In this sense, the separating off of the economy is the result of a utopia having transformed historical reality. This process has thus been strongly performative, giving rise to profound changes; in particular, since the nineteenth century it has engendered a neglect of the mutual imbrication between the economic, the social, and the environmental—a neglect that is constitutive of the ideology of progress and growth. Finally, the formal economy can claim self-sufficiency only because it ignores the functions that enable the reproduction of natural and human ecosystems over time (Passet 1996, 74).

To recognize this limitation is to acknowledge the strength of the institution of capitalism; but it is also to suggest that, over two centuries, economic reality has never amounted to capitalism alone. Many economic means have been mobilized to preserve these ecosystems. As Weber shows, economic action does not consist in formally purposive-rational action alone—i.e., action that makes no reference to values. Actors have introduced values (political, ethical, and religious) in order to carry out materially purposive-rational actions or economically oriented actions—i.e., actions oriented in principle toward other ends, but whose completion takes account of economic facts. Our analysis should therefore not simply view economic action as the result of a "calculation" performed through technical and purposive-rational means. We also need to take into account other possible goals in order to understand activity from a value-rational or materially purposive-rational angle. Today, as yesterday, there are many activities that do not fit within the coherent whole of the formal economy, since their economic efficacy is inextricably linked to the ethico-political principles that underpin them. But these activities cannot therefore be ignored by economic analysis. The problem they face is that of establishing their legitimacy.[11] The coup de force consists in reducing the entire economy to formally purposive-rational actions. In order to avoid a complete surrender to this narrow understanding of the economy, it is important for an institutionalist political economy[12] to encompass economic activities that combine, to various degrees, both monetary calculation and qualitative evaluation.

The Double Movement of the Economy's Institution

To prevent currently dominated economic forms and logics from being rendered invisible or invalidated, we need to understand how the process of the economy's institution has centered on the formal economy, while also being challenged constantly by other modes of institution. This process can be grasped through the two contradictory movements that, with varying degrees of intensity during different periods, have drawn the contours of the actual economy.

The first movement, by focusing on the formal definition of the economy, engages in a reductionism that spans three different levels:

> The separating off of the economic sphere, which is equated to the market, constitutes the first level. By obscuring the substantive meaning of the economy, this movement grants pre-eminence to the market economy. As the third sector approach illustrates, the market economy constitutes the means of satisfying needs, and other solutions can only be adopted if the market fails, as subsidiary solutions. This prioritization ends up being a self-fulfilling prophecy, since economists seek to "bring the real state of things closer to this order of abstract conceptions on which theoretical arguments can be based" (Cournot 1974, 38; on Cournot, see Vatin 2007, 37–47), proceeding by analogy with Newtonian mechanics (Maréchal 1997, chapter 2).

> The identification of the market with a self-regulating market constitutes the second level—a logical consequence of the first. The hypothesis of utility maximization, which consists in considering humans as self-sufficient beings endowed with reason, legitimates the study of the economy using a deductive method, through the aggregation of individual behaviors without any consideration of the institutional context in which they take shape. Considering the market as self-regulating—i.e., as the

mechanism for aligning supply and demand through prices—leads to the institutional changes that were necessary for its emergence being overlooked, and to the institutional structures that make it possible being forgotten. Explaining the market by appeal to utility maximization in a situation of scarcity masks the fact that it is an instituted process.

To these two levels, described by Polanyi, we can add a third level to which many authors—including Marx but also Mauss and Weber—have drawn attention: the identification of the modern enterprise with the capitalist enterprise. In a capitalist economy founded on private ownership of the means of production, the creation of goods depends on possible profit for those who possess capital. The enterprise engages in "capitalistic economic action . . . which rests on the expectation of profit by the utilization of opportunities for exchange" according to Weber, who adds that capital accounting constitutes the rational foundation of the capitalist economy since it makes it possible to calculate whether a surplus is produced in relation to "the estimated value of the material means of production used for acquisition in exchange" (Weber 2001, xxxii–xxxiii). The recognition of the joint-stock company provides the means for an unprecedented concentration of capital, since property rights can be exchanged without their holders needing to know each other, with the mediation of the stock exchange also guaranteeing the liquidity of their assets.

In contemporary societies, the market and capitalism are thus in league with one another, since it is the complementarity between self-regulating market and capitalist enterprise that creates the system. Finally, when it is treated as the combination of the self-regulating market and the capitalist company, the economy makes room for another development: the project of a society rooted in the workings of its own economy. When it knows no limits, the market economy leads to the market society, in which the market engulfs society and is sufficient to organize it. But this limiting case of the market society has proved impossible to achieve because it has profoundly threatened democracy. On the three levels that have just been mentioned, society has thus reacted so as to contain and circumscribe market capitalism.

Reciprocity and redistribution have both withstood attempts to reduce the economy to the market. Redistribution is the principle according to which production is assigned to a central authority that has responsibility for sharing it out. Reciprocity corresponds to the relationship established between groups or individuals through allocations that only have meaning insofar as they stem from a desire to demonstrate a social link between stakeholders. Reciprocity and redistribution are not solely found in premodern societies; these principles exist in contemporary societies. Reciprocity is exhibited in the first place within a "ground floor economy,"[13] in the absence of which the other floors could not be constructed. This material life made up of innumerable inherited gestures, accumulated pell-mell and repeated again and again until they take up a large proportion of human energy in tasks of reproduction—this is the sphere of the nonmonetary economy, of householding, without which no other production would be possible. If this economy—as vital as it is ignored—has largely receded with time under the grip of market capitalism, another economy has nonetheless unfurled: the nonmarket economy. This is the economy in which the circulation of goods and services is entrusted principally to public redistribution. It has come into being because the market economy has not been able to fulfil its own promise of social harmony. On the contrary, it became necessary to promote institutions capable of countering the effects of social fragmentation. As the first part of the book explained, it is around the welfare state that a modern form of redistribution, funded by compulsory deductions, has been constructed, through which payments are made on the basis of social rights. This operates largely through public services, whose rules are set by an authority subject to democratic control.

Against the assumption that the market is self-regulating, it has been placed under institutional control. If there exists a modern tendency toward "laissez-faire" when it comes to the market, this has been countered by the recurrent reactions of civil society seeking to "socialize" the market, that is, to embed it in a set of rules developed through a process of political deliberation.

Historically, the response to the promotion of the impersonal and abstract norm of the market has been the creation of regulatory institutions (see Verley 1999, 66–69). There are numerous concrete markets that depend on rules that frame and control the formulation—and the meeting—of supply and demand (see Gadrey 1999).

In addition, attempts have been made to establish noncapitalist enterprises and give them their due place. In the formal conception of the economy, as endorsed by neoclassical theory, the basic model of the enterprise is one where property rights are held by investors. The enterprise's objective is reduced to profit maximization, i.e. the accumulation of capital. Faced with this single model, it is important to remember the diversity of forms of ownership, that is, the diversity of people who can hold property rights and thus control an enterprise's objectives. The analysis of associations, cooperatives, and mutuals has highlighted, alongside enterprises in the hands of workers, those owned by consumers or savers. In the evaluation of economic activity, there are thus criteria other than the return on financial capital that are promoted: access to a job or service, the quality of service provision, and so on (Rose-Ackerman 1986).

The economy in democratic modernity is thus caught up in this double movement: a tendency toward disembedding and an inverse tendency toward democratic reembedding. Because they allow us to grasp the recurrent tensions connected to this double movement, the insights of Polanyi and Mauss can be interpreted as providing an analytic grid that clarifies the plural character of the real economy. It does so by highlighting the existence of a diversity of economic principles of distribution and production, as well as by attending to the various ways in which the market is institutionally embedded.

From Observation to Project, a Plural Economy

Extending Weber's inquiry into the economy's institution, Polanyi identifies the plurality of economic principles. This is not just an observation with historical relevance, but one that has heuristic value for contemporary societies. Extending Marx's inquiry into the ownership of the enterprise, Mauss recognizes the plurality of forms that enterprises can take, which does not imply the abolition of individual property restrictive of freedom, but the addition of "state ownership, collective or semi-collective ownership" on top of and alongside other forms of ownership (Mauss 1984, 356). In his view, "there are no exclusively capitalist societies . . . There are only societies that have a regime or rather—what is even more complicated—systems of regime . . . more or less arbitrarily defined by the predominance of one or other of these systems or institutions" (1984, 372). There is not a single way of organizing the economy that expresses a natural order, but a set of forms of production and redistribution that coexist. Individuals' ideas and beliefs give rise to collective action and social practices that institutions normalize through public policies; these public policies set the framework in which practices can unfold and, in turn, influence ideas. Institutions are changeable because they are social conventions that both express and delimit the field of possibilities: studying them can give us "precise awareness of facts and the apprehension of, if not certainty about, their laws"; it also helps us to detach ourselves from the "metaphysics" with which "-ism words" such as "capitalism" are laden. Asserting the existence of a capitalist society amounts to assuming perfect coordination of individual representations; in reality there is capitalist dominance since "an economic system is composed of contradictory institutional mechanisms, irreducible to one another."

Based on these proposals, it is possible to identify the mechanisms through which resistance to the naturalization of the self-regulating market and the capitalist enterprise appear. We can also study the complementarities, the tensions, and the conflicts between different economic logics and forms.

The performances of the market economy are nourished through resources provided to it by nonmarket and nonmonetary economies, but its enthusiasts deny this dependence in order to make the market economy into the sole home of wealth production and thus move toward a market society. This situation has already been exposed as untenable, and the inequalities that have resulted from it have given rise to a counterproject of subjecting the economy to political will, a "great transformation" that has taken the form of both fascism and communism. So as not to fall back into these totalitarian ruts, it is important to return to a transformation that is more respectful of democracy in its rejection of the brutal establishment of a new order: one that takes account of the plural reality of the economy in order to derive from this a project of extending this plurality. The concept of the plural economy lies at the crossroads between an analytic observation and a project of change. Orienting ourselves toward this plural economy entails principles of action that acknowledge complexity, accepting the market while rejecting the marketization of everything.

First of all, the market economy is not to be eliminated. In his debate with von Mises, Polanyi acknowledged the compatibility between socialism and the market; meanwhile Mauss wrote that "freedom of the market is the absolutely necessary precondition of economic life" (1984, 353). The solution is to be sought not in the abolition of the market but rather in its organization, its "domestication." Particularly important among the new forms of regulation that should be promoted are those based on social and environmental rules defined not just at the national level but also at the local and international levels.

Next, in addition to these market regulations, it is important to attack the dominant argument that attributes the monopoly over wealth creation to the market. Doing so requires the establishment of "modes of recognition of value of the goods produced" other than "market mechanisms." The "limitation" of the market will also be achieved "through the strengthening of a nonmarket sector,"[14] including public services and associations.[15] Against the image of the self-regulating market, it is crucial to demonstrate the variety of real markets, but this concern "does not preclude the observation, in the same situations, of the existence of specific forces that, as Weber saw perfectly well, tend toward impersonality and formal rationality" (Le Velly 2006, 339). Keeping this in mind is not to join in the moralizing critiques of the market mocked by Zelizer (1988, 614–34). Rather, it is to ask whether we can revive public debate about the economy, which must not be confined to a discussion about externalities while leaving the cultural representation of the market intact. It will only be possible for civil society to begin reappropriating the economy if economic diversity is not just preserved but increased.

Herein lies the importance of solidarity economy initiatives. Through their multifaceted presence, they contest developments that neoliberal ideology presents as inevitable. By activating a lived solidarity, they can moreover rekindle demands for solidarity clearly distinct from both aid and charity; in doing so, they can help socialize the welfare state. If these initiatives are capable of uniting beyond their sectoral boundaries, of reflecting more deeply on their causes and on their implications for public regulations, of allying themselves with forces and social movements that share their goals, then they can help realize a project of democratizing the economy and society. It is clear, however, that such capacity for change cannot stem from the mere presence of noncapitalist enterprises. The social economy came up against limits because the enterprises it brought together suffered from isomorphism: generally market isomorphism in the case of cooperatives, and generally nonmarket isomorphism in the case of mutuals and associations. Beyond the possibility of different enterprises, civil society should be mobilized to consolidate diverse socioeconomic principles and secure their recognition by the state.

The solidarity economy perspective is part of this conception of change, which calls on us to alter power relations so that the various types of economic activity in all their plurality might acquire their due place.

Reaffirming the Political

Confronted over time with an institutional isomorphism that spares them no more than it does other productive entities, the constituents of the solidarity economy can resist this isomorphism only by being firmly anchored in democratic solidarity. They can only avoid their initial projects being obliterated by attending to this dimension on two complementary levels.

Internally, participation must be maintained in productive processes by making sure that the different types of actors affected continue to have the capacity for—and a collective right to—expression. A solidarity economy perspective can only be maintained if there remain open micro public spheres that enable collective inquiry, in particular about "aspects of social conduct that previously went undiscussed, or were 'settled' by traditional practices" (Giddens 1994, 120).

Externally, those responsible for socioeconomic innovations must become engaged in meso public spheres that are intermediaries between civil society initiatives and the state, which are essential if these interventions are to result in "instituted processes of economic democratization" (Mendell 2007). Public engagement is all the more effective in generating change if it takes shape beyond each individual initiative.

Internal Functioning

Historically, the collective identity experienced in a group to which one belonged (workers, consumers) was the cement that partly explained the creation of social economy enterprises. These enterprises emanated from a homogeneous group. Those associations and cooperatives that appeared in the last quarter of the twentieth century, however, did not all form out of such a collective identity. The examples cited have shown "the very low homogeneity of the founding groups" (Defourny, Favreau, and Laville 1997, 31); these initiatives emerged from multiple stakeholders (users, volunteers, employees) coming together around a common cause, which, moreover, led to legislative changes in various countries. It is therefore less the satisfaction of the specific needs of one group that brings people together around the activity and more the aim of serving the community—that is, of pursuing positive effects for the community beyond the direct beneficiaries of production. This is the shift from common good to public good.

Faced with hugely complex problems, communication between various stakeholders (users, volunteers, employees) allows decision-making mechanisms to be established that are legitimate under the framework of "multilateral reciprocity" (Gardin 2006). What is crucial, from this point of view, is personal involvement in social networks mobilized around a common good. Thanks to these networks, and to their public dimension, the linking of usually separated orders and logics reconfigures problems, allows them to be approached in a different way, and brings to light other potentialities. The autonomy of these micro public spheres is key. Such spheres appeal to people as citizens and allow them to promote activities that respond to the problems they have identified. As a consequence, the survival of innovative associationalist initiatives is tied to their ability to preserve their public-sphere dimension in civil society, both to ensure the equal participation of diverse stakeholders and to preserve the originality of their economic activity.

The social economy approach—which by definition ignores this issue because it focuses on evaluating the influence of its organizations in the economy and on market relations—can only result in the recurrent observation of a "reversal of the relations between people and enterprises" (Vienney 1994, 114). Legal forms that respect equality between members, typical of the social economy, are necessary but not sufficient for democratic functioning. It is important not to keep conflating formal equality between people in statutes and democratic functioning; the trajectories of social economy organizations have shown that collective ownership of the means of production provides no guarantee that inequalities will not reappear. If we consider internal democracy a fundamental issue, it is crucial to look beyond the initiative's official legal status, investigating the effective means for those involved to actively participate in projects.

This is why we must attend to the management tools that promote the solidarity dimension through social (Perret 2001) and socioeconomic (Viveret 1989l) indicators, through social and societal audits, or through any other approach that encourages self-reflexivity. Because it requires direct participation,[16] the solidarity economy approach calls for modes of self-evaluation that encourage reflection by those involved, so that evaluation is not reduced to the pressure exercised by market and nonmarket economies through associated regulatory procedures (annual accounts, conventions, tax documents, certifications). Among the advances in this direction, we might mention different social-audit models (Pestoff 1998; Viviani 1995; Cooperative Union of Canada 1985), methodologies centered on the development of "capabilities,"[17] and operational diagnostics based on taking into account both the general project and its specific mode of organization (see Laville and Sainsaulieu 1997, 196). These tools are not cited as technical solutions to the problem of participation; they are only suggested possibilities mentioned. Whatever the means, the important thing is to survive over time or to reestablish the real possibility of voice that is not restricted to the start-up stage. By taking note of the marketization and bureaucratization processes that affect associations, these observations allow us concretely to identify how associationalism might be revitalized. Every association can, through the reappropriation of its history or the voice of its different constitutive groups, find resources capable of reactivating its public-sphere dimension. We might even hypothesize that the most institutionalized associations can only regain credibility through renewed democratic practices, without which they will be suffocated between the weight of public tutelage and the force of the private enterprise model. This is the position that the solidarity economy approach defends, but it is only sustainable if solidarity economy initiatives help change public institutional frameworks to their benefit.

The Relation to Institutionalization

The opportunities for associations to do this depend on the period: following Merrien (1990), we should distinguish "normal" periods in which a social paradigm—that is, a way of thinking about public intervention in society—has a certain hegemony, and "crisis" periods when the search for new paradigms becomes necessary because the pernicious effects of the old paradigm multiply. In a "normal" period of institutional stability, socioeconomic innovations struggle not to be condemned to marginality (Lévesque and Vaillancourt 1998). At times that can be described as "crisis" periods, the exhaustion of previous modes of public action encourages the search for new paradigms. Associations can then help determine new arrangements. The instituting force of associationalism can influence public action (Lévesque 1997). In other words, the balance of power can change between highly organized public spaces impregnated by power (Habermas 1988, 354) and autonomous public spheres (Habermas 1992, 186). Thus a new approach to institutionalization takes shape.

In the previous chapter, the theory of the social economy's approach to institutionalization was considered too simple, because it understood the consecration of pioneering initiatives to consist in their obtaining legal status. It is important to take account of more critical approaches in which institutionalization is seen as a process of "recuperation." Thus Loureau argues that "it is the negation of the institution by the instituted. Through institutionalization, a new form becomes equivalent to the other instituted forms" (1971, n.p.). But the critical approach is one-sided in its own way. As Marchat notes: "Without denying the power with which the established forms tend to curb the no lesser power of the 'negative' that troubles and threatens them . . . institutionalization does not seem doomed to pure reproduction. Historically, the proof of this has been the establishment of the democratic system, which cannot be understood as the 'equivalent' reproduction of prior social forms" (2001, 23). Institutionalization is ambivalent: it neither attests to the success of previously ignored initiatives nor does it curtail everything to fit within instituted forms. It must be analyzed as a complex process—one that subjects associationalism to systemic integration, but which is also able to partially recognize associationalism's instituting impact. We can therefore replace a clear-cut view of institutionalization with one that is more nuanced, in which practices are capable of both undergoing integration and altering a future that cannot be understood solely in terms of reproduction. It is this more nuanced view that has been adopted for solidarity-based services (Laville 1992) and work integration social enterprises in Europe[18]—with international comparison helping to identify the full range of possibilities. In the contemporary period of "crisis," the exhaustion of previous modes of public action is prompting the search for new paradigms. The development of public policy reflects the constraining effects of previous sociopolitical interventions; this is the path dependency highlighted in the second part.[19] But coming up against unprecedented challenges can also encourage a change of direction through multiple exchanges between public-policy makers and external networks. These exchanges are influenced by appeals to experts but can also involve reflection on local experiences.

Amid instability, the strategic importance of access to information becomes clear. Ultimately, the emergence of a new societal paradigm for public policy—which has to address problems that are simultaneously economic, environmental, and social—is one of the major issues facing democracies with an uncertain future. The content and construction of this paradigm seem to be linked firstly to the judgments, interests, and ideologies of the principal public-policy makers—to how they have previously intervened and drawn on the expertise and experience on which they rely. They then appear to be connected to the breadth of debate, which can either be confined to specialized circles of "decision makers" and professionals, or expanded to include other social actors. As long as we do not underestimate the obstacles to the spread of any initiative that does not conform to previous models, institutionalization can be problematized rather than being either lauded or reviled. It results from an interaction marked by inequality between social actors and public authorities, "whose respective weight in a negotiation process is reflected, at any given time, by legislation" (Bouchard, Carré, Côté, and Lévesque 1995, 214). Thus a study on the "institutionalization of the social economy in Quebec" (D'Amours 1999) reveals that the recognition by the state is very much linked to its employment objective. The antidotes to this tendency lie in strengthening "access to the public sphere," and in "links with social movements" and between the "different components of the social economy"; these are the unique features of the solidarity economy perspective that are called on to "repoliticize the social economy" (D'Amours 1999, 39–40). In order to influence institutional frameworks, it is therefore essential that civil society self-organizes so that it is able not only to represent social economy actors but also to bring them closer to other collective initiatives and social movements.

Beyond Economism, a Plural Democracy

Solidarity economy initiatives can only escape their confinement if public policies are introduced that counteract the negative discrimination they face. Yet the public officials in favor of this economy can only consolidate their action by legitimating it through the pressure exerted by forces organized within civil society. Policy change depends on the emergence of meso public spheres—spheres referred to earlier as intermediary because they hybridize participatory and representative forms of democracy.[20] They can help both to reconfigure the institutional framework and to deconstruct the most prevalent representations of the economy, on condition that solidarity economy actors do not withdraw into particular initiatives, on the one hand, and that politicians support their voice, on the other.

All in all, positive interaction with public authorities rests on the recognition of the solidarity economy's contribution on the economic and social levels as well as the political level. Their participatory component is valuable for moving toward a deliberative democracy that encourages the formation of considered and justifiable arguments. Democratic theory cannot ignore the fact that the current crisis of representation is accompanied by forms of public engagement that reflect a civic desire to improve everyday life. In these micro public spheres, forms of economic activity are being developed that result from civic participation, clearly in reaction to the grip of the market. But they can only result in stable activities if their protagonists also get involved in meso public spheres, that is, in groupings designed to fight for these

logics of heterodox action that are otherwise steamrolled by the orthodox conception of the economy.[21] The fundamental task is therefore the
co-construction of public policies.[22] Micro public spheres are no more
geared toward reconciliation than are meso public spheres; on the contrary, they sustain conflict through which "temporary consensuses are
constructed—definitions of the common good that are not present to
begin with in society and are literally the product of democratic debate"
(Thériault 2001, 147–48, cited by Lévesque 2001, 100). When reduced to
its outcomes in terms of employment or social cohesion, the solidarity
economy cannot become a priority on the political agenda. It can only
become so if these effects are connected to the public engagement it
gives rise to. Its recognition thus largely depends on the emergence of
a politics of the public sphere.

We must still free ourselves from an ideology of progress that has
placed economic growth at the heart of social functioning, thus evad-
ing the test of collective decisions (see Perret 1999). The political is subordinated to the economic when society's progress is equated to market
growth, whose untenability is highlighted by the worsening of social
and environmental problems. Resisting the sacralization of growth
thus appears necessary if we are to overcome the actual powerlessness
of politics.

Since the industrial revolution, growth has been synonymous with
progress because it has largely contributed to making everyday life less
arduous and helped emancipate people from traditional dependencies. But the increasing commodification of human existence renders
growth much more ambivalent. It is thus no accident that it is being
contested, in spite of its role in producing social cohesion. To confront
this contradiction, in 1961 Perroux distinguished between growth defined as "the sustained increase of an indicator" at national level, "the
gross or net global product in real terms," and development defined
as "the combination of mental and social changes in a population that
enables it to increase its real global product cumulatively and sustain-
ably" (see Maréchal 2001, 80–81). Understood in this way, the notion
of development acquires a qualitative dimension. It makes reference to
well-being and encompasses living conditions that cannot be reduced
to mere standard of living. "Capabilities," according to Sen (1987; 1999),
echo such an approach endorsed by the United Nations Development
Programme in its definition of human development as expanding the

range of choices open to individuals. Defending the idea that conflict between growth and development does not entail "zero growth," in 1987 the Brundtland report introduced sustainable development as a mode of development in which the use of resources, the choice of investments, the orientation of technological development, as well as institutional change, are determined by future as well as current needs. This World Commission on Environment and Development placed sustainable development on the agenda of international negotiations. In 1988, the Toronto Conference addressed global warming, resulting in the creation of the Intergovernmental Panel on Climate Change, whose report—presented in Geneva at the Second World Climate Conference in 1990—launched the process that culminated in the Earth Summit in Rio de Janeiro in 1992. The sustainable development advocated aimed to create the conditions for solidarity that was both horizontal—i.e., with those most impoverished at the time—and vertical—i.e., between generations. Solidarity, which had been the organizing principle of resistance to the market's unlimited expansion, had been expressed through protections linked to work in the form of salaried employment. But under current conditions, solidarity cannot be limited to this, given the obstacles to securing "dignified" work, any more than it can be obtained through redistribution indexed to market growth. The acceleration of social and environmental damage can only be combated through forms of intervention that involve transnational coordination.

The sustainable development approach has in turn been challenged by proponents of degrowth, who believe it remains trapped in the Western myth of development (Rist 1996). For its part, degrowth, or rather "a-growth," presented itself as "the rejection of the irrational and quasi-idolatrous cult of growth for growth's sake" (Latouche 2006, 11). There is certainly a danger of sustainable development being instrumentalized—a danger that the "degrowth objective" exposes by raising awareness of all the individual and collective behaviors that predate on social and ecological resources. But there is a symmetrical danger: that degrowth becomes a prophecy awaiting a catastrophe that will demonstrate its truth. The situation is serious enough not to aim at the wrong target: while proponents of sustainable development and degrowth may challenge each other out in the context of a legitimate debate, when their dialogue turns into confrontation, they forget their common adversary, which is the productivist model of development. Besides, as suggested

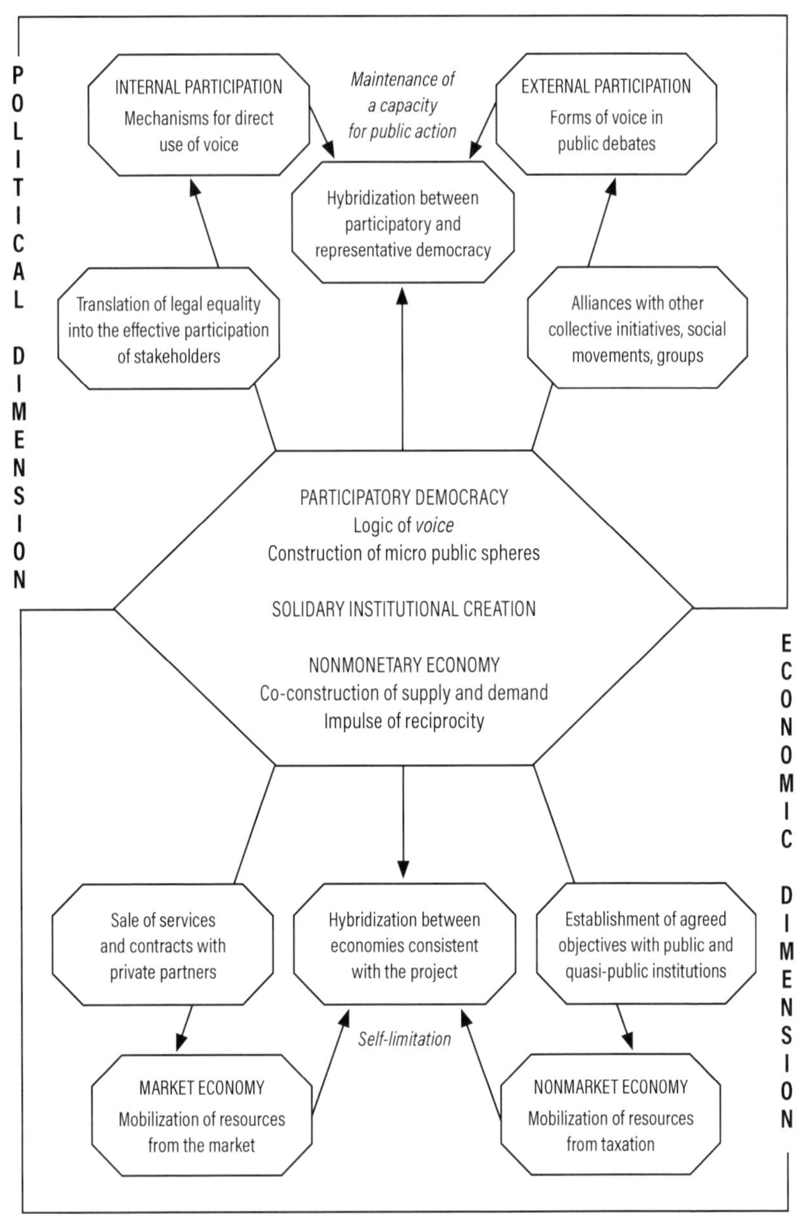

FIGURE 4. An explanation of the two dimensions of the solidarity economy.

in chapter 6, the oppositions are less entrenched among practitioners than among theorists. Despite the disagreements, alliances should be considered in order to attack the sacred figure that growth has become (see Bellet 1998), hindering even the slightest attempt at the economy's civic reappropriation.

Furthermore, the search for maximal growth is hampered by the rise of the tertiary sector and more particularly of relational services, which are based on direct interaction between provider and user. These services depend on fixed contact time and thus cannot yield significant gains in productivity. Since the human functions of assistance and intervention that they fulfil cannot be replaced by the use of information technologies except at the margins, such services even tend to slow down growth. This is visible in the gap between average rates of growth in the 1960s and those of the following decades in the so-called developed countries. We can thus ask what purpose it serves to keep referring to growth in an economy where two-thirds of jobs are found in services, and where relational services are gaining in importance. As Gadrey says, the notions of productivity and growth are connected to performance measures developed in Fordist industry, and we might ask ourselves whether Western countries are not "in search of a form of development after growth and intellectual tools to think about this post-growth development" (Gadrey 1996).

Solidarity initiatives are built on the observation that growth can no longer set the direction for a collective project. Economic activities cannot bypass the ends to which they refer. Put differently, it is the return of what has long been repressed: a political questioning of the economy. Today, this is carried out by an associationalism that has also become internationalized. In an echo of what happened in the nineteenth century, the challenge is to make room for an economy framed by the principles of preserving human communities and consolidated through democratic deliberation and regulation. The solidarity economy does precisely this, recognizing that a plural economy and a plural democracy are mutually dependent. The challenge may be formidable, but at least it does not suffer from the illusion that one can be realized without the other.

Conclusion

Associationalism's most important feature is that it challenges the atomistic conception of the individual through the lived experience of reciprocal solidarity, that common decency that for Orwell corresponded "to the concern to embed basic human virtues at the very foundation of socialist practice" (Michéa 2007, 139; also see Michéa 2000). To reappropriate this associationalist heritage is, in a certain sense, to reaffirm what Roland wrote in 1850: "From certain mistakes made within associations—which I neither claim to deny, nor to disguise, nor to minimize—the enemies of socialism purport to draw conclusions against a principle that they are increasingly keen to condemn the more they fear it."[1] It is above all to defend other conceptions of the economy, of politics, and of social change.

The reflections in this book lead us to conclude that the deepening of democracy through associationalism relies on our not yielding to "economic sophism"[2] and not endorsing the dominant premise of the "associative phenomenon's exteriority in relation to politics" (Fecteau 1992, 162). Envisaging the economy beyond the market and politics beyond the state is thus the very condition of a new approach to social change.

The Economy beyond the Market

As far as the economy is concerned, the contemporary debate on the different definitions covered in the last three chapters shows that civil society is beginning to be taken into account.

Nonetheless, while the label "third sector" gives a place to associations, it confines them to a supporting role. Constructed as a response to market and state failures, the notion of the third sector treats associations as supplementary service providers and largely ignores the social framework in which they take shape.

Conversely, the term "social economy" groups them together with other organizations: cooperatives and mutuals. The social economy approach thus has the merit of underlining that these different legal structures can contribute to associationalism in the generic sense of the term. These structures are not-for-profit and are concerned with the accumulation of collective wealth and the limitation of the power of those who hold capital. Unlike the third sector, the social economy does not ignore the tensions between the economic and the social. The French school of sociology has affirmed this consistently since Durkheim:[3] there is no economic activity that is not socially embedded and that lacks social ties. But while the social is dependent on the economic in the capitalist firm, social economy initiatives do not give it a subordinate role. The social economy approach aptly identifies a set of organizations in which the distribution of profit and the power of capital holders are limited. The solidarity economy approach shares this emphasis on the legal statuses of these noncapitalist enterprises; this allows us to not falsely conflate economic initiatives and capitalist organizations.

Another Economy

The solidarity economy perspective adds to this the observation that the economy is an institutional construction and not the mere matching of supply and demand by fixing a price. On this point it converges with the new economic sociology inspired by Granovetter (2008), which emphasizes that markets are embedded in networks and governed by rules, which leads him to talk of plural markets. Highlighting plural markets raises the possibility of institutionally framing markets through norms related to social justice and environmental protection. Authors such as Callon, Lascoumes, and Barthe (2001) emphasize such "framing-overflowings" of markets, with externalities subjected to public deliberation and then reinternalized through the modification of rules regulating market activities.[4]

But the solidarity economy approach proposes to take the critique further. While markets in all their concrete multiplicity do not conform to the abstract representation of the self-regulating market, this does not prevent the self-regulating market from having a performative character.[5] For this reason, the framing of markets does not by itself protect against "the political construction of an economic market society" (Polanyi 2007). To counteract such a construction, a further distinction must be added to the distinction between markets: that between the economy and the market.[6] An economy that strengthens democracy rather than threatening it cannot do without markets, but neither can it limit itself to them. The reinstatement of the economy as a means at the service of socially valued ends requires an institutional framing that makes space for several logics of economic action. Without contesting the legitimacy of the market economy, it is important not to interpret all economic forms in terms of material interest alone. It is not just markets that are plural but economic motives and, ultimately, the economy itself.

Mechanisms for regulating markets are necessary. They cannot, however, be sufficient for democratizing the economy. The preservation of markets and their decentralized arbitration must be accompanied by protections against their becoming too powerful. Respect for markets must be complemented by appeal to principles of redistribution and reciprocity. Redistribution should be revalued as a system for allocating resources for everything related to the public good. For its part, reciprocity should be regarded as the taking into account of the common good: in a largely immaterial and relational economy, trust based on mutual understanding can enable the codevelopment of initiatives with both creative and productive ends. It is important to fully rehabilitate the collective power that stems from reciprocity, which is learned and experienced in collective mobilizations (see Céfaï 2007), but which also has economic potential. The affirmation of a form of reciprocity that connects the "spirit of the gift" (Godbout 2000) with a concern for equality is, moreover, an antidote to the philanthropy that has been recruited to add a touch of soul to liberalism and that poses the threat of "giving without reciprocity" (Ranci 1990).

More specifically, this is not a matter of simply bringing collective enterprises into existence, as the social economy approach stipulates. Here again, the problematic of the solidarity economy extends the social economy approach by forcefully reintroducing the public dimension of collective actions emanating from civil society, whose aim is to democratize the economy. The existence of noncapitalist enterprises will have little impact unless it is accompanied by political action to change the institutional frameworks within which economic facts take shape. Legal statuses are not enough to ensure democratic functioning, and the importance of effective engagement in both internal practices and social debates must be emphasized in order to establish a plural economy strategy.

Democratic Solidarity after Social Democracy

Social democracy has weakened itself by conceding the monopoly over wealth creation to market capitalism. On the defensive for several decades, it believed it was saving what was most important by watering down its reference to solidarity. Adopting a line of reasoning that construed solidarity as more of a cost than a collective investment, it has been diluted in several different countries into a social liberalism that has allowed the incomes of the best-off to explode, while exacerbating the precarity and insecurity of the less affluent by reducing social provision and making it conditional. Far from combating the culture of aid, the so-called active welfare state (See Esping-Andersen 1989)—which has thus become more restrictive—is once again returning to that desire to regulate the conduct of the poor that one might have hoped had been surpassed. This is both a regression and a dead end. After a social democracy that relied on state redistribution alone to protect society, we must now, by contrast, reaffirm the strength of the principle of solidarity and rediscover the complementarity of the two forms of democratic solidarity, one based on rights and state redistribution, the other on equality and the civic bond (Théret 1999).

As Habermas remarks, the crisis of the welfare state can only be resolved by "a completely altered relationship between autonomous and self-organized public spheres on the one hand, and subsystems steered by money and administrative power on the other" (1986, 13–14). This means that both associations and the state should accept their mutual interdependence. In truth—in the past as in the present—the two are neither separable nor interchangeable.

Associations' renewal cannot be consolidated without state support for the spirit of civic responsibility, to take up the terms of the new citizenship program proposed by Barber (1984). Public policy must therefore include policies related to the public sphere in order to promote opportunities for citizens to come together around social issues. As for public services, they must accept "a form of service provision that is more participatory and decentralized, which leaves room for mutual assistance and local initiatives. Spontaneous socialization must be complemented by socialization stimulated by the state, that is, the democratic transformation of state services at the local level or the transfer of authority and resources to associations," in Walzer's view.[7] Gurvitch (1932) moves in the same direction when he argues for a social right that protects forms of self-organization that work toward justice.

The Political beyond the State

The challenge is not that of choosing between state and civil society; it is envisaging their reciprocal democratization. It is important not just to strengthen public and association-based services but to facilitate their mutual enrichment. The welfare state has promoted a conception of solidarity centered on individual rights and redistribution. It can only regain legitimacy if it starts to offer opportunities for participation among employees and users, and if it is strengthened by an association-alism infused with democratic solidarity. It is time to cross-fertilize public intervention and civil society.

But it would be pointless to call for such hybridization without opening up space for it to be realized. Now of course the revival of associationalism provides such a space. It can thus help relegitimize public regulation once the way in which such regulation is carried out has been rethought. The achievements of the welfare state—such as Keynesian policies—must be complemented by a concern for people's participation. This is the best way to fight against the rise of authoritarian demagogy.

Reinventing Public Action

This is why proponents of associationalism stress the importance of participatory democracy. But they refuse to allow it to be lost in consultations that have no real influence on decisions; to be credible, it must clearly be imbricated with action and connected to representative democratic bodies. Conversely, representative democracy can now be reinforced by forms of direct democracy that are not only granted by those in power but also achieved via collective action. This dovetailing of participatory and representative democracies is, however, inconceivable unless the fears of those in power that the establishment may be destabilized are outweighed by a belief in the urgent need for a more active citizenry. Revisiting the analysis of public policy's frames of reference, and citing the cases of Ireland and South Africa, Jobert notes that such a model is being sought—a model that would strengthen "civil society in the definition of the public interest" and would weaken "the pernicious effects of state action." This emerging model opposes neo-conservatism, but also distinguishes itself from welfare-statism and the "third way."[8] It promotes a project of the "renewal of public debate" and "more inclusive deliberative frames" that can be identified as plural democracy. Its future depends on the state's capacity to promote an open public sphere through "the inclusion of those with weak or vague interests" (Jobert 2009, 417–22) in a civil dialogue that respects, but is not limited to, the social dialogue between unions and management.

The foundations of a plural democracy exist. The international data[9] discussed in this book confirm that public engagement is not disappearing. It is recomposing and crystalizing, largely around what the people concerned consider to be their vital needs (food, housing, transport) and around what they defend as their common goods (access to resources, health, cultural dignity). What is highlighted is thus the complementarity between a plural democracy and a plural economy. The alter-globalization movement is the symbol of a critique of the economy that claims to be based on alternative expertise but which is also anchored in spaces of socialization that are defenses established in the face of generalized commodification (see Pleyers 2010). From these spaces emerge interactions between this movement and the recognition of solidarity initiatives. It is no accident that social forums—whether global, local, or continental[10]—are giving increasing prominence to solidarity initiatives, as they reconnect the political contestation of contemporary globalization with practices of economic citizenship. From these debates, it becomes clear that a form of public action that combines resistance and construction requires both the preservation of nonmarket economies, on the one hand, and the introduction of solidarity practices in the most common economic activities, on the other.

The practices that can carry us toward a plural economy and a plural democracy already exist; the question is what kind of social change they can bring about. When combined with our clarifications about the boundaries of the economic and the political, the comparison of contemporary conceptualizations of associationalism and the analysis of past experiences can allow us to rethink social change.

Reconsidering Social Change

At the end of the twentieth century, deregulated capitalism was presented as the only rational path. Any reluctance to accept this was only the product of backward-looking forms of resistance and would impede the inevitable march of progress. In the first decade of the twenty-first century, however, the sham was exposed. "The intrinsic unsustainability of the mode of development promoted by the actors of global capitalism" (Peemans 2002, 466) became obvious. Under these conditions, any attempt to make capitalism more ethical can only be trivial, a mere adjustment at the margins of a predatory system that continues to forge ahead while ignoring the question of limits. Instead, the challenge is to establish a new alliance between state and civil society against the excesses of capital.[11]

In order to realize this possibility—which is the only one likely to reduce the extent of social and environmental degradation—a plural economy and a plural democracy can be used as solid reference points. These notions help us reformulate social change in a way that avoids the pitfall of referring too easily to postcapitalism while forgetting to ask questions inherent to the transition. Twentieth-century approaches to social change were overly infused by fascination with a global alternative (Jullien 2011). Escaping the cycle of hopes and disillusions depends not on modeling a better world but rather on comprehensively addressing multiple practices. Thus the solidarity economy—as Allard and Matthaei write—"does not create practices in order to conform to principles, but creates principles in order to translate practices" (2008, 10). In doing so, it clearly situates itself in the associationalist tradition. The historical retrospective carried out in the first part of this book showed that associationalist experiences have distanced themselves from totalizing utopias' dream of universal harmony;[12] they have rejected the prospect of a society capable of being reconciled as soon as it has thrown off its capitalist fetters. True to these teachings, the associationalist revival mentioned in the second part assumes that there will be both cooperative and conflictual interaction with the market and the state. Nonetheless, it does not situate itself equidistant between these two poles; it acquires meaning through strengthening public and associative economies, as well as through their mutualization.[13] Associationalism is not just a "tool for fighting against marketization"; more fundamentally, it counteracts a "fatal opposition between the political and the economic," proposing a vision of society that moves beyond the "juxtaposition of the particular interest and the general interest" (see Peillon 2008, 51 and 115).

This is why the third sector approach is insufficient here: because the goal of social transformation is absent. This is not the case with the social economy perspective, which insists that noncapitalist enterprises have a market presence so that they are not locked in the domain of social action and can demonstrate their efficacy. But change cannot result from this strategy alone. Although it has been in operation for over a century, it has had hardly any effect on the economic order. Social economy enterprises cannot escape strong isomorphic tendencies when they are forced to adapt to the dominant conception of the economy. We must question their modes of institutionalization—but we must also recognize that their actors' collective expression is necessary to prevent a gradual loss of all originality. Their transformative impact is thus linked to citizens speaking up about what they can do together in the economy, as well as to a change in public regulations in favor of a different way of institutionalizing the economy.

To this end, the solidarity economy approach suggests influencing institutional frameworks from the perspective of a strong, reaffirmed conception of democratic solidarity. If the market and the capitalist enterprise can be subjected to social and environmental regulations, then they can also be restricted through the deployment of a democratic solidarity based on both state redistribution and egalitarian reciprocity. Solidarity does of course rest on the legal forms of the social economy, but it also constitutes—as an institutional logic distinct from that of interest—an asset for the dynamics of democratic socialization. This may be the case within public services through the input of users, or within associations, where the same concern is met through the adoption of internal rules that go further than statutes in guaranteeing rights to voice.

This position once again raises the arguments developed by Mauss and Polanyi. These two authors sketched the theoretical foundations of a plural approach to the economy, but they also initiated a discussion about social change that was not satisfied with ritual references to overthrowing the system. After the demise of associationalist socialism, the prevailing critique of capitalism long disdained the forms of resistance that opposed the dominant system's naturalization through concrete action. Too weak to oppose capitalism, they ended up serving its interests, distracting from the tasks prioritized by the revolution. It is this "Bolshevik" understanding of change that Mauss[14] and Polanyi rail against. For them, true transformation can only be sought through institutional innovations anchored in social practices; it is these innovations that can show us how to reembed the economy in democratic norms while avoiding a political voluntarism that results in authoritarianism. We can only advance thinking about the reconciliation of freedom and equality, which remains the nodal point of democracy in complex societies (see Polanyi 2008, 485–564), by taking account of answers that come from those societies themselves. This involves looking to practices themselves in order to learn about them, studying them, and strengthening them—in other words, starting from the "real economic movement" and not from a project of social reform stuck onto reality. From this perspective, the state's role is not to plan everything but rather to encourage and amplify society's democratic movements. Even if it is difficult to achieve, the recognition of associationalist practices in public policy would—as far as this view is concerned—be a major gain. Rather than sustaining a mythology that "assumes there are stark choices to be made between two contradictory forms of society," it is crucial to face up to the challenge of pluralism through the "construction of new groups and institutions alongside and beneath the old ones," as Mauss puts it (1977, 265).

Problematizing the Social and Solidarity Economy

It is around the defense of pluralism in both the economy and politics that—as the debate examined in the third part shows—we can see new rapprochements materializing. While the respective conceptions of the third sector, the social economy, and the solidarity economy have significant differences, as has been shown, the new fact is that it seems possible to minimize these differences around a pluralist framework that acknowledges the insufficiency of the market and the state.

As we have noted, the third sector perspective has focused on non-profit organizations. But recent writings on the topic have a different emphasis: a plural approach to the economy and to democracy but also to social welfare.[15] Instead of thinking of the third sector as composed of private organizations, they integrate the associational dimension of public voice that Hirschman stressed. The emphasis on combinations of institutional logics and institutional forms from "multiple contributors" (Pestoff 1998, cited by Trouvé 2003, 135) leads to the third sector being treated not as a sector per se but rather as a space "of mediation between various spheres and social logics" (Evers 2000, 57). This more open conception of the third sector as an intermediary space has a strong presence in Europe. Here it echoes that of the solidarity economy, whereas the opposition between the two concepts remains much more pronounced in South America, where the third sector is invoked by big businesses and the solidarity economy by social movements.

Another indicator of the trend toward the adoption of a pluralist framework—this time just as visible in America as in Europe—is that the expression "social and solidarity economy" is spreading. The reference to the plural economy has served as a shared foundation for this grouping. The social economy approach adopts it in order to talk about enterprises with a plurality of forms, while the solidarity economy approach—as mentioned previously—stresses the plurality of economic principles. Nonetheless, a shared vocabulary is emerging—with cultural implications. The identification of such a grouping does not eliminate the differences between one pole that is more focused on the volume of this grouping's activities, and another more concerned with its sociopolitical dimensions.[16] But it does subordinate these differences to the existence of a fundamental convergence in the general balance of power. The attractiveness of the social and solidarity economy (SSE) as a grouping is demonstrated by the fact that, since the start of the twenty-first century, more than thirty countries on different continents have adopted public policies or laws in this area. Not only has there been a resurgence of the practices initiated in the last third of the twentieth century, these practices are also now experiencing an unprecedented level of recognition. This does not mean, however, that the SSE has become definitively established. As argued earlier, it is important to analyze these institutionalization processes—which range from a loss of distinctiveness to social transformation—in all their complexity.[17]

A Political Issue in Need of Clarification

A few examples will suffice to illustrate the variety of paths these institutionalization processes take. Some countries are exceptions: this is true of Venezuela, where the state under Chávez promoted cooperatives; community associations for work, savings, and consumption; communally owned enterprises; and solidarity exchange groups. This ambitious program collided, however, "with the double obstacle of a bureaucratic state resistant to new policies, and a society lacking in sufficient organizations, which did not manage to make proposals independently" (Coraggio 2015a, 243). As Coraggio explains, significant resources derived from oil profits were invested to encourage the creation of cooperatives, but very few remain in operation. While such voluntarism remains exceptional,[18] some typical itineraries of institutionalization have emerged despite the disparity between different national processes.

The social economy—for the Kirchner administrations in Argentina—and the solidarity economy—for the Lula and Rousseff administrations in Brazil—were considered primarily as conduits for spreading the new social policies of an interventionist state. In this respect, the various elements of the Argentina Trabaja program play a role close to that of the *bolsa familia* ("family fund") in Brazil—that is, integrating into the labor market those previously excluded from it by means of a minimum income. Here the SSE remains a subeconomy designed for the poor, who can reintegrate themselves through it; it is nothing but an airlock designed to prepare them to return to the market economy, which continues to be equated with normality. As such, the SSE is bound up in controversies stemming from the revolt of the middle classes against antipoverty policies that are deemed too expensive, above all in Argentina. In Brazil, the short-term social assistance programs to which the SSE has been assigned by the most orthodox fringes of the national government have been the target of protests—both by the Solidarity Economy National Secretariat (SENAES), within the Ministry of Labour, and by the Brazilian Solidarity Economy Forum (FBES, a social movement bringing together solidarity entrepreneurs, networks, and civil-society supporters as well as public officials). The National Solidarity Economy Council—an advice and advocacy organization—was created in accordance with the 1988 constitution in order to encourage the liaison between SENAES officials and social actors from the FBES. This reflects a shared desire to co-construct public policy and a reaction against the uniform use of these initiatives as a tool of an interventionist welfare state.

In other countries—including Spain and France[19] in Europe—the SSE is viewed more as a sector composed of small and medium enterprises. Governments want to see such enterprises develop because the structure of their capital offers guarantees that they will remain permanently located in the places where they take root. However, the change of scale that it is hoped will result from a national legal reform can hardly generate the desired results: it remains infused with an "enterprise-ist" vision according to which the enterprises that have found market success are likely to promote this model by serving as examples. But as mentioned in chapter 8, this project of scaling-up has, historically, demonstrated its own limitations by resulting in cooperatives' and mutuals' loss of distinctiveness. Admittedly, it is important for collectively owned enterprises to prove they can establish themselves in competitive environments, but it is worth reiterating that a strategy based on this lever alone is put at risk by the strength of market isomorphism. So such a strategy cannot provide a basis for the SSE to properly flourish. This approach shows the inadequacy of neglecting nonmarket entities in favor of market ones. There is a real divergence here from the contemporary composition of the SSE, which is largely made up of associations—in France, for example, associations account for 80 percent of SSE jobs. This underestimation of the size of the associative component—and in particular of civic initiatives that appeared in the final decades of the twentieth century—can be explained partly by the "industrialist" bias pointed out by Demoustier (2001, 130). The industrialist bias leads us to ignore the importance of social action[20] in these projects, as well as their relationship to public policy. The definitions that equate the SSE with private enterprise—as Spanish and French law do—emphasize the relevance of social entrepreneurs, but these definitions also sideline the public dimension of initiatives that is such an important part of the solidarity economy. Although national frameworks are largely influenced by this traditional private-sphere perspective in social economy, they also have some positive aspects: the French framework, for example, reaffirms the legality of subsidies for associative financing or the recognition of innovations, as with the

Pôles Territoriaux de Coopération Économique [Local Networks for Economic Cooperation],[21] *circuits courts* (alternative food networks), and local currencies (Fourel 2015). These are all covered by policies implemented at the meso economic level, both regionally and locally: the Réseau des territoires pour l'économie solidaire [Network of Solidarity Economy Local Authorities][22] in France or the municipality of Barcelona in conjunction with the Xarxa d'economia solidaria [Solidarity Economy Network] (Fernandes and Miro 2016).

Ultimately, if the SSE's goal of social integration risks making it into a sub–public service, its identification with a set of enterprises with particular goals or ownership structures threatens to reduce it to a subsidiary element of an essentially unchanged market. In both cases, despite new dedicated policies, the SSE remains subservient to the state or the market. A true transformation requires us to abandon this dualism and opt for a new institutional architecture that grants civil society a legitimacy equal to that held by the market and the state.

This scenario's translation into institutional terms has begun already, in particular with the constitutions approved in Bolivia and Ecuador in 2008, whose originality lay in their turn away from maximal growth towards *vivir bien* ("living well"). This term, translated from indigenous languages (Aymara, Kichwa, Quechua), recalls that of "livelihood" used by Polanyi to refer both to subsistence and to the "good life" in Aristotle's sense. This perspective aims to achieve balance in four areas: within humans considered as persons, between human beings, between human beings and nature, and between collectivities of human beings (see Acosta 2016). According to the authors of Ecuador's constitution (Coraggio 2015b, 543), realizing this goal requires us to abandon the economic monopoly of a capitalism without limits that threatens the planet. This is why they adopt an explicit plural economic strategy. Against the total-market, they do not propose the total-state, but rather an economic system whose purpose is both social and solidary, in a plurality of forms: private and public enterprises, but also domestic units producing for self-consumption, family units including entrepreneurial initiatives, and autonomous self-employed entities. At the same time, the popular and solidarity economy is based on forms of organization that result from inherited or constructed ties: communities, cooperatives, associations. Furthermore, the solidarity economy is not limited to popular initiatives but is also expanding to encompass public entities. A top-down movement complements the bottom-up movement when local governments support food sovereignty or exchange networks that use local currencies.

Establishing a plural economy is inconceivable without a plural democracy that goes beyond mechanisms of representation—one that rejects both the perception of a civil society restricted to the market and the withdrawal of the state to its sovereign functions. In Ecuador, after a period of revolts, the state approached civil society in 2008, and fifty thousand proposals were made about what the new constitution should contain. The personalization of power resulted in these principles being abandoned. Nonetheless, a tight link remains between a plural economy and a plural democracy, which have a mutual influence on one another. Likewise, "the recognition of economic as well as cultural and political pluralism is affirmed as the foundation of the new Bolivian state and indeed appears as an indispensable condition for the deepening of democracy" (Hillenkamp 2015), in a context where there was a dramatic mobilization of society between 2003 and 2009. However much these two countries have drifted toward authoritarianism, there is nothing exotic about the Ecuadorian and Bolivian cases; rather, through their institutional recognition of a plural economy and a plural democracy, they help enrich the international tradition of thinking that advocates an innovative SSE. They demonstrate that the defense of pluralism cannot be conflated with a plea for a pacified society. Instead, it is a matter of social struggles: struggles to gain acceptance for the diversity of the real economy despite orthodox economics' domination at the theoretical level and that of the capitalist market economy at the practical level; struggles to anchor this diversity in public policies that institute participatory processes that make space for previously sidelined components of the economy; struggles against the power of multinationals and the bureaucratic tendencies of state intervention. In fact, European local collectivities have already explored paths that follow the same logic: invitations to tender containing social and environmental clauses; the funding of forums and conferences to support citizen participation; charters of mutual commitment with associative providers that take into account their contributions to employment but also to social cohesion and participatory democracy; procurement policies that favor fair trad; and so on. There is no lack of opportunities given that, for example, public contracts account for 15 percent of gross domestic product in the European Union.[23]

A Conceptual Task to Be Continued

In line with the emerging policies mentioned above, the SSE is conceptualized as a contribution to a plural framework of institutions, norms, values, and practices capable of strengthening democracy and structuring economic processes of production, distribution, circulation, and consumption in order to satisfy a population's needs and demands. The SSE approach is distinguished by its rejection of the compartmentalization of different spheres (economic, social, cultural, political). The goal is therefore clear: to reproduce human life and nature under conditions that guarantee the dignity of human beings and the protection of the environment. An SSE of this kind obviously cannot be reduced to the sum of the market and state redistribution. Reciprocity and householding are mixed to form complex combinations that aim to reconcile protection and emancipation. Fraser has observed that, by emphasizing civil society's protection against marketization, Polanyi perhaps neglected emancipation. We can hypothesize that the SSE would respond to marketization through actions that closely combine protection and emancipation, which is one of its principal characteristics. In order to understand these necessarily ambiguous arrangements, it is useful to engage in critical reflection—but this reflection must also redefine critique by cross-pollinating epistemologies from the North and the South. The practices of the solidarity economy have revitalized the social economy. And the various theorizations of the solidarity economy are also bringing about a regeneration, because they have appeared at the same time in America and in Europe, thus providing an unprecedented opportunity for South and North to contribute equally to these theorizations.

The epistemology of the North, whose principles are condensed in European critical theory from Marx to Bourdieu, emphasizes the phenomena of domination and reproduction inherent to the capitalist system. It therefore distrusts all attempts at resistance—which is doomed to be recuperated—and has a propensity to disregard civic initiatives. This tendency has become more pronounced since the second nineteenth century, with a focus on state seizure of power and trust in the avant-gardes.[24] Distrustful of the people, it ultimately results in "the radical critique of a radically unalterable situation" (Rancière 2003, 365). This impasse is manifested in its inability to predict the surge in demands for emancipation: neither those that led to the crumbling of Soviet power, nor those of the Arab Spring, nor those of indigenous peoples were anticipated. The "ghostly relation" (Sousa Santos 2011, 30) that thus formed between theory and practice should prompt Western authors to question their approach and execute a "turn" (Frère 2015) so that critique—rather than "preaching to an evacuated audience"— sees itself as having a role in "knitting together a global civil society," anchored in "actual existing utopias" in order to work toward a science "that is not frightened of reflecting on its value foundations nor of articulating them publicly." In line with the public sociology promoted by Burawoy, this approach "says that science without politics is blind, that critique without intervention is empty" (Burawoy 2007, 357–65).

Taking responsibility for its own choices in this way, it would then benefit from an exchange with an epistemology of the South that claims to have a different perspective on the world. This is an epistemology less obsessed with denunciation and more concerned with identifying absences and emergences[25]—that is, what has been "produced as nonexistent" and what "enlarges the present by adding to the existing reality the . . . possibilities" that emanate from those alternatives, which are both utopian and realistic, cited by Burawoy. As a global phenomenon, the SSE cannot content itself with a Northern perspective: the SSE of the South carries its own identities that are based on "real community springs," where initiatives are "born in the wake of social movements" and "rely on participatory dynamics that, like democracy, must be constantly re-nourished" (Defourny, Develtère, and Fonteneau 1999, 48–50).

In this respect, the challenge faced by the SSE is also epistemological. This can be invigorating as long as it avoids two pitfalls that Wanderley warns against (2015, 188–19). The first pitfall is to adopt a minimalist definition restricted to a set of noncapitalist statuses. This results in significant facts being evaded—for example, that most contemporary forms of the SSE across all continents have been initiated by women. Reducing them to mere business creations obscures their "explicit sociopolitical dimension" (Guérin, Hersent, and Fraisse 2011, 11)—as the example of the women's movement in Québec illustrates (Coté 2011). The second pitfall lies, conversely, in a maximalist definition that postulates the existence of a self-sufficient cooperative rationality and substitutes a utility-maximizing *Homo economicus* with an equally essentialized solidary *Homo sociologicus*. In contrast to an analysis that assumes a lack of ambiguity—one that results in an organizational or activist simplification of reality—it is vital to adopt a descriptive approach able to elaborate on existing initiatives' ambivalences and engage in a dialogue between researchers and actors. Connections must be reinforced between academic and political discourses in order to better understand the experiences of members of these initiatives, as well as to define the conditions conducive to associationalism in contexts that are largely unfavorable to it. Feminist research programs, such as those focused on provisioning and care, point to a methodological path that neither condemns nor idealizes practices. They identify hybridizations between economic principles, linking production and reproduction within an economy structured by gender relations. By understanding empirically observable mixes between different principles of economic integration, we can promote the reconciliation of emancipation and protection in practice. Doing so will involve detailing the ambiguities inherent to the imbrication between householding and reciprocity—between enclosure in private dependencies and openness toward ways of caring for others recognized by the collectivity (Hillenkamp, Guérin, and Verschuur 2014).

The SSE should be understood not through the lens of its national administrative boundaries but through an international comparison of the ways in which policies and institutional frameworks dovetail (Cary and Laville 2015, 23–37), with a view to social transformation and environmental transition. This way of understanding the SSE—which is the "pivotal actor in a bifurcation if the actions of civic initiatives are extended by big institutions" (Gadrey 2010, 169–74)—also requires us to refute the thesis that the SSE will only add a few activities combating exclusion to a social-economy base that it leaves unquestioned. On the contrary, the SSE is emerging because the solidarity economy is profoundly reconfiguring the legacy of the social economy by renewing the question of politicization or joint deliberation around economic practices—a question that was evaded throughout the twentieth century. This is why we must understand the characteristics of solidarity-economy practices in greater detail.

Theoretical Resources for Tomorrow

Today, there are various theoretical resources available for this purpose. They add to those centered on the public sphere—from Habermas and Fraser—and the substantive economy—from Mauss and Polanyi—discussed earlier in this book. The substantive examples whose importance is stressed by both Coraggio and Guerreiro Ramos (1989) are—for democracy as for the economy—furnished by South America and Europe. They provide a shared language for deepening and cross-referencing between different approaches in these two contexts. The singular contribution of South American authors on this topic consists in their ability to cross the boundaries between the political and economic spheres too often drawn by conceptions influenced by Arendt, who favors the autonomy of the political and is wary of its perversion by the economic. Extending Fraser's observation that popular public spheres necessarily address socioeconomic questions, the epistemology of the South details the processes of delegitimization faced by initiatives that seek to improve everyday life through democratization. The sociology of absences and emergences thus seems capable of renewing critical theory. It allows us to oppose "a hermeneutic of skepticism [. . .] that ends up dismissing any kind of social experimentation suspected of being contaminated by the existing system." Valuing alternatives that are too often rejected or neglected in the North, it emphasizes and develops their "emancipatory traits in order to reinforce their visibility and credibility. The hermeneutic of emergence does not thereby give up on rigorous and critical analysis. But rather than undermining their potential, it aims to consolidate these alternatives" (Garavito and Sousa Santos 2013, 130–34). Political philosophers like Avritzer (2002) and Munera Ruiz (2008) expand the political process, in a substantive sense, to areas where emphasis is placed on intersubjectivity in the formation of opinions and decisions. They thus attach great importance to popular public spheres.

Research on the SSE can also be informed by Dewey's pragmatism (1929; 1954), according to which social inquiries should be conducted by the public involved in the problems raised (Charles 2016). He thus insists on the interaction between experience and deliberation—which is the only approach suited to complex societies. Opposing the ideology of expertise defended by Lippmann, Dewey claims that such public inquiry—which is open to everyone and converts collective action into collective intelligence—is the most appropriate response to complexity. He therefore warns against the practices through which public officials seek to control the activities they are supposed to oversee. Dewey's remarks—which have the advantage of challenging technocracy and its propensity to think for but without the people—can also help alert SSE actors to the illusion that democratic functioning might be provided by the mere existence of formal equality between members. This formal equality is only relevant if it forms the basis for acting together. Dewey's message is valuable: only shared experience allows for movement toward real equality and, in this process, public valuation (Dewey 2011, 37–171) must be preferred to technicist evaluation since it makes the emergence of a transformative collective power more likely. He thus suggests a reconfiguration of public action to which the SSE can contribute if it is not shaped in an economistic mold, but instead cultivates its "commendable democratic specificities" (Bloch-Lainé 1994) on two levels. First, the SSE provides fertile ground for deliberations in "local public spheres" (Eme and Laville 1994, 155–94) that it can encourage by facilitating internal discussions, the confrontation of different points of view, and the formulation of solutions that emerge from experience. Second, the SSE participates in "the constitution of public problems," and even helps push for institutional changes in "intermediary" public spheres where it stands up to the established powers (Cefaï 1996, 43–66). Research into this public domain shows that the SSE can be one of the places where deliberative potentialities—or, to take up Dacheux and Goujon's (2020) apt term, a "deliberalism"—takes shape. Since it belongs to a deliberative paradigm, the SSE differs from liberalism and its aggregative paradigm based on the expression of individual preferences and the choice between several options by vote. Within the aggregative paradigm, preferences are exogenous to the political process. This gives rise to a confusion between behaviors appropriate for the market and those appropriate for the forum; the first are devoted to the pursuit of efficacy, the second to the pursuit of the correct definition. In addition, it is assumed that the choices expressed reflect real preferences without acknowledging that actors may have reasons to mask these preferences or to adapt to an unfavorable context. Above all, by ignoring the specificity of the forum,[26] the aggregative paradigm is unable to grasp the meaning of the very idea of the public sphere—a view that Habermas confirms by deconstructing the neoliberal line of argument. According such a significant place to deliberation must not, however, result in a search for consensus. As Mouffe and Tassin remind us, democracy rejects the idea of ultimate reconciliation. The time has come not to limit democracy but to extend it through "the activity of the state and more broadly any activity linked to a public sphere that depends on reference to a common good" (Laborier and Trom 2003, 11).

Such a reference to the common good opens up another heuristic path—that of research that investigates overlaps between the commons, on the one hand, and the social and solidarity economy, on the other. Like the SSE, "the return of the commons" (Coriat 2015) demonstrates the inadequacy of market–state dualism: it recommends a triangulation between market, state, and civil society in which civil society constitutes a productive force thanks to informal cooperation in various forms of the collaborative economy. This return resembles the resurgences within the long history of an associationalism where collective action has been oriented around a common good (see chapters 4 and 5).

The social economy approach does not really take into account this common good, which is conflated either with members' mutual interest or with the general interest.[27] The slide from *the common* toward *interest* endorsed a functionalization of social economy entities at the very moment when state communism was also erasing the common.[28] The new solidarity spirit rehabilitates this vocabulary of the common—which adopts the perspective of civil society—as stated in the 1991 Italian law on social cooperatives: Article 1 stipulates that they work for the community, either by providing health, social, and educational services, or through employment integration. It is in fact their involvement of multiple stakeholders (employees, volunteers, users, etc.) that leads them to abandon a focus on interest in favor of a politics of the common. Where the collaborative economy is torn between being coopted by the new capitalism and creating a continuum between the commons and the state, the SSE is able to put its weight behind the latter solution thanks to new forms of cooperative. It thus provides opportunities insofar as it promotes open dialogue and does not become a closed-off stronghold whose defense by specialists amounts to a new form of corporatism.

The Contribution of Historical and International Perspectives

The discourse on the beneficial consequences of growth and the liberalization of trade is undermined by the facts. Since the nineteenth century, the justification that market integration is capable of eradicating poverty has served to disqualify associative actors. In the dominant discourses, their "salvation could only come through external help," unless they left behind their "assisted status" in order to enter the game of competition. The SSE's specificity lies in its rejection of this subservience to the market, as it seeks to reestablish a public debate on the economy—that is, a fight for a plural economy.

The SSE is not merely a sector of economic activity. Those involved in it engage in activity at the point where the political and economic spheres connect. It is expressed in the ideas of a plural democracy and a plural economy. Placing it in historical context supports the hypothesis that these two ideas might provide the framework for renewed thinking about the "equality of difference."[29]

The SSE would also be limited in scope if it were only a mode of undertaking economic activity. It takes on another meaning through the two advances that this book has made: "recollection," to use Benjamin's term, and "intercultural translation," to use Sousa Santos's. The combination of these two advances enables the present to be situated in its historical and international context.

When we follow the seemingly chaotic trajectory of associationalism, once-buried continuities come to the surface, for instance between the economic reordering of the second nineteenth century and the second wave of neoliberalism. In both cases, reference to an unchallengeable economic system is complemented by the use of philanthropy in order to defuse demands for democratization. This examination of the relations between economy and society from the perspective of practices themselves then gives rise to a rereading of major theoretical contributions. We must place the innovative character of the SSE in perspective; this is what a reconstruction of the associationalist tradition—as the introduction recommended—enables us to do. "Working on historical discontinuities is to rediscover the traces of invisible continuities" (Riot-Sarcey

2016, 335) and revisit thinkers whose ideas have been put on a pedestal—for example those of Durkheim and Arendt.

As we saw in the introduction, we cannot follow Durkheim too closely because of his evolutionism, but his insistence on the morality of "special secondary groups" and on "collective effervescence" (Durkheim 1997)—which is far from any moralization—remains insightful. "What is moral," he notes, "is everything that is a source of solidarity, everything that forces man to take account of other people, to regulate his actions by something other than the promptings of his own egoism, and the more numerous and strong these ties are, the more solid is the morality."[30]

For her part, Arendt writes that the workers' movement carries the hope of "a new public space with new political standards" (Arendt 2018, 219). When she then dissociates this movement from trade unions and parties defending strict economic and social class interests (Chanial 2003, 48), she falls into a paradox: "She first emphasizes coordinated action that must come from argumentation and agreement. Then she creates a surprising division—which is untenable—between the public domain on the one hand, and the economic and social domains on the other," as Fraser notes (Interview with Hersent, Laville, and Saussey, 2015, 257). The separation between political and social is no guarantee of the purification of the political, but rather a construction of liberal thought intended to curb attempts at emancipation, since "social policy" is "at the heart of the workers' tradition" (Riot-Sarcey 2016, 338), just as it is at the heart of contemporary solidarity initiatives. The escape from economic determinism thus does not lie in the preeminence of the political, but in the integration of economic decisions into the "space of democratic decisions," which "amounts simply to reconnecting, or else reinterpreting, the economic and political spheres" (Floris 2003, 129–36). The excesses of capital reach such a level that, despite this "constellation of manifestations of the rejection of norms and practices of domination" across the globe—of which the SSE is part—the paths toward a rebalancing of power in favor of citizens remain steep: "The task is immense and cannot be undertaken without collective reflection on the scale of the five continents from this point forward" (Sousa Santos and Garavito 2013). It relies on each continent becoming aware of its own tendencies.

In this respect, Europe—which has relied particularly heavily on the regulatory virtue of the state—finds it difficult to free itself from statism: this is only possible if it enters into a debate with other regions, intercultural translation being understood as "the procedure that creates a mutual intelligibility between the different experiences of the world" (Sousa Santos 2011, 40). It is no accident that authors claiming allegiance to an epistemology of the South have a less condescending view of solidarity initiatives than do their occidental colleagues. For them, these initiatives "are not just economic: their emancipatory potential and their prospects of success depend in large part on their ability to integrate processes of economic transformations with social, cultural, and political dynamics" (Sousa Santos and Garavitos 2013, 138). This gap in perceptions between North and South would benefit from further scrutiny, even if it is beginning to narrow.

The Beginnings of a Fruitful Dialogue

Thanks to new dialogues, another history is taking shape—one that is not part of the march of progress that has long promised a glorious future. The annexations that Lutz calls "interior" and "exterior" (as quoted in chapter 2) have been asymmetrical faces of the popular economy's exclusion. The rediscovery of 1848 and, more broadly, of the first nineteenth century, combined with approaches focused on "decoloniality" and "living well," allows for a better understanding of processes that have hitherto been hidden. They become visible via a heuristic decentering: "To the extent that it becomes possible for the South to consider itself through terms other than the South, it is possible for the North to think about itself with terms other than the North" (Sousa Santos 2011, 46). Critical and possibilist analyses now allow us to rehabilitate a forgotten past and to open up the range of possibilities that "are built on a renewal of individual freedom and collective freedom in society" (Riot-Sarcey 2013, 338).

Alliances are being woven between actors and researchers despite being prohibited by scientism. Thus, for the future of the "Earth system"—which concerns us all—past and present resistance to anthropogenic action teaches us that "it is by connecting the endeavors and commitments of scientists with initiatives—reflections, struggles, sociotechnical alternatives—emanating from all sectors of global society that there may be some hope of 'transition' in the face of global environmental disarray" (Bonneuil and Fressoz 2013, 265). The same observation can be made for culture and civil society. The tragedy today is the gaping abyss that separates civic initiatives from public policy. The roots of this problem are old, but it is because they tackle this problem that the SSE's forms of institutionalization are important. They can either endorse a movement toward uniformity or increase institutional diversity in order to shore up economic and political plurality.

A Matter of Democracy

For the SSE to be more than just a "mobilizing linguistic artefact,"[31] numerous obstacles still need to be overcome. They can stem from various solidarity economy actors who justifiably complain about a lack of institutional recognition, but who maintain this through a strongly anti-institutional culture of alternativism. They can also stem from beliefs about the economy among elected representatives who support productivism while contradictorily declaring the need for sustainable development. Finally, they stem from the anxieties of some social economy leaders who want to protect their position by restricting the solidarity economy to a secondary role. For them, the solidarity economy is only a segment of the social economy, born principally from the fight against exclusion. But when we consider what has been discussed in this book, we can see that this position is manifestly incorrect. The solidarity economy cannot be understood as a set of specific organizations; its role is different: it contributes to a new problematization, that of the SSE.

The synergy envisaged between the social economy and solidarity economy approaches must be based on respect for their distinct identities, as well as on an openness to mutual critique. In sum, the social and solidarity economy might be nothing but a tactical compromise—one that is temporary and superficial—but it might also give rise to a new dynamic. Collaboration between instituted structures and instituting processes on concrete projects; dialogue with the state and social movements—trade unions in particular; combined pressure for a place in academic research: there are many areas in which there is work to be done in concert.

Will it be possible to move in this direction? The answer must come from different protagonists—state and association officials in the first instance. Either they are able to initiate a new culture of public action or they will simply come to support a capitalism that remains unchallenged. It is on their self-reflexive capacities—to which researchers concerned with a political economy that makes space for associations may contribute—that the future configuration of the political and economic spheres largely depends.

In the current system, the plurality of forms of wealth production and circulation is limited by demands for returns on invested capital and market development. It is important to expand the field of activities that are not subject to such imperatives. But while the economy cannot be conflated with the market alone, social solidarity cannot be conflated with the state alone. The SSE approach by no means has all the virtues—it can often drift toward the commercial and the bureaucratic—but it gives form to social practices that cannot find a home elsewhere. For this reason, it can give politics a place that economism refuses to give it, without thereby focusing on the state. Moving beyond small-scale initiatives, a plural economy and a plural democracy reinforce each other. They transform the activities of associations and their institutionalization into phenomena that are simultaneously economic and democratic.

In this book, I have argued that these phenomena should be given the attention they deserve. Running counter to those analyses that establish watertight separations, both past and present experience shows that the reciprocal democratization of civil society and the state is congruent with an economy based on the plurality of economic principles and forms of ownership. By discussing practices that aim to democratize the economy, we can concretely attack the absolutization of the market economy and, in doing so, no longer withdraw economic decisions from public debate. While preserving the analytic distinction between political and economic spheres, we should acknowledge that the continuation of democratization processes in contemporary societies calls for a democratization of the economy, which depends both on renewed public regulation and the penetration of democratic principles into activities of production, trade, commerce, savings, and consumption. Without rebalancing economic conditions, political equality cannot be preserved. In the twenty-first century, we should fight the ideology of risk by once again taking up the project of a solidarity society.

Notes

Introduction to the English Edition

1. In his analysis, Laville incorporates hundreds of years of history, extensive referencing, and engagement with the various theoretical traditions, from classic sociological theory to contemporary organization and science and technology theorists. It's understandable why the book cannot be more comprehensive in its spatial scope. The book primarily focuses on experiences in Europe, North America, and South America. It is worth noting, however, that the social and solidarity economy movement is global, and many movement participants live and work in Asia, Africa, and Oceania, which are left unexplored in this volume.

Introduction

1. According to the 2021 IPCC report

2. According to Peemans 2002, chap. 3.

3. Polanyi warns against this double threat throughout his work. See in particular Polanyi 1944 and 2014.

4. According to Gauchet 2005, 18.

5. Using Habermas's terms (1997, 58–60).

6. See Habermas's (1991) responses to criticism that he neglects the plebeian public sphere, in the preface to the seventeenth German edition of *The Structural Transformation of the Public Sphere* (iii–ix).

7. Habermas 1991, i–xxxv.

8. Habermas 1991, xxxi, refers to C. Offe. See also Cohen and Arato 1994.

9. Habermas 1991.

10. Durkheim 1997. The discussion about solidarity is often framed by the Durkheimian distinction between mechanical and organic solidarity. But this typology is implicitly evolutionist, which is why the key difference that will be used is between democratic solidarity defined in the first chapter and philanthropic solidarity defined in the second.

11. As written by C. Gide, quoted by Penin 1998, 61 and 300.

12. As emphasized by Servet (2006, 448).

13. This evocative image of the "first" and "second" 19th centuries will be used throughout this book.

14. According to Habermas (1978, 219), this dichotomy can be inferred from Arendt's reflections because she "stylizes the image she has of the Greek polis to the essence of politics as such. This is the background to her favored conceptual dichotomies between the public and the private, between state and economy, freedom and welfare."

15. Considering the economy as an institutionalized process is one of the characteristics of Polanyi's (1977) methodology.

16. Which, as Honneth (1995, chapter 5) reminds us, constitute two models of intersubjective recognition.

17. To use Fournière's (2009) expression. For a general definition of associationalism, see Chanial and Laville 2006, 46–55.

18. Reported by Penin 1998, 51 and 276–78.

19. Sousa Santos 2011, 29. For a more complete presentation of his point of view, see Sousa Santos 2016.

20. Negt 2007 drew on Aristotle and Xenophon to propose the notion of the "integral household." In his view, Arendt's distinction between the economic and political spheres establishes a "radical dichotomy between oïkos and polis that did not really exist in antiquity" (235).

21. The argument supporting this point is developed in the introduction of Hillenkamp and Laville 2013, 7–36.

1. Democracy and Solidarity-Based Associationalism

1. As the notes will show, this chapter makes particular reference to the work of E. Brooks Higginsbotham, K. D. McCarthy, M. P. Ryan, and H. Zinn for North America; J. L. Coraggio, A. Quijano, B. de Sousa Santos, L. Razeto, and G. Santana Jr. for South America; and H. Desroche, R. Gassez, E. J. Hobsbawm, M. Riot-Sarcey, and W. J. Sewell for Europe.

2. These ideas came from France and Scotland, respectively, according to Hirschman (1984, 12).

3. According to the metaphor of the invisible hand (Smith 2002, 184–85, IV.1.10).

4. In the words of Razeto 1993.

5. For a more complete synthesis of his theoretical approach, see Coraggio 1999, 2006.

6. Here Coraggio (2006) shares Bourdieu's (2005) critique.

7. For an in-depth examination of these variants and developments, see Santana Junior 2005.

8. Such as "La natillera, el montepio, la minga, el convite, la ayuda mutual comunitaria, la acción comunal," as cited by Moreno 2001.

9. This description is based on Nyssens's (1994) work, which was largely inspired by Salazar (1989 and 1991). See also Grez 1990.

10. This word is used in Colombia to designate farmworkers and artisans.

11. This point is made by Mingione (1991a).

12. Abigail Adams, letter to John Adams, May 7, 1776. Cited in McCarthy 2003, 36.

13. These groups continued in various forms. For the end of the nineteenth century, see Clemens 1993. For the contemporary period, see Evans 1980.

14. Unless otherwise indicated, the passages in quotation marks about England have been taken from E. P. Thompson's book (1971), which has become a classic; in particular chapters 5 to 12.

15. For another example that illustrates this point, see the case of Quebec in Petitclerc 2007.

16. Spanish discussion groups that focused on subjects such as equality and popular education. See Sola 1978.

17. This project was then transformed from social workshops to national workshops organized by the state. For more information about the events of 1848, see *La Revue du MAUSS* 2000, 217–328.

18. These quotations appear in Desroche 1981, 58 and 66.

19. According to Fourier, cited by Chanial 2001.

20. If we use the terms from Wright 2010.

2. Capitalism and the Moralization of the Poor

1. According to J. S. Mill, cited by Habermas 1991, 129–40.

2. According to Malthus 1872, 417.

3. Comments reported by G. Salazar, cited by Nyssens 1994, 19.

4. Nyssens 1994, chapter 2. The expressions "productive social fabric" and "industry imposed from above" are borrowed from Nyssens.

5. This conception of development in terms of "stages" is central in liberalism, as explained by Meek 1976.

6. Understood as the domination of the imaginary, in the words of Castoriadis 1975, 218–24.

7. According to Lutz (1990), these two "annexations" are similar in many ways.

8. The notion of moral economy was introduced by E. P. Thompson in studies of workers and extended to peasants by J. C. Scott (1976).

9. For more about Douglass, a former slave, see Scott 1976, 163–93; McCarthy 2003, 161–64.

10. According to the paradox mentioned by E. P. Thompson (1960, 212) and explained from at 213–308.

11. Chevassus-Au-Louis 2006, in particular chapter 10, "*Historiagraphical Rehabilitation.*"

12. The quotations in this paragraph (Audiganne, Thiers) have been taken from J.-F. Marchat's highly original thesis (1989).

13. C. Coquelin, quoted by J,-F. Marchat (1989, 203).

14. According to Abensour in his preface to the 1988 French translation of E. P. Thompson (viii).

15. Laval 2007, 315. Cf. Foucault 1995 and 2010.

16. Expression borrowed from Gide and Rist 1926.

17. Bastiat 1682–1864, 411, 622, and 626; cited by Gide and Rist 1926. A strange similarity can be noted between the expressions used by Bastiat and Fourier when reading the following lines from Bastiat: "The general laws of the world are 'harmonic': they contribute in every sense to the improvement of humanity" (387).

18. Chapter 3 in Blais (2007, 74–106) is devoted to the ideas of C. Pecqueur and P. Leroux.

3. The Welfare State and the Social Economy

1. According to J. Lewis (1997, 6).

2. The history of European countries shows how much associations have been hindered in their economic activities. See the contributions of C. Borzaga for Italy, V. Pestoff for Sweden, P. Chanial and J.-L. Laville for France, and P. Dekker for the Netherlands in Evers and Laville 2004.

3. These findings have led to the proposal of a typology, not only for welfare states but also for the relationship between states and associations in social services. See Laville and Nyssens 2001b, chapter 15.

4. In reference to J. Guesde, a socialist politician, and J. Allemane, pioneer of trade unionism and political leader.

5. "A la recherche de l'unité perdue," the title of chapter 3 of Blais 2007.

6. For a critique of this approach, see Ruby 1997, 73–74.

7. Using C. Ruby's expression (1997, 63–74).

8. See Marx 1965, especially in the Parisian Manuscripts of 1844.

9. In his economic writings: Marx 1963; Marx and Engels 1973.

10. Of which Mauss articulated a strong critique as early as 1924 (103–32); Mauss 1997, 537–66.

11. As Lefort reminds us in his "rereading of the *Communist Manifesto.*" See Lefort 1986, 195–212.

12. This is the subtitle of the book by Riot-Sarcey, already quoted.

13. See also, among others, Gribaudi 2014, Bouchet et al. 2015, and Gribaudi and Riot-Sarcey 2008.

14. According to Sousa Santos (2016). For "decoloniality," see Quijano 1998.

15. Which, according to Arendt (2018, 184), is based on a mechanistic philosophy.

4. Associative Metamorphoses

1. For more on the changes affecting associations in France see, for example, Ion 1997 and Barthélémy 2000, 60–67.

2. See, for example, Baudrillard 1974, 35–41.

3. Their theoretical approach is based on multiple studies. See Touraine 1981; Touraine, Hegedus, and Wieviorka 1980; Touraine, Wieviorka, and Dubet 1984.

4. As expounded by Schumpeter (1943).

5. The title of Friedmann's 1956 book on the breaking up of work into "crumb" ("miettes")-sized pieces.

6. To use the names given by Mothé (2006, 53–60).

7. In the words of Mothé (1980), these different meanings of autogestion can be perceived in the evolution of the review *Autogestion et Socialisme,* which became *Autogestion,* then *Autogestions.*

8. It is difficult to pick out the data among the mass of available statistics. See Rock and Klinedinst 1992.

9. The arguments specifying the neoliberal project are discussed in the introduction and conclusion of Laville and Salmon 2015.

10. This general trend was observed in companies by Alter and Uhalde (2006, 347).

11. It is the title of one of the first books dedicated to the analysis of workers takeovers: Paton 1989.

12. Among the best known were *The Scottish Daily News,* KME, and Meridien in the United Kingdom (known as "Benn" cooperatives because they were supported by Labor Minister Tony Benn), Clems in Italy, and Tricofil in Quebec.

13. Manufrance was a workers takeover project strongly supported by the trade union in the period of left government in France. It was a high-profile failure affecting the image of the cooperative movement.

14. In contrast to the previous period, when nonagricultural employment growth was much higher than that of the urban population—87 percent and 12 percent respectively between 1925 and 1950. See Santana Junior 2005.

15. When it was introduced by Hart (1973).

16. *Talleres laborales* in Spanish. See Razeto, Klenner, Ramirez, and Urmeneta 1983.

17. In the *assentamentos* experiments—that is, occupations of unused land—cooperatives form the Sistema de Cooperativismo dos Assentados.

18. See their debate: Navarro 2002, 189–232, and de Carvalho 2002, 233–60.

19. See the argument developed in Fonteneau, Nyssens, and Fall 1999, 159–78. See also Larraechea and Nyssens 2007, 145–88.

20. Fonteneau, Nyssens, and Fall 1999, 165. The following references from Zaoual and Latouche are cited in the same article, page 166.

21. Thus Sarria Icaza (2005 and 2008) shows how public policies in Porto Alegre and the Rio Grande do Sul region continue to value cooperative take-overs by male workers more than other more feminized components of the popular economy.

22. On the denaturalization of these notions inherent in the capitalist and patriarchal economy, see, for example, Faria and Nobre 1999.

5. Local and International Initiatives

1. The term *community* is often used in English (see for instance Healy, Heras, and North 2023). So we chose to translate *services de proximité* by community-based services because it is more understandable by Anglo-American readers, but it was also translated in other texts as *solidarity-based services*; see for instance Laville and Nyssens 2000

2. On this phenomenon, see Gadrey 2003; Laville 2005.

3. On the dual dimension of changing and restoring multiple practices, see Laville, Levesque, and Mendell 2007, 155–80.

4. For a summary of the paradoxes of integration based on the example of France, see Eme 2005. For an international review of initiatives, see Defourny, Favreau, and Laville 1997; Gardin, Laville, and Nyssens 2012. The wide range of integration initiatives in Europe is described in these texts, along with different development scenarios.

5. See also Folbre 1997. This has to do with the question of care.

6. For a more detailed discussion, see Guérin 2003 and Méda 2001.

7. As Gorz (1997, 70–91) already warned.

8. An economic sociology focused solely on networks and markets has endorsed this equation; see Laville 2008b, 43–58. The conclusion of this book also addresses the relationship between economic sociology and the social and solidarity economy.

9. See the chapters on these topics in Hersent and Palma Torres 2014.

10. Thus, as *Agir ici* shows, 70 percent of broiler-chicken farms in Senegal have disappeared due to the mass importation of European cuts. See *Campagne d'Agir ici* 68 (October 2004).

11. According to FINE, a group of four international organizations representing fair trade as listed below.

12. Again, according to FINE.

13. According to figures from the Fair Trade Platform.

14. As in the collective De l'éthique sur l'étiquette in France.

15. Which, in addition to debates about commercialization, has given rise to debates about the balance between volunteers and professionals.

16. On responsible and solidarity-based consumption, see Pleyers 2010.

17. This data is taken from J.-M. Servet's reference book (2006, 9–10).

18. In this respect, the strategies of cooperative and mutual banks diverge because, while some are returning to their original objectives, others are adopting behaviors similar to those of their competitors. The difficulties of the trajectories of these organizations are described in chapter 8 in this book.

19. The origin of this section's title, which is borrowed from Servet 1999.

20. On complementary currencies, see Blanc 2006; 2013, 241–70.

21. On the relationship between trade, markets, and social cohesion, see the distinction between trade and the market put forward by Polanyi 1968; see also the discussion on the "marketplace" and "customer relationships" in Servet 2006, 314–317.

22. On SEL and LETS, see Blanc, Ferraton, and Malandrin 2004.

23. As pointed out by J. Blanc (2006, 460–67).

24. See the website of the Programme Autoproduction et Développement Social: www.pades.autoproduction.org.

25. According to Cérézuelle 2004, 101–8.

26. This economic dynamic emerging from local communities is discussed in Franca Filho et al. 2013, 115–31.

27. According to Vidal 1992.

6. In the Face of Crises

1. "Public action," as Drèze and Sen define it, refers to "not merely the activities of the state, but also social actions taken by members of the public—both 'collaborative' (through civic cooperation) and 'adversarial' (through social criticism and political opposition) . . . the reach of public action goes well beyond the doings of the state, and involves what is done *by* the public—not merely *for* the public" (1989, vii).

2. On this relationship between financialization and employment, see Deakin, Hobbs, Konselmann, and Wilkinson 2001.

3. Several debates about the type of production among the workers are presented in Paton 1989.

4. The opprobrium that supporters of these two theoretical approaches may direct at one another does not correspond to the reality of the initiatives, which may be very similar while claiming to follow one or another of these approaches; here again, considering practices themselves provides

some perspective on the oppositions that are exaggerated in some of the literature. For balanced presentations of degrowth and sustainable development, see Roustang 2006 and Maréchal 2006. On degrowth, see the works of Georgescu-Roegen 1994, Latouche 1991, and Cheynet 2008.

5. "On the one hand, it became increasingly difficult for parents to find the time to help run nurseries and the money to self-finance this, and on the other hand, the importance of the stability of a paid job became apparent." This and the previous quote are from Passaris 1984, 2.

6. On social enterprise, see Defourny and Borzaga 2001; Nyssens 2006; see also OCDE 1999.

7. For a summary of local initiatives in Europe, see Gardin and Laville 2007; Gardin 2006.

8. For a summary of research on social utility, see Gadrey 2006, 641–51. On indicators, see Gadrey and Jany-Catrice 2006.

9. This question is developed further in Laville 1995, 32–54; resumed in Laville 1997.

10. Such positions are granting the monopoly of economic action to capitalist companies.

11. The notion of path dependency is borrowed from the work of the economic historian David 1985, 332–37. It has been used with regard to welfare states; see Merrien 1990, 29–44. This notion emphasizes the historical continuities fostered by institutional legacies.

12. The general idea of the Danish Social Development Project (SUM) was to deinstitutionalize social services in order to meet inherently unpredictable human needs. The objective was to strengthen local initiatives and preventive social work. The SUM supported 4,000 requests and 1,800 projects, mainly related to community services. The main impact identified by the heads of county and municipal social services was an improvement in quality among 70 percent of services and greater inventiveness in their implementation among 87 percent, thanks to new services and methods that placed citizens at the center.

13. On the genesis and content of this movement of thought, see Maréchal 2005 and 2008.

14. The role of the new public management is important in this perspective (Mongkol 2011).

15. These statistics are taken from Maréchal 2008, 9–40. Piketty (2014) is the more commented book about the links between capitalism and unequalities.

16. In the United States, foundations benefit from the equivalent of one-third of the federal budget, or 2 percent of national income, thanks to a tax relief system.

17. See the difference between regular philanthropy and *venture philan-thropy* in Abélès 2002.

18. See the experiences of work integration social enterprises discussed in Nyssens 2006.

19. The perverse effects of governance modeled on private for-profit enterprises are described in Laville and Sainsaulieu 1997, then in Hoarau and Laville 2008.

20. To take the title of one of the workshops of the MEDEF Summer University in 2008.

21. On the transition from one to the other, see Frère's 2009 analysis of the content of the review *Autrement*.

22. On the comparison between microcredit and solidarity finance, see Servet 2007.

23. The quotes in this paragraph are from Yunus 2008.

24. The literature on social business has two main characteristics: the small number of examples and the dearth of independent data. In the rare cases where the results were not controlled by the studies' sponsors, the success stories have been refuted, see Humberg 2011.

25. This is the argument of Fontaine 2014b; a response is given in Hillenkamp and Servet 2015.

26. This unequivocal conclusion is probably due to the method Boltanski and Chiapello adopt to identify the new spirit of capitalism. Examining management discourse from the 1970s onward leads them to assign the demand for authenticity to the 1960s movement, ignoring the fact that this demand had already appeared in reactionary writings (see Salmon 2009). Focusing on business alone leads to a neglect of the sporadic movements that do indeed connect the "artistic critique" and the "social critique" (see Lazzarato 2008), as well as art and culture groups that link creativity and solidarity to the need for an alternative economy (see Colin and Gautier 2008).

7. The Third Sector

1. The findings for France are presented in Archambault 1996—the French contribution to the Johns Hopkins project.

2. For instance, in France they make less than 5 percent of all service providers. For an international review, see Laville and Nyssens 2001b.

3. For the gap between discourse and job creation in France, see Devetter, Jany-Catrice, and Ribault 2009, 24–41.

4. Resistance that is prevalent in care services. See the dossier produced by the *Revue française de socio-économie*, 2008.

5. According to Smouts 1988.

8. The Social Economy

1. These are respectively the *ideell förening,* that came out of the popular movement, and the *ekonomisk förening.* The term *ideell* is difficult to translate because it refers both to the basis of values and to unpaid work or work without personal material benefits.

2. See chapters 3, 5, and 6 of Pestoff, Taylor, Bode and Evers, in Evers and Laville 2004.

3. Procacci traces the history of the term (1993, 163–69).

4. The French term *l'économie sociale* translates into English as both "the social economy" (i.e. a type of economy) and "social economy" without the definite article (i.e. an academic discipline akin to political economy).

5. From 1904 and in 1909, to name the collection he edited. See Bidet 2001, 88.

6. Thus formulating a "unitary theory," according to Vienney (1994, 97).

7. We have seen the importance of this in the previous chapter on nonprofit sector analyses such as Hansmann's. See also Ortmann and Schlesinger 1997.

8. Champagne 1998; the following references are taken from Bidet 2003, 162–78.

9. Mandel 1974; Oppenheimer 1914; Webb and Webb 1914; with this theory, the authors concur with the law of oligarchy whose formulation is associated with Michels 2009 (reprint of the first text translated into French in 1914).

10. In the words of Desroche (1983).

11. A definition given by by DiMaggio and Powell 1993, 49.

12. This quotation and the two that precede it are taken from Vienney 1994, 114.

13. Bélanger and Lévesque 1990. The importance of adding the institutional dimension to the organizational dimension in the analysis of associations is detailed in Laville and Sainsaulieu 2013.

14. The French Social Economy Charter, a declaration of Comité national de liaison des activités mutualistes, coopératives et associatives, May 10, 1995, cited in Jeantet 2006, 45.

15. In Anglo-Saxon countries, the second half of the nineteenth century was marked by *scientific charity,* which brought about *case work* as a working method, as noted by Castel 1995, 248–49.

16. On Buret, see Vatin 2007. On Le Play, see Savoye 1994.

17. To use the term of Worms 1898, reported in Castel 1995, 245.

18. According to Hatzfeld 1971; also see Dreyfus 2001.

19. According to the parliamentary debates of 1849 and 1864, respectively, cited Le Goff 1985.

20. This is the thesis defended by Gueslin in his previously cited work.

21. In doing so Develtère follows Giddens, and adopts a social movement perspective. Develtère 1998, 40–59.

22. In a book entitled *Quatre Écoles d'économie sociale: Conférences de Genève* (1890), in Archives de sciences sociales de la coopération et du développement, no. 82 (1987).

9. The Solidarity Economy

1. As F. Espagne, 1999, says, *stakeholders* become *shareholders*.

2. The other characteristics that the EMES network has retained in the definition of social enterprise taken up internationally (see OECD 1999) are already included in those of the third sector and the social economy.

3. See chapters by A. Evers, J.-L. Laville and M. Nyssens in C. Borzaga, J. Defourny (eds.), 2001.

4. It is by doing so that it becomes part of economic sociology, if, as Cusin and Benamouzig say, it "does not remain subordinated to the problematics of economic theory" and encourages "more general reflection on the role of the economy in modern societies" (2004, 12).

5. This passage draws in particular on the preface and the three first chapters of Polanyi 1977.

6. See Polanyi 1977, chapter 1, republished in a revised translation in 2007.

7. Reinforced by the absence of an English translation of Menger's posthumous work. As Polanyi notes, by describing this book as "fragmentary and disorderly"—and thereby justifying its lack of translation—Hayek engaged in an editorial maneuver aimed at discrediting it.

8. Among whom are Bartoli 1977; Maréchal 2001; Passet 1996; Perroux 1970.

9. Too often, disembedding is interpreted as a process by which the market is placed beyond state regulation, but reading Polanyi more carefully we see that he is referring to a kind of state intervention in favor of the economy understood in its formal sense.

10. This is why Granovetter's critique—which alleges that Polanyi has an undersocialized conception of economic action—should be reconsidered. Granovetter began to do this himself in his introduction to French readers in Granovetter 2008. Several senses of disembedding can be distinguished, and Polanyi cannot be criticized for neglecting the reticular disembedding of economic action since he did not study this type of action's insertion in social networks. What Polanyi does is quite different: he analyses the social consequences of the emergence of a formal conception of the economy. For an account of the different types of disembedding, see Laville 2008b.

11. On the question of the legitimacy of economically oriented activities, see Roulleau-Berger 2001.

12. Which could constitute the "banner" under which various schools of a nonstandard and nonorthodox approach to the economy might operate. See *La Revue du MAUSS semestrielle* (2007).

13. What Braudel labeled "material life"; see Braudel 1980; 1985.

14. These quotations from Renault 2004 allow us to underline our convergence with his position (see 215–33 and particularly 218–19).

15. On this point we should note the incompleteness of a "new economic sociology" that focuses on markets, such as that presented by Steiner 2005.

16. In its "double dimension of expression and interpellation," according to Blondiaux 2008, 82.

17. Inspired by Sen's theorization (1987 and 1999).

18. Cf.id., A.Lemaître, M.Nyssens, 2006.

19. On this topic, Mingione (2004) is right to underline the importance of path dependency.

20. This is the question of the link between these two forms of democracy, raised by Blondiaux 2008; also see Revel, Blatrix, Blondiaux, Fourniau, Hériard Dubreuil, Lefebvre 2007. A research program on this topic could compare the effects generated by solidarity initiatives with those engendered by the various other models of participatory democracy. Using the example of Porto Alegre, Sonia Icaze examines the relationship between participatory budgeting and the solidarity economy.

21. On the respective roles of local public spheres and intermediary public spheres, see the conclusion of Laville, Magnen, de França Filho, and Medeiros 2005, 365–76, where the authors offer a transversal reflection based on studies of the Brazilian and French cases.

22. On this point see Vailancourt 2008.

Conclusion

1. Letter by P. Roland from 18 May 1850, cited in Guépin 1850.

2. In the words of Polanyi 2011, 37–54.

3. Contrary to what Chantelat proposes, the attention paid by the French school's founders—Mauss in particular—to the gift and to reciprocity never implies the negation of social links in market relations.

4. M.Callon, P.Lascoumes, Y.Barthe, 2001.

5. Drawing support from Weber, Le Velly (2006) has shown that the "new economic sociology's" analysis of markets can can miss out analysis of their progressive enclosure of a modern economy understood as rational and capitalist. This results in the delegitimation of nonmarket forms.

6. The need for this distinction between different economic realities has been explained in Mingione 1991a and 1991b, and Borghi and Magatt 2002.

7. Walzer 2000, 20–21. In his "critical associationalism," Walzer (1991) defends that "only a democratic state can create a democratic civil society ; only a democratic civil society can sustain a democratic state" (302–3).

8. As presented by Giddens 1999.

9. Those mentioned in this book converge with those gathered by Peemans 2002. Note how close his conclusion (chapter 15) is to this one.

10. The theme of the solidarity economy was included in the 2002 World Social Forum and from then on its importance has only increased, up to the point where the Belem Forum, attended by 133,000 people, gave the solidarity economy a prominent place.

11. Which is advocated by Beck 1992.

12. To put it in the terms used by Giust-Desprairies 2003 and Enriquez 1967, the collective imaginary of utopians is an "enriched imaginary" that turns into a "deluded imaginary" when its prophets wish to constrain reality to fit their project, slipping either into the interpersonal confrontation between followers, as in Cabet's *Icaria,* or into paternalism, as with the Familistère de Guise founded by the industrialist Godin. On the Familistère, see Draperi 2008 and Lallement 2009.

13. Something on which Renault (2004, 218–19) insists.

14. The text by Mauss (9884, 331–74), already mentioned in the third chapter, is essential reading on this topic.

15. For an overview, see Evers and Laville 2004.

16. This polarization is reproduced in emerging movements such as fair trade. For example, Max Havelaar's desire to increase the role of fair trade in international trade brings it into line with to a social economy strategy; Artisans du Monde and Minga follow a solidarity economy strategy by combining economic activities, educational activities to raise consumers' awareness, and public interventions promoting fair trade regulations across all trade.

17. Extending the methodology tested by D'Amours (1999) in his previously cited book on Quebec.

18. At least in the current context, because it recalls the cooperatives orchestrated in the past by communist states in Eastern Europe and Africa, which permanently tarnished these organizations' credibility.

19. A comparison of the SSE's institutionalization processes in Brazil and in France, reviewed by researchers, network actors, and public officials, has been conducted: see Laville, Magnen, França Filho, et al. 2005.

20. Which is nonetheless the primary sector of the SSE by a long way, accounting for one in every three employees, as is reported at regional level by the Observatory of the Social and Solidarity Economy in the Île-de-France.

21. For PTCEs and local food networks, see the SSE laboratory's website: http://www.lelabo-ess.org/.

22. See the RTES's website: http://rtes.fr/.

23. In France, almost all regions include the social and solidarity economy in their regional economic development plans (SRDE); see Fraisse 2006.

24. This epistemological problem of the European left is described in Laville 2016.

25. Sousa Santos 2016, 184. At the end of chapter 3, I noted how solidarity associationalism could be reconsidered through the lens of a sociology of absences.

26. According to Elster 2002.

27. This is why a social economy approach like that of Gui (1992a; 1992b)—which categorizes organizations according to how they are related to the mutual or general interest—is incomplete.

28. According to Dardot and Laval 2014, 79–93.

29. To return to the concern that Le Bras-Chopard considered primordial in Leroux, see Le Bras-Chopard 1986. This is also the question posed by liberal socialism; see Audier 2006. It is also notable that a political philosophy of pluralism has taken shape in the United Kingdom, according to Gauchet 2007, 90. See Nicholls 1989; Runciman 1997.

30. Durkheim 1997, 331; on this matter also see Chanial 1999–2000, 79–95.

31. To use Jérôme's expression (2008, 18).

References

Abélès, M. 2002. *Les Nouveaux Riches: Un ethnologue dans la Silicon Valley.* Paris: Odile Jacob.

Abensour, M. 1988. "La passion d'Edward P. Thompson," in *La formation de la classe ouvrière anglaise* by E. P Thompson. Paris: Seuil-Gallimard.

Acosta, A. 2016. "Le bien vivre comme alternative au développement." In *Les Gauches du XXIe siècle. Un dialogue Nord-Sud,* ed. J.-L. Laville, J.-L. Coraggio. Lormont: Le Bord de l'eau.

Aglietta, M. and A. Rébérioux. 2004. *Dérives du capitalisme financier.* Paris: Albin Michel.

Albo, X. and F. Barrios . 2006. *Por una Bolivia plurinacional y intercultural con autonomias.* La Paz, PNUD: Documento de Trabajo, Informe nacional sobre Desarollo humano en Bolivia.

Alcolea-Bureth, A.-M. 2004. *Pratiques et théories de l'économie solidaire: Un essai de conceptualization.* Paris: L'Harmattan.

Allard, J., C. Davidson, and J. Matthaei. 2008. Introduction to *Solidarity Economy: Building Alternatives for People and Planet.* Chicago: Change-Maker Publications.

Alpha, A., M. François, and D. Lagrandé. 2008. *Le Commerce équitable en France en 2007,* étude commanditée par le ministère des Affaires étrangères et européennes, Direction générale de la coopération internationale et du développement, et par la Plate-Forme pour le commerce equitable. Paris: GRET.

Alphandéry, C., L. Fraisse, and T. Ghezalit. 2009. "50 propositions pour changer de cap," Paris: Le Labo de l'économie sociale et solidaire.

Alter, N., and M. Uhalde. 2006. "Modernisation et mouvement de crise." In *Sociologie du monde du travail,* ed. N. Alter. Paris: PUF.

Alvarez, A., E. Dagnino, and A. Escobar, eds. 1998. *Culture of Politics, Politics of Culture,* Boulder, Colo.: West View Press.

Anheier, H. K. 1995. "Pour une révision des théories économiques du secteur sans but lucrative," *Revue des études coopératives mutualistes et associatives* 74, no. 257.

Archambault, E. 1996. *Le Secteur sans but lucratif: Associations et fondations en France.* Paris: Economica.

Arendt, H. 2018. *The Human Condition,* 2d ed. Chicago: University of Chicago Press.

Arensberg, C., H. Pearson, and K. Polanyi. 1957. *Trade Markets in History and Theory.* New York: The Free Press.

Arnsperger, C. 2005. *Critique de l'existence capitaliste.* Paris: Le Cerf.

Audier, S. 2006. *Le Socialisme liberal.* Paris: La Découverte.

Audier, S. 2007. *Léon Bourgois: Fonder la solidarité.* Paris: Michalon.

Audier. S. 2008. *La Pensée anti-68: Essai sur les origines d'une restauration intellectuelle.* Paris: La Découverte.

Audiganne, A. 1860. *Les Populations ouvrières et les Industries en France.* Paris: Capelle.

Auroi, C., and I. Yepez del Castillo, ed. 2006. *Économie solidaire et commerce equitable: Acteurs et actrices d'Europe et d'Amérique latine.* Genève: Presses universitaires de Louvain-Institut universitaire d'études du développement.

Autogestions. 1981. "Les habits neufs du président Tito: Critique sociale, répression politique et luttes ouvrières en Yougoslavie." Toulouse: Privat, no. 6.

Avare, P., and S. Sponem. 2008. "Le managérialisme et les associations." In *La Gouvernance des associations: Économie, sociologie, gestion,* ed. C. Hoarau, J.-L. Laville. Toulouse: Érès.

Avritzer, L. 2002. *Democracy and the Public State in Latin America.* Princeton, N.J.: Princeton University Press.

Azam, G. 2001. "Partie 1: L'invention de l'économie sociale." *De l'économie sociale au tiers secteur: Les theories économiques à l'épreuve de la théorisation marchande,* PhD thesis, Université des sciences sociales, Toulouse 1.

Azam, G. 2007. "La connaissance une merchandise fictive." *La Revue du MAUSS semestrielle,* 29, no. 1: "Avec Karl Polanyi contre la société du tout marchand."

Azoulay, G. 2002. *Les Théories du développement: Du rattrapage des retards à l'exclusion des inégalités.* Rennes: Presses universitaires de Rennes.

Badelt, C. 1990. "Institutional Choice and the Nonprofit Sector," in *The Third Sector: Comparative Studies of Nonprofit Organizations,* ed. H. K. Anheier, W. Seibel. New York: De Gruyter.

Barber, B. 1984. *Strong Democracy: Participatory Politics for a New Age.* Berkeley: University of California Press.

Barber, B. 1996. *Jihad vs. McWorld.* New York, Ballantine Books.

Barel, Y. 1982. *La Marginalité sociale.* Paris: PUF.

Barel, Y. 1990. "Le grand intégrateur." *Connexions* 56.

Barthélémy, M. 1994. *Les Associations dans la société française: Un état des lieux.* Paris: Centre d'étude de la vie politique française, Fondation nationale des sciences politiques, CNRS.

Barthélémy, M. 2000. *Associations: Un nouvel âge de la participation?* Paris: Presses de Sciences Po.

Bartoli, H. 1977. *Économie et création collective.* Paris: Economica.

Bastiat, F. 1862–1864. *Œuvres complètes.* Paris: Guillaumin et Cie.

Baudrillard, J. 1974. *La Société de consummation.* Paris: Gallimard.

Baudrillard, J. 2017. *The Consumer Society,* trans. Ian Hamilton Grant, rev. ed. London: Sage Publications.

Beck, U. 1992. *The Risk Society: Towards a New Modernity,* trans. Mark Ritter London: Sage Publications.

Bélanger, P., and B. Lévesque. 1990. *La Théorie de la regulation: Du rapport salarial au rapport de consommation.* Montréal: UQAM.

Bell, D. 1998. *The Cultural Contradictions of Capitalism.* New York: Basic Books.

Bellet, M. 1998. *Le Sauvage indigné.* Paris: Desclée de Brouwer.

Benevides Pinho, D. 1979. "Anatomie du mouvement coopératif brésilien." *Communautés: Archives de sciences sociales de la coopération et du développement* 50 (October–November).

Benjamin, W. 2006. "On the Concept of History." In *Selected Writings, Vol. 4, 1938–1940,* ed. Howard Eiland and Michael W. Jennings. Cambridge, Mass.: Belknap Press, 2006.

Ben-Ner, A., and T. Van Hoomissen. 1991. "Nonprofit Organizations in the Mixed Economy: A Demand and Supply Analysis." *Annals of Public and Cooperative Economy* 62.

Berger, A., L. Fraisse, and M. Hersent. 2000. "Femmes et économie solidaire." *Sciences de l'homme et sociétés: Cultures en mouvement* 31 (October).

Bergthold, L., C. R. Estes, and A. Villanueva. 1998. "Public Light and Private Dark: The Privatization of Home Health Services for the Elderly in the US." *Home Health Care Services Quarterly* 11, no. 341 (July).

Berlin, I. *Liberty: Incorporating Four Essays on Liberty,* ed. Henry Hardy. Oxford: Oxford University Press, 2002.

Besson, M. 2008. "Commerce équitable dans la grande distribution, un leurre." *Naturellement,* January.

Besson, M. 2014. "Andines, coopérative pour une économie equitable." In *L'Économie solidaire en pratiques,* ed. M. Hersent and A. Palma Torres. Toulouse: Erès.

Beveridge, W. 1948. *Voluntary Action.* London: Allen & Unwin.

Bidet, E. 1997. *L'Économie sociale.* Paris: Le Monde Éditions.

Bidet, E. 2001. "Économie sociale et tiers secteur en Corée du Sud." PhD diss., Université Paris-X-Nanterre.

Bidet, E. 2003. "L'insoutenable grand écart de l'économie sociale: isomorphisme institutionnel et économie solidaire." *La Revue du MAUSS semestrielle,* "L'alter-économie, quelle 'autre mondialisation'?" 1, no. 21.

Blais, M.-C. 2007. *La Solidarité: Histoire d'une idée.* Paris: Gallimard.

Blanc, J., ed. 2006. *Exclusion et liens financiers: Monnaies sociales, rapport 2005–2006*, Paris: Editions Economica.

Blanc, J. 2013. "Penser la pluralité des monnaies à partir de Polanyi: un essai de typologie." In *Socioéconomie et démocratie: l'actualité de Karl Polanyi,* ed. I. Hillenkamp and J.-L. Laville. Toulouse: Erès.

Blanc, J., C. Ferraton, and G. Malandrin. 2004. "Les systèmes d'échange local." *Hermès* 36, "Économie solidaire et démocratie," ed. E. Dacheux and J.-L. Laville.

Bloch-Lainé, F. 1994. "Identifier les associations de service social." *Revue des études coopératives, mutualistes et associatives* 49, no. 251.

Bloch-Lainé, F. 1996. "Perfectionner le pacte associatif." *Revue internationale de l'économie sociale* 75, no 251.

Bloch-Lainé, F., ed. 1999. *Faire société: Les associations au cœur du social.* Paris: Syros.

Blondiaux, L. 2008. *Le Nouvel Esprit de la Démocratie: Actualités de la démocratie participative.* Paris: Seuil.

Bode, I. 2000. "De la solidarité au marché? En France et en Allemagne, nouveaux défis pour les organismes d'assurance-maladie à but non lucratif." *Revue internationale de l'économie sociale* 79, no. 278.

Bode, I., and A. Evers. 2004. "From Institutional Fixation to Entrepreneurial Mobility? The German Third Sector and Its Contemporary Challenge." In *The Third Sector in Europe,* ed. A. Evers and J.-L. Laville. Cheltenham, UK: Edward Elgar.

Boltanski, L., and E. Chipello. 2018. *The New Spirit of Capitalism,* trans. Gregory Elliot. New York: Verso.

Boltanski, L. and L. Thévenot. 2006. *On Justification: Economies of Worth,* trans. Catherine Porter, Princeton Studies in Cultural Sociology. Princeton. N.J.: Princeton University Press.

Bonneuil, C., and J.-B. Fressoz. 2013. *L'Événement Anthropocène: La Terre, l'histoire et nous.* Paris: Seuil.

Bonneuil, C., and J.-B. Fressoz. 2017. *The Shock of the Anthropocene: The Earth, History, and Us,* trans. David Fernbach. New York: Verso.

Borgetto, M., and R. Lafore. 2000. *La République sociale: Contribution à l'étude de la question démocratique en France.* Paris: PUF.

Borghi, V., and M. Magatti, ed. 2002. *Mercato e societa: Introduzione alla sociologia economica.* Rome: Carocci.

Borzaga, C. 2004. "From Suffocation to Re-emergence: The Evolution of the Italian Third Sector." In *The Third Sector in Europe,* ed. A. Evers and J.-L. Laville. Cheltenham, UK: Edward Elgar.

Borzaga, C., and J. Defourny. 2001. *The Emergence of Social Enterprise.* London: Routledge.

Bouchard, M., G. Carré, D. Côté, and B. Lévesque. 1995. "Pratiques et législations coopératives au Québec: un chassé-croisé entre coopératives et État." In *Coopératives, marchés, principes coopératifs,* ed., A. Zevi and J.-L. Monzon Campos. Brussels: De Boeck.

Bouchet, T., V. Bourdet, E. Castleton, L. Frobert, and F. Jarrige, eds. 2015. *Quand les socialistes inventaient l'avenir, 1825–1860.* Paris: La Découverte.

Bouglé, C. 2007. *Les Idées égalitaires.* 1902; Latresnes: Le Bord de l'eau.

Bourdieu, P. 2005. *The Social Structures of the Economy,* trans. Chris Turner. Cambridge: Polity.

Bourgeois, L. 2008. *Solidarité: L'idée de solidarité et ses conséquences sociales.* 1902; Latresnes: Le Bord de l'eau.

Bouvier, P. 2005. *Le Lien social.* Paris: Gallimard.

Boyte, H. C. 1981. *The Backyard Revolution: Understanding the New Citizen Movement.* Philadelphia: Temple University Press.

Braudel, F. 1973. *Capitalism and Material Life: 1400–1800,* trans. Miriam Kochan. New York: HarperCollins.

Braudel, F. 1980, *Civilisation matérielle, économie et capitalism.* Paris: Armand Collin.

Braudel, F. 1985. *La Dynamique du capitalism.* Paris: Arthaud.

Breaugh, M. 2007. *L'Expérience plébéienne: Une histoire discontinue de la liberté politique.* Paris: Payot.

Bressand, A. 1994. "Réseaux et marchés-réseaux." In *Relations de services, marchés de services,* ed. J. de Bandt and J. Gadrey. Paris: CNRS Editions.

Brooks-Higginbotham, E. 1990. *Righteous Discontent: The Women's Movement in the Black Baptist Church, 1880–1920.* Cambridge, Mass.: Harvard University Press.

Brugère, F. 2019. *Care Ethics: The Introduction of Care as Political Category,* trans. Brian Hefferman. Leuven: Peeters.

Bry, F. de. 2006. "Du paternalisme à la responsabilité sociale." *European Journal of Economic and Social Systems* 19, no. 1, "Éthique, économie et société: une affaire de politique ?" ed. J.-P. Galavielle and A. Salmon.

Burawoy, M. 2005. "2004 American Sociological Association Presidential Address: For a Public Sociology." *British Journal of Sociology* 56:259–94.

Burawoy, M. 2007. "Public Sociology vs. the Market." *Socio-Economic Review* 5. https://doi.org/10.1111/j.1468-4446.2005.00059.x.

Caffareti, J. 2003. *Fabricas y empresas recuperada: Protesta social, autogestion y rupturas en la subjectivida.* Buenos Aires: IMFC.

Caillé, A. 1993. *La Démission des clercs: La crise des sciences sociales et l'oubli du politique* Paris: La Découverte.

Caillé, A. 2000. *Anthropologie du don: Le tiers paradigm.* Paris: Desclée de Brouwer.

Caillé, A. 2010. "Gift." In *The Human Economy: A Citizen's Guide,* ed. K. Hart, J.-L. Laville, and A. D. Catttani. Cambridge: Polity.

Caillé, A. 2020. *The Gift Paradigm: A Short Introduction to the Anti-Utilitarian Movement in the Social Sciences.* Chicago: Prickly Paradigm Press.

Callon, Michel, Pierre Lascoumes, and Yannick Barthe. 2009. *Acting in an Uncertain World: An Essay on Technical Democracy.* Cambridge, Mass.: MIT Press.

Carvalho, G. de F. F. 2002. "A emancipação do movimento no movimento de emancipação continuada (resposta a Zander Navarro)." In *Producir para viver: Os caminhos da produção nao capitalista,* ed. B. de Sousa Santos. Rio de Janeiro: Civilização Brasileira.

Cary, P. and J.-L. Laville. 2015. "L'économie solidaire: entre transformations institutionnelles et chantiers théoriques." *Revue française de socio-économie* 15, no. 1.

Castel, O. 2005. *Histoire des faits économiques: La dynamique de l'économie mondiale du XIXe siècle à nos jours.* Rennes: Presses universitaires de Rennes.

Castel, R. 1995. *Les Métamorphoses de la question sociale.* Paris: Fayard.

Castoriadis, R. 1975. *L'Institution imaginaire de la société.* Paris: Seuil.

Castoriadis, C. 1998. *The Imaginary Institution of Society,* trans. Kathleen Blamey. Cambridge, Mass.: MIT Press.

Cefaï, D. 1996. "La constitution des problèmes publics: Définitions de situations dans des arènes publiques." *Réseaux,* no. 75.

Cefaï, D. 2007. *Pourquoi se mobilise-t-on? Les théories de l'action collective.* Paris: La Découverte.

Cérézuelle, D. 2004. "Autoproduction et développement social." *Hermès* 36, "Économie solidaire et démocratie."

Cette, G., P. Héritier, D. Taddéi, and M. Théry. 1998. "Stratégie de développement des emplois de proximité." In *Emplois de proximité,* report from the Conseil d'analyse économique, no. 12.

Chambost, I., C. Hoarau, N. Largo, P. Pons, P. Roturier, and E. Tarrière. 2008. *Financiarisation des entreprises et dialogue social.* Paris: Syndex.

Champagne, P. 1998. "Les administrateurs de coopératives agricoles sont-ils indispensables?" *Revue internationale de l'économie sociale* 77, no. 269.

Chanial, P. 1999–2000. "Le projet utopique des sciences sociales, le paradigme de l'association." *Quaderni* 40 (Winter).

Chanial, P. 2001. *Justice, don et association: La délicate essence de la démocratie.* Paris: La Découverte.

Chanial, P. 2003. "Les trésors perdus du socialisme associationnisme français." *Hermès* 36, "Économie solidaire et démocratie."

Chanial, P., and J.-L. Laville. 2005. "L'économie sociale et solidaire en France." In *Action publique et économie solidaire,* ed. J.-L. Laville, J.-P. Magnen, G. C. de França Filho, and A. Medeiros. Toulouse: Érès.

Chanial, P., and J.-L. Laville. 2006. "Associationnisme." In *Dictionnaire de l'autre économie,* ed. J.-L. Laville and A. D. Cattani. Paris: Gallimard.

Chantelat, P. 2002. "La nouvelle sociologie économique et le lien marchand." *Revue française de sociologie* 43, no. 3 (July–September).

Charles, J., 2016, *La Participation en actes: Entreprise, ville, association.* Paris: Desclée de Brouwer.

Chavassus-Au-Louis, N. 2006. *Les Briseurs de machines: De Ned Ludd à José Bové.* Paris: Seuil.

Cheynet, V. 2008. *Le Choc de la décroissance.* Paris: Seuil.

Chiffoleau, Y. 1999. "Je ne vais pas aux AG et pourtant j'ai des idées: pour une coopération rurale en Languedoc-Roussillon." *Revue internationale de l'économie sociale* 78, no. 253.

Chomel, A. 2000. "La coopération d'épargne et de crédit et microcrédit: Kafo-Jiginew, au Mali-Sud." *Revue internationale de l'économie sociale* 78, no. 271.

CIRIEC. 2000. *The Enterprises and Organizations of the Third System: A Strategic Challenge for Employment.* Pilot action "Third System and Employment" of the European Commision, Liège. https://www.uv.es/uidescoop/TSE-DGV-CIRIEC-Full%20text-English.pdf.

CIRIEC. 2013. *The Social Economy in the European Union.* Brussels: Report for the European Economic and Social Committee, https://www.eesc.europa.eu/sites/default/files/resources/docs/12_368-gr3-env2.pdf.

Clemens, E. S. 1993. "Organizational Repertoires and Institutional Change: Women's Groups and the Transformation of US politics, 1890–1920." *American Journal of Sociology* 98.

Clerc, D. 2008. *La France des travailleurs pauvres.* Paris: Grasset.

Cohen, J. L. and A. Arato. 1994. *Civil Society and Political Theory.* Cambridge, Mass.: MIT Press.

Colin, B. and A. Gautier, eds. 2008. *Pour une autre économie de la culture.* Toulouse: Érès.

Collombson, J.-M., S. Barlet, and D. Ribier, eds. 2004. *Tourisme solidaire et développement durable,* Agridoc, dossier thématique. Paris: Éd. du Gret.

Constant, B. 1988. *Political Writings.* Cambridge: Cambridge University Press.

Cooperative Union of Canada. 1985. *Social Auditing: A Manual for Cooperative Organizations.* Toronto: CUC Social Audit Task Force.

Coquelin, C. "Des sociétés commerciales en France et en Angleterre." *Revue des Deux Mondes,* August 1843.

Coraggio, J.-L. 1998. *Economia popular urbana: Une nueva perspectiva para el desarollo local.* Buenos Aires: Universidad de General Sarmiento.

Coraggio, J.-L. 1999. *Politica social y economia de trabajo.* Madrid and Buenos Aires: Minio y Davila Editores.

Coraggio, J.-L. 2000. *La economia del trabajo ante el tercer sector.* Multiday workshop "Perspectives et rivalités du tiers secteurs en Amérique latine et Europe," organized by Arci and Lenoc. Buenos Aires, July 11–13.

Coraggio, J.-L., 2006, "Economie du travail" in J-L. Laville, AD. Cattani, *Dictionnaire de l'autre économie.* Paris: Gallimard.

Coraggio, J.-L. 2010. "Labor Economy." In *The Human Economy: A Citizen's Guide,* ed. J.-L. Laville and A. D. Cattani. Cambridge, UK: Polity.

Coraggio, J.-L. 2015a. "L'économie sociale et solidaire et son institutionnalisation en Amérique latine: cinq pays, cinq processus." *Revue française de socio-économie* 15, no. 1.

Coraggio, J.-L. 2015b. "De la mobilisation citoyenne à la Constitution et au gouvernement: la trajectoire de l'économie solidaire en Équateur." In *Associations et action publique,* ed. J.-L. Laville and A. Salmon. Paris: Desclée de Brouwer.

Coriat, B. 2015. *Le Retour des communs.* Paris: Les liens qui libèrent.

Corpet, O. 1982. "Collectifs d'intervention et mouvements alternatifs." *Communautés: Archives de sciences sociales de la coopération et du développement* 62 (October–December).

Corpet, O., M. Hersent, J.-L. Laville. 1986. "Le savoir sans privileges." *Revue internationale d'action Communautaire.* Montréal: 15/5.

Coté, D. 2011. *Difficiles convergences: mouvements de femmes et économie sociale, l'expérience québécoise.* In *Femmes, économie et développement,* ed. I. Guérin, M. Hersent, and L. Fraisse. Toulouse: Erès.

Cournot, A. 1974. *Recherches sur les principes mathématiques de la théorie des richesses.* Paris: Calmann-Lévy.

Coutrot, T. 2005. *Démocratie contre capitalisme.* Paris: La Dispute.

Crozier, M., S. Huntington, and J. Watanuki. 1975. *The Crisis of Democracy: Report on the Governability of Democracies to the Trilateral Commission.* New York: New York University Press.

Cunha Dubeux, A. M. 2004. *Éducation, travail et économie solidaire: Le cas des incubateurs technologiques de coopératives populaires au Brésil.* PhD diss. Paris: Université Paris-I, Institut d'études du développement économique et social.

Cusin, F., and D. Benamouzig. 2004. *Économie et Sociologie.* Paris: PUF.

Dacheux, E., and D. Goujon. 2020. *Défaire le capitalisme, refaire la démocratie: les enjeux du délibéralisme.* Toulouse: Erès.

Dahrendorf, R. 1959. *Class and Class Conflict in Industrial Society.* Stanford, Calif.: Stanford University Press.

Dahrendorf, R. 1972. *Classes et conflits de classes dans la société industrielle.* Paris-La Haye: Mouton.

Dalton, R. J., and M. Knechler, dir. 1990. *Challenging the Political Order.* Cambridge, UK: Polity Press.

D'Amours, M. 1999. *Processus d'institutionnalisation de l'économie sociale au Québec.* Montréal: Université du Québec à Montréal.

Dardot, P., and C. Laval. 2014. *Commun.* Paris: La Découverte.

David, P. 1985. "Clio and the Economics of QWERTY." *American Economic Review* 75, no. 2.

Deakin, S., R. Hobbs, S. Konselmann, and F. Wilkinson. 2001. *Partner, Ownership, and Control: The Impact of Corporate Governance on Employment Relations.* Working paper 200. Center of Business University of Cambridge. June.

De Certeau, M. 1984. *The Practice of Everyday Life, Vol. 1,* trans. Steven F. Rendall. Berkeley: University of California Press.

Defourny, J. 1983. "The Emergence of Workers' Cooperatives in Belgium." *Review of International Cooperation,* no. 3.

Defourny, J., and C. Borzaga, eds. 2001. *The Emergence of Social Enterprise.* London: Routledge.

Defourny, J., P. Develtère, and B. Fontenau, eds. 1999. *L'Économie sociale au Nord et au Sud,* Paris-Bruxelles: De Boeck.

Defourny, J., L. Favreau, and J.-L. Laville. 1997. *Insertion et nouvelle économie sociale.* Paris: Desclée de Brouwer.

Defourny, J., and J.-L. Laville. 2007. "Pour une économie sociale revisitée." *La Revue nouvelle* 1–2.

Develtère, P. 1998. *Économie sociale et développement: Les coopératives, associations et mutuelles dans les pays en développement.* Brussels: De Boeck.

Demoustier, D. 2001. *L'Économie sociale et solidaire.* Paris: La Découverte.

Demoustier, D., D. Rousselière, J.-M. Clerc, and B. Cassier. 2003. "L'entreprise collective: unité et diversité de l'économie sociale et solidaire." *Revue internationale de l'économie sociale* 82, no. 290.

De Soto, H. 1987. *The Other Path: The Invisible Revolution in the Third World.* New York: Harper and Row.

Desroche, H. 1976. *Le Projet coopératif.* Paris: Éd. Ouvrières.

Desroche, H. 1981. *Solidarités ouvrières 1: Sociétaires et compagnons dans les associations coopératives (1831–1900).* Paris: Éd. Ouvrières.

Desroche, H. 1983. *Pour un traité d'économie sociale.* Paris: Coopérative d'information et d'édition mutualiste.

Devettere, F.-X., F. Jany-Catrice, and T. Ribault. 2009. *Les Services à la personne.* Paris: La Découverte.

Dewey, J. 1920. *Reconstruction of Philosophy.* New York: Henry Holt & Company.

Dewey, J. 1929. *The Quest for Certainty.* New York: Milton Balch and Co.

Dewey, J. 1939a. "Creative Democracy: The Task Before Us." In *The Later Works 1925–1953,* vol. 14. Carbondale: Southern Illinois University Press.

Dewey, J. 1939b. *Theory of Valuation.* Chicago: University of Chicago Press.

Dewey, J. 1954. *The Public and Its Problems.* Chicago: Swallow Press.

Dewey, J. 2011. *La Formation des valeurs.* Paris: Les Empêcheurs de penser en rond–La Découverte.

Di Maggio, P., and W. W. Powell. 1993. "The Iron Cage Revisited: Institutional Isomorphism and Collective Rationality in Organizational Fields." *American Sociological Review* 48 (April).

Dockès, P., and J.-M. Servet. 1992. "Les lecteurs de l'armée morte: Notes sur les méthodes en histoire de la pensée économique." *Revue européenne des sciences sociales* 30.

Donzelot, J. 2003. *Faire société: La politique de la ville aux États-Unis et en France.* Paris: Seuil.

Draperi, J.-F. 1998. "L'économie sociale, un ensemble d'entreprises aux formes infiniment variées." *Revue internationale de l'économie sociale* 268.

Draperi, J.-F. 2008. *Godin, inventeur de l'économie sociale.* Valence: Repas.

Dreyfus, M. 2001. *Liberté, égalité, mutualité, mutualisme et syndicalisme, 1852–1967.* Paris: Éd. de l'Atelier et Mutualité française.

Dreze, J., and A. Sen. 1989. *Hunger and Public Action.* Oxford: Oxford University Press.

Dubois, P., and M. Abhervé. 2009. "Les banques cooperatives: Du pire au meilleur pour le développement de l'économie sociale." Available at www .idies.org, "Entreprise et pluralisme."

Duflo, E. 2009. *Expérience, science et lutte contre la pauvreté: Leçons inaugurales du Collège de France.* Paris: Fayard.

Duguit, L. 1922. *Souveraineté et Liberté.* Paris: Alcan.

Dumont, J.-P. 1995. "Mutualité, Sécurité sociale et compagnies d'assurances." *Revue internationale de l'économie sociale* 74, no. 257.

Dumont, L. 1977. *Homo aequalis: Genèse et épanouissement de l'idéologie économique.* Paris: Gallimard.

Duprat, C. 1993. *"Pour l'amour de l'humanité": le temps des philanthropes— La philanthropie parisienne des Lumières à la monarchie de Juillet.* Paris: Éd. du Comité des travaux historiques et scientifiques.

Duriez, B. 1996. "L'aide familiale à domicile: entre le respect et la transformation de l'organisation familiale." In *Faire ou faire-faire. Familles et services,* ed. J.-C. Kaufmann. Rennes: Presses universitaires de Rennes.

Duriez, B., and J. Nizey. 1990. *Les Services d'aide familiale du Mouvement populaire des familles: Du mouvement confessionnel à l'action sociale spécialisée.* Rapport MIRE. Villeneuve-d'Ascq-Saint-Étienne: CLERSE-CRESAL.

Durkheim, E. 1997. *The Division of Labor in Society.* Trans. W. D. Halls. New York: The Free Press.

Durkheim, E. 2008. *Elementary Forms of Religious Life.* Trans. Carol Cosman. Oxford: Oxford University Press.

ECOTEC. 2003. *Guidance on Mapping Social Enterprise: Final Report to the DTI Social Enterprise Unit.* London: DTI.

Eley, G. 1992. "Nations, Publics, and Political Cultures." In *Habermas and the Public Sphere,* ed. G. Calhoun. Cambridge, Mass.: MIT Press.

Elster, J. 2002. "The Market and the Forum: Three Varieties of Political Theory." In *Debates in Contemporary Political Philosophy,* ed. D. Matravers and J. Pike. London: Routledge.

Eme, B. 1996. "Éléments de contribution à une analyse des différentes conceptions d'un nouveau secteur d'activités." In *Société civile, État et économie plurielle,* ed. J.-L. Laville, L. Favreau, Y. Vaillancourt. Montréal: Université du Québec-Cnrs.

Eme, B. 2005. *Sociologie des logiques d'insertion: Processus sociopolitiques et identités.* PhD diss. Paris: Institut d'études politiques.

Eme, B., and J.-L. Laville, ed. 1994. *Cohésion sociale et emploi.* Paris: Desclée de Brouwer.

Enjolras, B. 1995a. *Le Marché-providence: Aide à domicile, politique sociale et création d'emploi.* Paris: Desclée de Brouwer.

Enjolras, B. 1995b. "Comment expliquer la présence d'organisations à but non lucratif dans une économie de marché? L'apport de la théorie économique." *Revue internationale de l'économie sociale* 44.

Enjolras, B. 1996. "Associations et isomorphisme institutionnel." *Revue des études coopératives mutualistes et associatives* 75, no. 261.

Enriquez, E. 1967. "Imaginaire social, refoulement et répression dans les organisations." *Connexions,* no. 3.

Espagne, F. 1999. "Les coopératives à but social et le multisociétariat." *Revue internationale de l'économie sociale* 78, no. 274.

Espagne, F. 2002. "Sur l'économie sociale et solidaire." *Revue internationale de l'économie sociale,* no. 286.

Esping-Andersen, G. 1989. *The Three Worlds of Welfare Capitalism.* London: Polity.

Estivill, J. 2015. "Le mouvement associatif en Espagne: permanence historique et ouverture démocratique." In *Associations et action publique,* ed. J.-L. Laville and A. Salmon. Paris: Desclée de Brouwer.

Etzioni, A. 1988. *The Moral Dimension: Toward a New Economics.* New York: The Free Press.

European Commission. 1993. *Growth, Competitiveness, Employment: The Challenges and Ways Forward in the 21st Century.* https://op.europa.eu/en/publication-detail/-/publication/0d563bc1-f17e-48ab-bb2a-9dd9a31d5004.

European Commission. 1995. *A European Strategy for Encouraging Local Development and Employment Initiatives.* http://aei.pitt.edu/2785/.

European Commission. 1996. *The First Report on Local Development Initiatives: Lessons for Territorial and Local Employment Pacts.* http://aei.pitt .edu/35690/.

European Commission. 2010. *Second Biennial Report on Social Services of General Interest.* Brussels. http://aei.pitt.edu/45910/1/SEC_(2010)_1284_ final.pdf.

Evans, S. 1980. *Personal Politics. The Roots of Women's Liberation in the Civil Rights Movement and the New Left.* New York: Vintage Books.

Evers, A. 1993. "The Welfare Mix Approach: Understanding the Pluralism of Welfare Systems." In *Balancing Pluralism: New Welfare Mixes in Care for the Elderly,* ed. A. Evers and I. Svetlik. Vienna and Aldershot, UK: European Center for Social Welfare Policy and Research and Avebury Press.

Evers, A. 2000. "Les dimensions socio-politiques du tiers secteur: Les contributions théoriques européennes sur la protection sociale et l'économie plurielle." *Sociologie du travail* 42, no. 4 (October–December). Special issue, "Qu'est-ce que le tiers secteur? Associations, économie solidaire, économie sociale," ed. M. Lallement and J.-L. Laville.

Evers, A. 2001. "The Significance of Social Capital in the Multiple Goal and Resource Structure of Social Enterprises." In *The Emergence of Social Enterprise,* ed. C. Borzaga and J. Defourny. London: Routledge.

Evers, A., I. Bode, S. Gronbach, and A. Graf. 1999. *The Enterprises and Organisations of the Third System: A Strategic Challenge for Employment—National Report Germany.* Liège: CIRIEC, Working Group 1.

Evers, A. and J.-L. Laville. 2004. *The Third Sector in Europe.* Cheltenham, UK: Edward Elgar.

Falk, R. 1999. *Predatory Globalization: A Critique.* Malden, Mass.: Polity Press.

Faria, N. and M. Nobre, ed. 1999. *Economia feminista.* São Paulo: SOF.

Fauquet, G. 1965. *Œuvres completes.* 1935; repr., Paris: Éd. de l'Institut des études coopératives.

Faure, A., and J. Rancière. 2007. *La Parole ouvrière.* 1976; repr., Paris: La Fabrique.

Favereau, O. 1989. "Marchés internes, marchés externes." *Revue économique,* no. 2.

Fecteau, J.-M. 1992. "État et associationnisme au XIXe siècle québécois: éléments pour une problématique des rapports État / société dans la transition au capitalism." In *Colonial Leviathan: State Formation in Mid-Nineteenth Century Canada,* ed. A. Geer and I. Radforth. Toronto: University of Toronto Press.

Fernandez, A. and I. Miro. 2016. *L'Economia social i solidaria a Barcelona.* Barcelona: Commissionat d'Economia Cooperativa, Social i Solidaria.

Ferrara, M. 1996. "The Southern Model of Welfares in Social Europe." *Journal of European Social Policies* 6.

Ferraton, C. 2007. *Associations et Coopératives: Une autre histoire économique.* Toulouse: Érès.

Ferry, J.-M. 1987. *L'Éthique de la communication.* Paris: PUF.

Flahault, F. 2005. *Le Paradoxe de Robinson: Capitalisme et société.* Paris: Mille et Une Nuits.

Fleurbaey, M. 2006. *Capitalisme ou Démocratie? L'alternative du XXIe siècle.* Paris: Grasset.

Fleury, C. 2005. *Les Pathologies de la démocratie.* Paris: Fayard.

Floris, B. 2003. "Espace public et sphère économique." *Hermès,* no. 36. Issue on "Économie solidaire et démocratie."

Folbre, N. 1997. *De la différence des sexes en économie politique.* Paris: Éd. des Femmes.

Fontaine, L. 2014a. *The Moral Economy: Poverty, Credit, and Trust in Early Modern Europe.* Cambridge: Cambridge University Press.

Fontaine, L. 2014b. *Le Marché: Histoires et usages d'une enquête sociale.* Paris: Gallimard.

Fonteneau, B., M. Nyssens, and A. S. Fall. 1999. "Le secteur informel: creuset de pratiques d'économie solidaire." In *L'Économie sociale au Nord et au Sud,* ed. J. Defourny, P. Develtère, and B. Fonteneau. Paris: De Boeck.

Foucault, M. 1995. *Discipline and Punish,* trans. Alan Sheridan. New York: Vintage Books.

Foucault, M. 2010. *The Birth of Biopolitics: Lectures at the Collège de France (1978–1979),* trans. Graham Burchell. New York: Picador.

Fouillée, A. 1928. *Les Éléments sociologiques de la morale.* 3d ed. 1905; repr., Paris: Félix Alcan.

Fourel, C., J.-P. Magnen, and N. Meugnier. 2015. *D'autres monnaies pour une nouvelle prospérité.* Lormont: Le Bord de l'eau.

Fournière, E. 2009. *Essai sur l'individualisme.* 1901; repr., Lormont: Le Bord de l'eau.

Fraisse, G. 2000. *Les Deux Gouvernements: La famille et la cité.* Paris: Gallimard.

Fraisse, L. in collaboration with A. Berger, J. Berger, J. Meunier, and A. L. Frederici. 2006. *Première Synthèse des résultats de l'étude du Mouvement pour l'économie solidaire: Appréciation des représentants des structures territoriales d'économie sociale et solidaire sur les politiques regionals.* Mouvement pour l'économie solidaire, Réseau des territoires pour l'économie solidaire. Marseille: Conseil régional Provence-Alpes-Côte d'Azur.

Fraisse, L., L. Gardin, and J.-L. Laville, ed. 2000. *Le Fonctionnement socio-économique du troisième système.* Recherche européenne pour la direction de l'emploi et des affaires sociales de la Commission des communautés européennes.

Fraisse, L., V. Lhuillier, and F. Petrella. 2007. "Une proposition de typologie des régimes de gouvernance à partir des évolutions observées dans les services d'accueil des jeunes enfants en Europe." EMES Working Papers, Brussels, no. 07/ 01.

França Filho, G. C., A. Scalfoni Rigo, and J. Torres Silva Junior. 2013. "Micro-crédit policies in Brazil: an Analysis of Community Development Banks." In. *Securing Livelihoods Informal Economy Practices and Institutions,* ed. I. Hillenkamp, F. Lapeyre, and A. Lemaître. Oxford: Oxford University Press.

Fraser, N. 1990. "Rethinking the Public Sphere: A Contribution to the Critique of Actually Existing Democracy." *Social Text* 25/26: 56–80.

Fraser, N. 2015. Interview done by M. Hersent, J.-L. Laville, M. Saussey, *Revue française de socio-économie* 15: 255–62.

Frégier, H.-A. 1840. *Des classes dangereuses de la population dans les grandes villes et des moyens de les rendre meilleures,* 2 volumes. Paris, n.p.

Frémeaux, P. 2009. "Banques coopératives: qu'allaient-elles faire dans cette galère?" *Alternatives économiques,* no. 281 (June).

Frère, B. 2009. *Le Nouvel Esprit solidaire.* Paris: Desclée de Brouwer.

Frère, B., ed. 2015. *Le Tournant de la théorie critique.* Paris: Desclée de Brouwer.

Friedman, M. 2020. *Capitalism and Freedom.* Chicago: University of Chicago Press.

Friedmann, G. 1961. *The Anatomy of Work: Labor, Leisure, and the Implications of Automation,* trans. Wyatt Wilson. New York: Free Press.

Friedmann, G., and J.-R. Tréanton. 1962. "Sociologie du syndicalisme, de l'autogestion ouvrière et des conflits du travail." In *Traité de sociologie,* ed. G. Gurvitch. Paris: PUF.

Fukuyama, F. 1992. *The End of History and the Last Man.* New York: Free Press.

Gadrey, J. 1996. *Services: La productivité en question.* Paris: Desclée de Brouwer.

Gadrey, J. 1999. "La gauche et le marché: une incompréhension plurielle." *Le Monde,* March 10.

Gadrey, J. 2002. *New Economy, New Myth.* London: Routledge.

Gadrey, J. 2003. *Socio-économie des services.* Paris: La Découverte.

Gadrey, J. 2006. "Utilité sociale." In *Dictionnaire de l'autre économie,* ed. J.-L. Laville and A. D. Cattani. Paris: Gallimard.

Gadrey, J. 2010. *Adieu à la croissance: Bien vivre dans un monde solidaire.* Paris: Les Petits Matins-Alternatives économiques.

Gadrey, J., and F. Jany-Catrice. 2006. *The New Indicators of Wellbeing.* London: Palgrave Macmillan.

Garcia Jané, J. 2009. "La economia solidaria en el Estado español." In *Crisis capitalista y economia solidaria,* ed. J.-L. Laville and J. Garcia Jané. Barcelona: Icaria Editorial Nordan.

Gardin, L. 2006. *Les Initiatives solidaires.* Toulouse: Érès.

Gardin, L., and J.-L. Laville. 2007. "L'économie solidaire en Europe: initiatives locales et services de proximité." In *L'Économie solidaire: Une perspective internationale,* ed. J.-L. Laville. Paris: Hachette Littératures.

Gardin, L., J.-L. Laville, and M. Nyssens, ed. 2012. *Entreprise sociale et insertion: Une perspective international.* Paris: Desclée de Brouwer.

Gardin, L., J.-L. Lavile, and E. Roussel. 2005. "L'économie sociale et solidaire dans la région Nord-Pas- de-Calais." In *Action publique et économie solidaire,* ed. G. C. de Franca Filho, J.-L. Laville, and J.-P. Magnen. Toulouse: Erès.

Gauchet, M. 1998. "Essai de psychologie contemporaine." *Le Débat,* no. 99 (March–April).

Gauchet, M. 2005. *La Condition politique.* Paris: Gallimard.

Gauchet, M. 2007. *La Crise du libéralisme.* Paris: Gallimard.

Gendron, C. 2006. "Mouvements sociaux." In *Dictionnaire de l'autre économie,* ed. J.-L. Laville and A. D. Cattani. Paris: Gallimard.

Généreux, J. 2001. *Les Vraies Lois de l'économie.* Paris: Seuil.

Généreux, J. 2006. *La Dissociété.* Paris: Seuil.

Genestier, P., and J.-L. Laville. 1994. "Au-delà du mythe républicain." *Le Débat* (December).

Georgescu-Roegen, N. 1994. *La Décroissance (1970–1982).* Paris: Sang de la terre.

Gibaud, B. 1986. *De la mutualité à la Sécurité sociale: Conflits et convergences.* Paris: Éd. Ouvrières.

Giddens, A. 1994. *Beyond Left and Right: The Future of Radical Politics.* Cambridge, UK: Polity Press.

Giddens, A. 1999. *The Third Way: The Renewal of Social Democracy.* Cambridge, UK: Polity.

Gide, C. 1890. *Quatre Écoles d'économie sociale.* Paris: Librairie Fishbascher.

Gide, C. 2000. *Principes d'économie politique.* 1931; repr., Paris: L'Harmattan.

Gide, C. and C. Rist. 1926. *Histoire des doctrines économiques.* Paris: Librairie du recueil Sirey.

Gijselinckx, C., P. Develtère, and P. Raymackers. 2005. *The Cooperative Sector in the United Kingdom and the Case of the Cooperative Group.* Louvain: Katholicke Universiteit Leuven, Hoger Instituut voor der arbeid.

Gijselinckx, C., P. Develtère, and P. Raymackers. 2007. *Renouveau coopératif et développement durable.* Louvain: Katholicke Universiteit Leuven, Hoger Instituut voor der arbeid.

Giullari, S., and J. Lewis. 2005. "The Adult Worker Model Family, Gender, Equality, and Care: The Search for New Policy Principles, and the Possibilities and Problems of a Capabilities Approach." *Social Policy and Development Program Paper,* no. 19. United Nations Research Institute for Social Development.

Godbout, J.-T. 2000. *Le Don, la dette et l'identité: Homo donator vs homo œconomicus* Paris: La Découverte.

Goodspeed, T., and D. Kenyon. 1993. "The Nonprofit Sector's Capital Constraint: Coes It Provide a Rationale for the Tax Exemption Granted to Nonprofit Firms." *Public Finance Quarterly* 21, no. 4.

Gorz, A. 1988. *Métamorphoses du travail. Quête de sens.* Paris: Gallilée.

Gorz, A. 1989. *Critique of Economic Reason,* trans. Gillian Handyside and Chris Turner. London: Verso.

Gorz, A. 1997. *Misères du present. Richesse du possible.* Paris: Gallilée.

Gossez, R. 1967. *Les Ouvriers de Paris, Livre premier: l'organisation, 1848–1851; Société d'histoire de la révolution de 1848.* Paris: Bibliothèque de la révolution de 1848, t. 24.

Granovetter, M. 2008. *Sociologie économique.* Paris: Seuil.

Gréau, J.-L. 2005. *L'Avenir du capitalism.* Paris: Gallimard.

Grez, S. 1990. *Les Mouvements d'ouvriers et d'artisans en milieu urbain au Chili au XIXe siècle,* 2 vol. PhD diss., École des hautes études en sciences sociales.

Gribaudi, M. 2014. *Paris, ville ouvrière: Une histoire occultée, 1789–1848.* Paris: La Découverte.

Gribaudi, M., and M. Riot-Sarcey. 2008. *1848: la révolution oubliée.* Paris: La Découverte.

Guépin, A. 1850. *Philosophie du socialisme, ou étude sur les transformations dans le monde et dans l'humanité.* Paris: Gustave Saudré.

Guérin, I. 2003. *Femmes et économie solidaire.* Paris: La Découverte.

Guérin, I., M. Hersent, and L. Fraisse. 2011. *Femmes, économie et développement.* Toulouse: Erès.

Gueirrero Ramos, A. 1989. *A nova ciencia das organzaçoes: una reconceituaçao da riqueza das naçoes.* Rio de Janeiro: Editoria da Fundaçao Getulio Vargas.

Gueslin, A. 1987. *L'Invention de l'économie sociale.* Paris: Economica.

Gueslin, A. 1998. "Colloque sur la charte de mutualité (1898): rapport général de synthèse." *Revue internationale de l'économie sociale* 77, no. 259.

Gui, B. 1992a. "The Economic Rationale for the 'Third Sector': Non-profit and Other Noncapitalist Organization." *Annals of Public and Cooperative Economics* 62, no. 4.

Gui, B. 1992b. "Fondement économique du tiers secteur." *Revue des études coopératives, mutualistes et associatives,* no, 44–45.

Gui, B. 2000. "Beyond Transactions: On the Interpersonal Dimension of Economic Reality." *Annals of Public and Cooperative Economics* 71, no. 2.

Giust-Desprairies, F. 2003. *L'Imaginaire collectif.* Toulouse: Érès.

Gurvitch, G. 1932. *L'Idée du droit social.* Paris: Sirey.

Gutmann, A. (ed.), 1988, Freedom of Associations, Princeton, Princeton University Press.

Habermas, J. 1978. "Hannah Arendt's Communications Concept of Power." *Social Research* 44, no. 1.

Habermas, J. 1985. *The Theory of Communicative Action, Vol. 1: Reason and the Rationalization of Society,* trans. Thomas McCarthy. Boston: Beacon Press.

Habermas, J. 1989. *The Theory of Communicative Action, Vol. 2: Lifeword and System,* trans. Thomas McCarthy. Boston: Beacon Press.

Habermas, J. 1986. "The New Obscurity: The Crisis of the Welfare State and the Exhaustion of Utopian Energies," trans. Phillip Jacobs. *Philosophy & Social Criticism* 11, no. 2: 1–18.

Habermas, J. 1988. "Vingt ans après: la culture politique et les institutions en RFA." *Le Débat,* (September–October).

Habermas, J. 1989. "La souveraineté populaire comme procedure: Un concept normatif d'espace public," *Lignes* 7 (September).

Habermas, J. 1990. *Écrits politiques.* Paris: Le Cerf.

Habermas, J. 1991. *The Structural Transformation of the Public Sphere: An Inquiry into Bourgeois Society,* trans. Thomas Berger. Cambridge, Mass.: MIT Press.

Habermas, J. 1992. "L'espace public, trente ans après." *Quaderni,* no. 18 (Autumn).

Habermas, J. 1997. "Popular Sovereignty as Procedure." *Deliberative Democracy: Essays on Reason and Politics,* ed. J. Bohman and W. Rehg. Cambridge, Mass.: MIT Press.

Hansmann, H. B. 1980. "The Role of Nonprofit Enterprise." In *The Economic of Nonprofit Institution: Studies in Structure and Policy,* ed. S. Rose-Ackerman. New York: Oxford University Press.

Hansmann, H. B. 1981. "The Effect of Tax Exemption and Other Factors on the Market Share of Nonprofit versus For-profit Firms." *National Tax Journal* 40, no. 1.

Hansmann, H. B. 1987. "Economic Theories of Nonprofit Organizations."

In *Between the Public and the Private: The Nonprofit Sector,* ed. W. W. Powell. New Haven, Conn: Yale University Press.

Hansmann, H. B. 1996. *The Ownership of Enterprise.* Cambridge, Mass.: Harvard University Press.

Hart, K. 1971–1973. "Informal Income Opportunities and Rrban Employment in Development Studies." Text dating from 1971 and published in 1973. *Journal of Modern African Studies* 2, no. 1.

Harvey, D. 2006. *Paris: Capital of Modernity.* New York: Routledge.

Harvey, D. 2012. *Paris, capital de la modernité.* Paris: Les Prairies ordinaires.

Hatzfeld, H. 1971. *Du paupérisme à la Sécurité sociale, 1850–1940.* Nancy: Presses universitaires de Nancy.

Hayek, F. A. 1973. *Law, Legislation, and Liberty, Vol. 1: Rules and Order.* Chicago: University of Chicago Press.

Healy, S., A.-I. Heras, and P. North. 2023. "Community Economies." In *Social and Solidarity Economy Encyclopedia.* Cheltanham, UK: Edward Elgar.

Héber-Suffrin, C. 1992. *Échanger les savoirs.* Paris: Desclée de Brouwer.

Héber-Suffrin, C. 1998. *Les Savoirs, la réciprocité et le citoyen.* Paris: Desclée de Brouwer.

Herman, R. D. 1984. *Why Is There a Third Sector? Bringing Politics Back in School of Business and Public Affairs.* Kansas City: University of Missouri Press.

Hernes, H. 1987. *Welfare State and Woman Power: Essays in State Feminism.* Oslo: Norwegian University Press.

Hersent, M., J.-L. Laville, and M. Saussey. 2015. "Entretien avec Nancy Fraser." *Revue française de socio-économie,* no, 15 (1st quarter).

Hersent, M., and A. Palma Torres, ed. 2014. *L'Économie solidaire en pratiques.* Toulouse: Erès.

Hillenkamp, I. 2009. *Formes d'intégration de l'économie dans les démocraties de marché: Une théorie substantive à partir de l'étude du mouvement d'économie solidaire dans la ville d'El Alto (Bolivie).* PhD diss. in Development Studies, Université de Genève, Institut des hautes études internationales et du développement.

Hillenkamp, I. 2015. "Association, économie plurielle et État plurinational en Bolivie." In *Associations et action publique,* ed. J.-L. Laville and A. Salmon. Paris: Desclée de Brouwer.

Hillenkamp, I., I. Guérin, C. Verschuur. 2014. "Économie solidaire et théories féministes: pistes pour une convergence necessaire." *Revue d'économie solidaire,* no. 7.

Hillenkamp, I., I. Guérin, C. Verschuur. 2015. *Une économie solidaire peut-ele être féministe? Homo oeconomicus, Mulier solidaria.* Paris: L'Harmattan.

Hillenkamp, I., and J.-L. Laville, eds. 2013. *Socioéconomie et démocratie. L'actualité de Karl Polanyi.* Toulouse: Erès.

Hillenkamp, I., and J.-M. Servet, eds. 2015. *Le Marché autrement—Marchés réels et marchés fantasmés.* Paris: Garnier.

Hirschman, A. O. 1970. *Exit, Voice, and Loyalty.* Cambridge, Mass.: Harvard University Press.

Hirschman, A. O. 1971a. *Face au déclin des entreprises et des institutions.* Paris: Éd. ouvrières.

Hirschman, A. O. 1971b. "Political Economics and Possibilism." In *A Bias for Hope: Essays on Development and Latin America.* New Haven, Conn.: Yale University Press.

Hirschman, A. O. 1977. *The Passions and the Interests: Political Arguments for Capitalism before Its Triumph.* Princeton, N.J.: Princeton University Press.

Hirschman, A. O. 1980. *Les Passions et les Intérêts.* Paris: PUF.

Hirschman, A. O. 1981. *Essays in Trespassing: Economics to Politics and Beyond.* Cambridge: Cambridge University Press.

Hirschman, A. O. 1984. *L'Économie comme science morale et politique.* Paris: Gallimard-Seuil.

Hirschman, A. O. 1986a. "In Defense of Possibilism." In *Rival Views of Market Society and Recent Essays.* New York: Viking-Penguin.

Hirschman, A. O. 1986b. *Vers une économie politique élargie.* Paris: Minuit.

Hirschman, A. O. 1995. *Défection et prise de parole.* Paris: Fayard.

Hirst, P., and V. Bader. 2001. *Associative Democracy: The Real Third Way.* London: Franck Cass.

Hoarau, C., and J.-L. Laville. 2008. *La Gouvernance des associations: Économie, sociologie, gestion.* Toulouse: Érès.

Hobsbawm, E. J. 1962. *The Age of Revolution, 1789–1848.* London: Weidenfeld & Nicolson.

Hobsbawm, E. J. 1975. *The Age of Capital, 1848–1875.* London: Weidenfeld & Nicolson.

Hobsbawm, E. J. 1987. *The Age of Empire, 1875–1914.* London: Weidenfeld & Nicolson.

Honneth, A. 1995. *The Struggle for Recognition: The Moral Grammar for Social Conflicts,* trans. Joel Anderson. Cambridge, Mass.: MIT Press.

Huber, J. 1981. "Projets auto-organisés et réseaux d'entraide." *Futuribles,* no. 40 (January).

Humberg, K. 2011. *Poverty Reduction through Social Business: Lessons Learnt from Grameen Joint Venture in Bangladesh.* Munich: Oekom.

Humbert, M., and A. Caillé, ed. 2006. *La Démocratie au péril de l'économie.* Rennes: Presses universitaires de Rennes.

Inglehart, R. 1977. *The Silent Revolution: Changing Values and Political Styles among Western Democracies.* Princeton, N.J.: Princeton University Press.

Ion, J. 1989. "Lien social, groupements volontaires et representation." In *Le Lien social: Actes du XIIIe colloque de l'Association internationale des sociologues de langue française,* Geneva: Université de Genève, t. I.

Ion, J. 1997. *La Fin des militants.* Paris: L'Atelier.

IPCC. 2021. *Climate Change 2021. The Physical Science Basis, Report,* https://www.ipcc.ch/report/ar6/wg1/#FullReport.

Jackson, G., M. Höpner, and A. Kurdelbusch. 2004. *Corporate Governance and Employees in Germany: Changing Linkages, Complementaries, and Tensions.* RIETI Discussion Papers, series 04-E-008 (January).

James, E. 1987. "The Nonprofit Sector in Comparative Perspective." In *The Nonprofit Sector,* ed. W. W. Powell. New Haven, Conn.: Yale University Press.

James, E. 1990. "Economic Theories of the Nonprofit Sector: A Comparative Perspective." In *The Third Sector: Comparative Studies of Nonprofit Organizations,* ed. H. K. Anheier and W. Seibel. New York: De Gruyter.

Jeantet, T. 1999. *L'Économie sociale européenne ou la tentation de la démocratie en toutes choses.* Paris: CIEM.

Jeantet, T. 2001. "Une économie sociale unique et invisible?" *Revue internationale de l'économie sociale,* no. 281 (July).

Jeantet, T. 2006. *Économie sociale: La solidarité au défi de l'efficacité.* Paris: La Documentation française.

Jérôme, V. 2008. "L'économie sociale et solidaire: Une autre manière d'être dans l'économie." *Les Pratiques,* no. 4.

Joas, H. 1996. *The Creativity of Action,* trans. J. Gaines and P. Keast. Chicago: University of Chicago Press.

Jobert, B. 2009. Postface to "Des référentiels civils." In *Politiques publiques et démocratie,* ed. O. Giraud, P. Warin. Paris: La Découverte.

Jouen, M. 1995. *A European Strategy for Encouraging Local Development and Employment Initiatives.* http://aei.pitt.edu/2785/.

Jullien, F. 2011. *The Silent Transformations,* trans. K. Fijalkowski and M. Richardson. London: Seagull Books.

Karpik, L. 1996. "Dispositifs de confiance et engagements crédibles." *Sociologie du travail,* no, 4.

Kaufman, J. 2003. *For the Common Good? American Civic Life and the Golden Age of Fraternity.* Oxford: Oxford University Press.

Keane, J. 1988. "Three Views of Associationalism in the 19tth-Century America." *American Journal of Sociology* 104, no. 5 (March 1999): 1296–345.

Kendall, J. 2001. "Grande-Bretagne: une économie plurielle de soins bouleversée par les 'quasi-marchés.'" In *Les Services sociaux entre associ-

ations, État et marché: L'aide aux personnes âgées, ed. J.-L. Laville and M. Nyssens. Paris: La Découverte.

Kirkham, M. 1973. *Industrial Producer Cooperation in Britain: Three Case Studies.* Sheffield, UK: University of Sheffield.

Kish Sklar, K. 1973. *Catharine Beecher: Study in American Domesticity.* New Haven, Conn.: Yale University Press.

Klausen, K. K., and P. Selle. 1996. "The Third Sector in Scandinavia." *Voluntas* 7, no. 2.

Koulytchizky, S., and R. Mauget. 2003. "Le développement des groupes coopératifs agricoles depuis un demi-siècle, à la recherche d'un nouveau paradigm." *Revue internationale de l'économie sociale,* no. 287.

Krashinski, M. 1986. "Transaction Costs and a Theory of the Nonprofit Organization." In *The Economic of Nonprofit Institution: Studies in Structure and Policy,* ed. S. Rose-Ackerman. New York: Oxford University Press.

Laborier, P., and D. Trom. 2003. *Historicités de l'action publique.* Paris: PUF.

Lafore, R. 1992. "Droit d'usage, droit des usagers: une problématique à dépasser." In *Les Usagers entre marché et citoyenneté,* ed. M. Chauvière and J.-T. Godbout. Paris: L'Harmattan.

Lallement, M. 2009. *Le Travail de l'utopie: Godin et le familistère de Guise.* Paris: Les Belles Lettres.

Larraechea, I., and M. Nyssens. 2007. "L'économie solidaire, un autre regard sur l'économie populaire au Chili." In *L'Économie solidaire: Une perspective internationale,* ed. J.-L. Laville. Paris: Hachette.

Lascoumes, P., and P. Le Galès. 2007. *Sociologie de l'action publique.* Paris: Armand Colin.

Latouche, S. 1991. *La Planète des naufragés.* Paris: La Découverte.

Latouche, S. 2006. *Le Pari de la décroissance.* Paris: Fayard.

Lautier, B. 2006. "Économie informelle." In *Dictionnaire de l'autre économie,* ed. J.-L. Laville and A. D. Cattani. Paris: Gallimard.

Laval, C. 2007. *L'Homme économique.* Paris: Gallimard.

Laville, J.-L. 1995. "La crise de la condition salariale." In *Le travail, quel avenir?* Paris: Gallimard.

Laville, J.-L. ed. 1997. *Les Services de proximité en Europe.* Paris: Syros.

Laville, J.-L. 2005. *Sociologie des services.* Toulouse: Érès.

Laville, J.-L. 2008a. *Le Travail: une nouvelle question politique.* Paris: Desclée de Brouwer.

Laville, J.-L. 2008b. "Services aux personnes et sociologie économique pluraliste." *Revue française de socio-économie,* no. 2.

Laville, J.-L. 2009. "Services aux personnes: le rôle des associations." In *Traité de sociologie économique,* ed. P. Steiner and F. Vatin. Paris: PUF.

Laville, J.-L. 2015. "La théorie critique: de l'impasse au renouveau—Écoles de

Francfort, sociologies pragmatique et publique, épistémologies du Sud." In *Le Tournant de la théorie critique,* ed. B. Frère. Paris: Desclée de Brouwer.

Laville, J.-L. 2016. "Gauche européenne et épistémologie du Sud." In *Les gauches du XXIe siècle: Un dialogue Nord–Sud,* ed. J.-L. Laville and J.-L. Coraggio. Lormont: Le Bord de l'eau.

Laville, J.-L., and J.-L. Coraggio, ed. 2016. *Les Gauches du XXIe siècle: Dialogue Nord-Sud.* Lormont: Le Bord de l'eau.

Laville, J.-L., A. Lemaître, and M. Nyssens. 2006. "Public Policies and Social Enterprises in Europe: The Challenge of Institutionalization." In *Social Enterprise: Between Market, Public Policies, and Civil Society,* ed. M. Nyssens. London: Routledge.

Laville, J.-L., B. Lévesque, and M. Mendell. 2007. "The Social Economy: Diverse Approaches and Practices in Europe and Canada." In *The Social Economy, Building Inclusive Economies,* ed. A. Noya and E. Clarence. Paris: OCDE.

Laville, J.-L., J.-P. Magnen, G. C. de França Filho, and A. Medeiros. 2005. *Action publique et économie solidaire.* Toulouse: Érès.

Laville, J.-L., and M. Nyssens. 2000. "Solidarity-Based Third Sector Organizations in the 'Proximity Services' Field: A European Francophone Perspective." *Voluntas: International Journal of Voluntary and Nonprofit Organizations* 11:67–84.

Laville, J.-L., and M. Nyssens. 2001a. "The Social Enterprise: Towards a Theorical Socio-economic Approach." In *The Emergence of Social Entreprise,* ed. C. Borzaga and J. Defourny. London: Routledge.

Laville, J.-L., and M. Nyssens, ed. 2001b. *Les Services sociaux entre associations, État et marché: L'aide aux personnes âgées.* Paris: La Découverte.

Laville, J.-L., and R. Sainsaulieu. 1997. *Sociologie de l'association.* Paris: Desclée de Brouwer.

Laville, J.-L., and R. Sainsaulieu. 2013. *L'Association: Sociologie et économie.* Paris: Fayard.

Laville, J.-L., and A. Salmon. 2015. *Associations et action publique.* Paris: Desclée de Brouwer.

Lazzarato, M. 2008. *Le Gouvernement des inégalités: Critique de l'insécurité néolibérale.* Paris: Éd. Amsterdam.

Lebaron, F. 2000. *La Croyance économique: Les économistes entre science et politique.* Paris: Seuil.

Le Blanc, G. 2011. *Que faire de notre vulnérabilité?* Paris: Bayard.

Le Bras-Chopard, A. 1986. *De l'égalité dans la différence: Le socialisme de Pierre Leroux.* Paris: Presses de la Fondation nationale des sciences politiques.

Lefort, C. 1986. *Essais sur le politique, XIXe-XXe siècles.* Paris: Seuil.

Le Goff, J. 1985. *Du silence à la parole: Droit du travail, société, État (1830–1989)*. Quimper: Calligrammes.

Le Grand, J., and W. Bartlett. 1993. *Quasi-Markets and Social Policy*. London: Macmillan.

Leichsenring, K. 1997. *The Role of the Labour Market Service in Supporting Non-Statutory Childcare Providers*. Vienna: European Center for Social Welfare Policy and Research.

Leira, A. 1992. *Models of Motherhood: Welfare State Policy and Scandinavian Experiences of Everyday Practices*. Cambridge: Cambridge University Press.

Lemaître, A. 2009. *Organisations d'économie sociale et solidaire: Lecture de réalités Nord et Sud à travers l'encastrement politique et une approche plurielle de l'économie*. PhD diss., Paris-Louvain, CNAM- Université catholique de Louvain-la-Neuve.

Leonardis, O. de. 1997. "Declino della sfera pubblica e privatismo." *Rassegna italiana di sociologia* 38, no. 2.

Leroux, P. 1863. *La Grève de Samarez*. Paris: E. Dentu, t. I.

Leroux, P. 2007. *Anthropologie de Pierre Leroux*. Latresnes, Le Bord de l'eau. (New edition of B. Viard, *P. Leroux. À la source perdue du socialisme français*. Paris, Desclée de Brouwer, 1997.)

Le Velly, R. 2006. "Le commerce équitable: des échanges marchands contre et dans le marché." *Revue française de sociologie* 47.

Le Velly, R. 2012. *Sociologie du marché*. Paris: La Découverte.

Lévesque B. 1997. "Démocratisation de l'économie et économie sociale: un scénario radical pour de nouveaux partages." *Cahiers du CRISES*, no. 9705. Collectif de recherche sur les innovations sociales dans les entreprises et les syndicats. Montreal: Université du Québec.

Lévesque B. 2001. "Économie sociale et solidaire dans un contexte de mondialisation: Pour une démocratie plurielle." Paper presented at the second international conference on the Globalisation of solidarity, October 9–12, 2001, *Cahiers du CRISES*, Montreal.

Lévesque B. 2015. "Un nouveau modèle de service public par les associations: la garde de la petite enfance au Québec." In *Associations et action publique*, ed. J.-L. Laville and A. Salmon. Paris: Desclée de Brouwer.

Lévesque B., and D. Côté. 1995. "Le changement des principes coopératifs à l'heure de la mondialisation, à la recherche d'une méthodologie." In *Coopératives, marchés, principes coopératifs*, ed. A. Zevi and J.-L. Monzon-Campos. Brussels: De Boeck.

Lévesque B., and B. Ninacs. 1997. *L'Économie sociale au Canada. L'expérience québécoise*. Paris: OCDE.

Lévesque B., and Y. Vaillancourt. 1998. *L'Institutionnalisation de la nouvelle économie sociale au Québec: Une diversité de scénarios dans un contexte institutionnel relativement favorable.* Montreal: Université du Québec.

Lewis, J. 1992. *Women in Britain since 1945.* London: Blackwell.

Lewis, J. 1997. "Le secteur associatif dans l'économie mixte de la protection sociale." In *Produire les solidarités: La part des associations.* Paris: MIRE Rencontres et Recherches, in collaboration with Fondation de France.

Lipietz, A. 1996. *La Société en sablier.* Paris: La Découverte.

Lipietz, A. 2001. *Pour le tiers secteur.* Paris: La Découverte-La Documentation française.

Lorendahl, B. 1997. "Integrating the Public Sector and Cooperative Social Economy—Towards a Swedish New Model." *Annals of Public and Cooperative Economics* 68, no. 3.

Lourau, R. 1971. *L'Analyse institutionnelle.* Paris: Minuit.

Lutz, B. 1990. *Le Mirage de la croissance marchande.* Paris: Maison des sciences de l'homme.

Magnani, E. 2003. *El Cambio silencioso: Empresas y fabrica recuperadas en la Argentina.* Buenos Aires: Promoteo.

Makhaïski, J. W. 1979. *Le Socialisme des intellectuels,* trans. A. Skirda. Paris: Seuil.

Malo, M.-C. 2002. "Une lecture québécoise: une œuvre qui transcende les époques." In *Coopération et économie sociale au second XXe siècle: Hommage à Claude Vienney.* Les Cahiers de l'économie sociale 1. Paris: L'Harmattan.

Malthus, R. 1872. *An Essay on the Principle of Population.* London: Reeves and Turner.

Mandel, E. 1974. "Self-management, Dangers and Possibilities." *International* 2/3.

Marbeau, J.-B.-F. 1844. *Études sur l'économie sociale.* Paris: Comptoirs des imprimeurs unis.

Marchand, P. 2009. "La société cooperative européenne à l'épreuve des principes coopératif." In *L'économie sociale et solidaire aux prises avec la gestion,* ed. J.-L. Laville and P. Glémain. Paris: Desclée de Brouwer.

Marchat, J.-F. 1989. *L'Apprentissage de l'expérimentation sociale: Contribution à l'analyse et à la pédagogie institutionnelles de l'entreprise.* Phd. Diss., Université Paris VIII.

Marchat, J.-F. 2000. "L'expérimentation sociale à l'épreuve de l'État- providence." *La Revue du MAUSS semestrielle,* no. 16.

Marchat, J.-F. 2001. *Engagement(s) et intervention au CRIDA: recherche et espace public démocratique.* Paris: CRIDA-LSCI-CNRS.

Marchetti, R., and M. Pianta. 2006. *Transnational Networks in Global Social Movements.* Urbino: Université d'Urbino.

Maréchal, J.-P. 1997. *Le Rationnel et le Raisonnable: L'économie et l'environnement.* Rennes: Presses universitaires de Rennes.

Maréchal, J.-P. 2001. *Humaniser l'économie.* Paris: Desclée de Brouwer.

Maréchal, J.-P. 2005. *Éthique et Économie: Une opposition artificielle.* Rennes: Presses universitaires de Rennes.

Maréchal, J.-P. 2006. "Économie, éthique et politique." In *La démocratie au péril de l'économie,* ed. M. Humbert and A. Caillé. Rennes: Presses universitaires de Rennes.

Maréchal, J.-P. 2010. "Sustainable Development." In *The Human Economy: A Citizen's Guide,* ed. J.-L. Laville and A. D. Cattani. Cambridge: Polity.

Mariategui, J.-C. 1979. *7 Ensayos de Interpretacion de la Realidad Peruana.* Caracas: Biblioteca Ayacucho.

Martins de Carvalho, H. 2002. "A emancipaçao do movimiento no movimiento de emancipaçao social continuada." In *Produzir para viver, os caminhos da produçao nao capitalista,* ed. B. de Souza Santos. Rio de Janeiro: Civilizaçao Brasilira.

Marx, K. 1963. *Le Capital.* In *Œuvres: Économie I.* Paris, Gallimard.

Marx, K. 1965. *La Guerre civile en France* et *Le 18 Brumaire de Louis Bonaparte.* In *Œuvres: Politique I.* Paris: Gallimard, "Bibliothèque de la Pléiade."

Marx, K. 1986. *Karl Marx: A Reader,* ed. J. Elster. Cambridge: Cambridge University Press.

Marx, K. 2014. *The Civil War in France.* Eastford, Conn.: Martino Fine Books.

Marx, K. 2018. *The Eighteenth Brumaire of Louis Bonaparte,* trans. Daniel DeLeon. New York: Origami Books.

Marx, K., and F. Engels. 1973. *Œuvres,* 8 vol. Paris: Éd. Sociales.

Maucourant, J. 2005. *Avez-vous lu Polanyi?* Paris: La Dispute.

Mauss, M. 1899. "L'action socialiste." *Le Mouvement socialiste,* October 15.

Mauss, M. 1924. "Appréciation sociologique du bolchevisme." *Revue de métaphysique et de morale* 31, no. 1.

Mauss, M. 1984. "A Sociological Assessment of Bolshevism (1924–5)." *International Journal of Human Resource Management* 13, no. 3: 331–74.

Mauss, M. 1997. *Écrits politiques,* ed. M. Fournier. Paris: Fayard.

Mauss, M. 2001. *Sociologie et Anthropologie.* Paris: PUF.

McCarthy, K. D. 2003. *American Creed: Philanthropy and the Rise of Civil Society, 1700–1865.* Chicago: University of Chicago Press.

Méda, D. 2001. *Le Temps des femmes: Pour un nouveau partage des rôles.* Paris: Flammarion.

Meek, R. 1976. *Social Science and the Ignoble Savage.* Cambridge: Cambridge University Press.

Meister, A. 1974. *La participation dans les associations.* Paris: Editions ouvrières.

Melo, D. 2005. *Bibliografia seleccionada e anotada de associacionismo voluntario portugues.* Lisbonne: OBS 15.

Mendell, M. 2007. "Karl Polanyi et le processus institué de démocratisation économique." *Interventions économiques,* http://www.teluq.uquebec.ca/interventionseconomiques.

Mendell, M. 2013. "La démocratisation économique comme processus isntitué." In *Socioéconomie et démocratie: L'actuaité de Karl Polanyi,* ed. I. Hillenkamp and J.-L. Laville. Toulouse: Erès.

Menger, C. 1923. *Grundsätze der Volkwirstschaftslehre.* Vienne: Carl Menger.

Merrien, F.-V. 1990. "Etat et politiques sociales: contribution à une théorie néoinstitutionnaliste." *Sociologie du travail* 32, no. 3.

Michéa, J.-C. 2007. *Orwell, anarchiste Tory.* Paris: Climats.

Michels, R. 2009. *Les partis politiques: Essai sur les tendances oligarchiques des démocraties.* Brussels: Editions de l'université de Bruxelles.

Milgrom, P., and J. Roberts. 1992. *Economics, Organization, and Management.* London: Pearson.

Mingione, E. 1991a. *Fragmented Societies: A Sociology of Economic Life beyond the Market Paradigm.* Oxford: Basil Blackwell.

Mingione, E. 1991b. *Sociologia delle vita economica.* Rome: Carocci.

Mingione, E. 2004. "Embeddedness/Encastrement." In "La sociologie économique européenne: Une rencontre franco-italienne," ed. M. La Rosa and J.-L. Laville. *Sociologia del lavoro,* no 93.

Mongkol, K. 2011. "The Critical Review of New Public Management and its Criticism." *Research Journal of Business Management* 5, no. 1: 35–43.

Montesquieu, C. de. 1950. *Œuvres completes.* Paris: Gallimard, t. I.

Moreno, J. del C. 2001. *Economia solidaria: Origen, filosofia, desarrollo, proyecciones.* Santa Fe de Bogotá: Primera Edicion.

Moss, B. H. 1976. *The Origins of the French Labor Movement, 1830–1914: The Socialism of Skilled Workers.* Berkeley: University of California Press.

Mothé, D. 1980. *L'augestion goutte à goutte.* Paris: Editions du Centurion.

Mothé, D. 1982. "L'anorexie idéologique des alternatifs." *Autogestions,* no. 8–9.

Mothé, D. 2006. "Autogestion." In *Dictionnaire de l'autre économie,* ed. J.-L. Laville and A. D. Cattani. Paris: Gallimard.

Mouffe, C. 2016. *L'Illusion du consensus.* Paris: Albin Michel.

Munera Ruiz, L. 2008. *Normalidad y excepcionalidad en la politica.* Bogota: Université nationale de Colombie.

Navarro, Z. 2002. "'Mobilizaçao sem emancipaçao'–as lutas sociais dos sem-terra no Brasil." In *Produzir para viver: Os caminhos da produçao nao capitalista,* ed. S. Boaventura de Sousa. Rio de Janeiro: Civilizaçao Brasileira.

Negt, O. 2007. *L'Espace public oppositionnel.* Paris: Payot.

Neveu, E. 1996. *Sociologie des mouvements sociaux.* Paris: La Découverte.

Nicholls, D. 1989. *The Pluralist Theory of the State.* London: Blackwell.

Noguès, H. 2004. "Le positionnement de l'économie sociale et solidaire: un enjeu théorique et politique." In *Économie solidaire, économie sociale et tiers secteur: Le débat en Amérique latine et en Europe,* dossier no. 2: "Les approches en termes d'économie sociale," International Seminar, Paris, CNAM, January 12 and 14.

Nyssens, M. 1994. *Quatre Essais sur l'économie populaire urbaine: Le cas de Santiago du Chili.* Louvain-la-Neuve, université catholique de Louvain, faculté des sciences économiques, sociales et politiques, nouvelle série, no. 231.

Nyssens, M. 2000. "Les approches économiques du tiers secteur: Apports et limites des analyses anglo-saxonnes d'inspiration néoclassique." In "Qu'est-ce que le tiers secteur?" special issue, ed. M. Lallement and J.-L. Laville. *Sociologie du travail* 42, no. 4 (October–November).

Nyssens, M., ed. 2006. *Social Enterprise: At the Crossroads of Market, Public Policies, and Civil Society.* London: Routledge.

Nyssens, M. 2008. "Les analyses économiques des associations." In *La Gouvernance des associations: Économie, sociologie, gestion,* ed. C. Hoarau and J.-L. Laville. Toulouse: Érès.

OECD. 1999. *Social Enterprises.* Paris: OECD.

OECD. 2015. *In It Together: Why Less Inequality Benefits All.* Paris: OEDC Publishing.

O'Connor, J. S. 1996. "From Women in the Welfare State to Gendering Welfare State Regimes." *Journal of International Sociological Association* 44, no. 2 (Summer).

Oppenheimer, F. 1914. *Économie pure et économie politique.* Paris: Giard et Brières.

Orléan, A. 2002. "Pour une nouvelle approche des interactions financières: l'économie des conventions face à la sociologie économique." In *La Construction sociale de l'entreprise: Autour des travaux de Mark Granovetter,* ed. I. Huault. Paris: EMS.

Ortiz, H., and I. Munoz. 1998. *Globalizacion de la solidaredad: Un reto para todos.* Lima: SES-CEP.

Ortmann, A., and M. Schlesinger. 1997. "Trust, Repute, and the Role of Nonprofit Enterprise." *Voluntas* 8, no. 2.

Paine, T. 1951. *The Rights of Man* New York: E. P. Dutton.

Parodi, M. 1984. "Tiers secteur, économie sociale et crise." *Revue des études coopératives, mutualistes et associatives,* no. 12.

Passaris, S. 1984. *La Participation parentale dans les modes d'accueil de la petite enfance,* 4 vols. Paris: CIRED-École des hautes études en sciences sociales.

Passet, R. 1996. *L'Économique et le Vivant.* Paris: Economica.

Paton, R. 1989. *Reluctant Entrepreneurs: The Extent, Achievements, and Significance of Worker Takeovers in Europe.* New York: Open University Press.

Pecqueur, C. 1839. *Économie sociale: Des intérêts du commerce, de l'industrie et de l'agriculture et de la civilisation en général sous l'influence des implications de la vapeur: machines fixes, chemins de fer, bateaux à vapeur, etc.,* 2 vol. Paris: Dessart.

Peemans, J.-P. 2002. *Le Développement des peuples face à la modernisation du monde: Les théories du développement réel dans la seconde moitié du XXe siècle.* Louvain-la-Neuve, Belgium: Academia Bruylant-L'Harmattan.

Peillon, V. 2008. *La Révolution française n'est pas terminée.* Paris: Seuil.

Pénin, M. 1998. *Charles Gide, 1847–1932: L'esprit critique.* Paris: L'Harmattan.

Perec, G. 2010. *Things: A Story of the Sixties,* trans. D. Bellos. Boston: Verba Mundi.

Perraudin, C., H. Petit, and A. Rébérioux. 2007. *Marché boursier et gestion de l'emploi: Analyse sur données d'entreprises françaises.* Paris: Documents de travail du Centre d'économie de la Sorbonne, September.

Perret, B. 1999. *Les Nouvelles Frontières de l'argent.* Paris: Seuil.

Perret, B. 2001. *Indicateurs sociaux: État des lieux et perspectives.* Paris: Centre d'étude des revenus et des coûts.

Perret, B., and G. Roustang. 1993. *L'Économie contre la société: Affronter la crise de l'intégration sociale et Culturelle.* Paris: Seuil.

Perret, B., and G. Roustang. 2001. *L'Économie contre la société.* Paris: Seuil.

Perroux, F. 1960. *Économie et Société: Contrainte-échange-don.* Paris: PUF.

Perroux, F. 1970. "Les conceptualisations implicitement normatives et les limites de la modélisation en économie." *Économie et Société: Cahiers de l'ISEA* 4, no. 12 (December).

Pestoff, V. 1998. *Beyond the Market and the State: Social Enterprises and Civil Democracy in a Welfare Society.* Aldershot, UK: Ashgate.

Pestoff, V. 2004. *The Development and Future of the Social Economy in Sweden.* Cheltenham, UK: Edward Elgar.

Pestoff, V., M. Taylor, I. Bode, and A. Evers. 2004. "Defining the Third Sector in Europe." In *The Third Sector in Europe,* ed. A. Evers and J.-L. Laville. Cheltenham: Edward Elgar.

Petitclerc, J.-M. 2007. *"Nous protégeons l'infortune": Les origines populaires de l'économie sociale au Québec.* Montreal: VLB.

Petrella, F. 1996. "Libéralisation des services et régulation des services à la personne: contours et enjeux pour l'économie sociale." *Cahiers de la solidarité,* no. 9.

Piketty, T. 2013. *Le Capital au XXIe siècle.* Paris: Seuil.

Piketty, T. 2014. *Capital in the Twenty-First Century,* trans. Arthur Goldhammer. Cambridge, Mass.: Harvard University Press.

Pleyers, G. 2010. *Alter-Globalization—Becoming Actors in the Global Age.* Cambridge: Polity Press.

Polanyi, K. 1944. *The Great Transformation.* Boston: Beacon Press.

Polanyi, K. 1957. "The Economy as Instituted Process." In *The Sociology of Economic Life,* ed. M. Granovetter and R. Swedberg. Boulder, Colo.: Westview Press.

Polanyi, K. 1968. *Primitive, Archaic, and Modern Economic.* Boston: Beacon Press.

Polanyi, K. 1975. "L'économie comme procès institutionnalisé." In *Les Systèmes économiques dans l'histoire et la théorie,* ed. C. Arensberg and H. Pearson. Paris: Larousse.

Polanyi, K. 1977. *The Livelihood of Man,* ed. H. V. Pearson. New York: Academic Press.

Polanyi, K. 1983. *La Grande Transformation: Aux origines politiques et économiques de notre temps.* Paris: Gallimard.

Polanyi, K. 2007. "Le sophisme économiciste." *La Revue du MAUSS semestrielle* 29, no. 1.

Polanyi, K. 2008. *Essais.* Paris: Seuil.

Polanyi, K. 2011. *La Subsistance de l'homme: La place de l'économie dans l'histoire et la société.* Paris: Flammarion.

Polanyi, K. 2014. *For a New West: Essays, 1919–1958.* Cambridge: Polity.

Prahalad, C. K. 2004. *The Fortune at the Bottom of the Pyramid: Eradicating Poverty through Profits.* London: Person Prentice Hall.

Procacci, G. 1993. *Gouverner la misère: La question sociale en France, 1789–1848.* Paris: Seuil.

Proudhon, P. J. 1924. "De la capacité politique des classes ouvrières." In *Œuvres completes.* Paris: Marcel Rivière.

Prouteau, L., ed. 2003. *Les Associations entre bénévolat et logique d'entreprise.* Rennes: Presses universitaires de Rennes.

Prouteau, L. 2004. "Apports et limites des analyses économiques du secteur sans but lucrative." In *Associations et coopératives face aux marchés et aux pouvoirs publics: Y a-t-il un modèle européen?* Paris: CNAM.

Putnam, Robert D. 2000. *Bowling Alone: The Collapse and Revival of American Community.* London: Simon & Schuster.

Quijano, A. 1988. *Modernidad, identitidad y utopia en America Latina.* Lima: Sociedad y politica ediciones.

Quijano, A. 1998. *La Economia popular y sus caminos en America Latina.* Lima: Mosca Azul Editores.

Quijano, A. 2007. "Sistemas alternativas de produccion." In *La economia social desde la periferia: Constituciones latinoamericanas.* ed. J. L. Coraggio. Buenos Aires: Altamira.

Quinqueton, T. 1989. *Saul Alinsky, organisateur et agitateur.* Paris: Desclée de Brouwer.

Ranci, C. 1990. "Doni senza reciprocità: La persistenza dell'altruismo sociale nei sistemi complessi." *Rassegna italiana di sociologia* 31, no. 3 (July–September).

Rancière, J. 1981. *La Nuit des prolétaires.* Paris: Fayard.

Rancière, J. 2003. *Les scènes du people.* Lyon: Horlieu Editions.

Rancière, J. 2012a. *Proletarian Nights,* trans. J. Drury. London: Verso.

Rancière, J. 2012b. "The Ethics of Sociology." In *The Intellectual and His People: Staging the People, Vol. 2.* London: Verso.

Razeto, L. 1993. *Empresas de trabajadores y economia de mercado.* Santiago, Chile:, Programa de Economia del Trabajo, Academia de Humanismo Cristiano.

Razeto, L. 2000. *Dimensión economica del tercer sector en America Latina, Redefinición del Desarrollo.* Buenos Aires: Ediciones Unidas.

Razeto, L., A. Klenner, A. Ramirez, and R. Urmeneta. 1983. *Las Organizaciones economicas populares: La experiencia de las nuevas organizaciones economicas en Chile, Situacion y perspectivas.* Santiago, Chile: Programa de Economia del Trabajo, Academia de Humanismo Cristiano.

Renault, E. 2004. *L'Expérience de l'injustice: Reconnaissance et clinique de l'injustice.* Paris: La Découverte.

Revue du MAUSS semestrielle. 2000. "L'autre socialisme: Entre utilitarisme et totalitarisme." *Revue du MAUSS semestrielle* 16, no. 2.

Revue du MAUSS semestrielle. 2007. "Avec Karl Polanyi, contre la société du tout-marchand." *Revue du MAUSS semestrielle* 29, no. 1.

Revue française de socio-économie. 2008. "Le *care:* entre transactions familiales et économie des services." *Revue française de socio-économie* 2.

Revel, M., C. Blatrix, L. Blondiaux, J.-M. Fourniau, B. Hériard Dubreuil, and R. Lefebvre, ed. 2007. *Le Débat public: Une expérience française de démocratie participative.* Paris: La Découverte.

Richez-Battesti, N., P. Gianfaldoni, G. Gloukoviezoff, and J.-R. Alacaras. 2006. *Quelle contribution des banques coopératives à la cohésion sociale des territoires? Une approche en termes d'innovation sociale,* XXe colloque de l'ADDES, Paris, 7 March.

Ricoeur, P. 1986. *Ideology and Utopia.* New York: Columbia University Press.

Riot-Sarcey, M. 2016. *Le Procès de la liberté: Une histoire souterraine du XIXe siècle en France.* Paris: La Découverte.

Rist, G. 1996. *Le développement. Histoire d'une croyance occidentale.* Paris: Les Presses de Dacheux.

Rizza, R. 2004. "Néo-institutionnalisme sociologique et nouvelle sociolo-gie économique: quelles relations?" In "La sociologie économique européenne: Une rencontre franco-italienne," ed. M. La Rosa and J.-L. Laville. Special issue, *Sociologia de lavoro* 93.

Rizza, R., and J. Sermasi, ed. 2008. *Il Lavoro recuperato. Imprese e autogestione in Argentina.* Milan: Bruno Mondadori.

Rocard, M. 1999. *Mission mutualité et droit communautaire,* rapport au Premier minister. Paris: La Documentation française.

Roche, D. 1999. "Leçon inaugurale." Lecture delivered November 19, Collège de France, chaire d'histoire de la France des Lumières, Paris.

Rock, C. P., and M. Klinedinst. 1992. "In Search of the 'Social Economy' in the United States: A Proposal." In *The Third Sector: Cooperative, Mutual, and Nonprofit Organizations,* ed. J. Defourny and J. L. Monzon Campos. Brussels: De Boeck.

Rodriguez, C. 2002. "A procura de alternativas economicas em tempos de globalizaçao: o caso das cooperativas de reculadores de lixo na Colombia." In *Produzir para viver: Os caminhos da produçao nao capita- lista,* ed. S. Boaventura de Sousa. Rio de Janeiro: Civilizaçao Brasileira.

Rosanvallon, P. 1979. *Le Capitalisme utopique: Critique de l'idéologie économique.* Paris: Seuil.

Rosanvallon, P. 2004. *Le Modèle politique français: La société civile contre le jacobinisme de 1789 à nos jours.* Paris: Seuil.

Rosanvallon, P. 2006. *La Contre-démocratie: La politique à l'âge de la defi-ance.* Paris: Seuil.

Rose-Ackerman, S., ed. 1986. *The Economic of Nonprofit Institution: Studies in Structure and Policy.* New York: Oxford University Press.

Rostow, W. W. 2017. *The Stages of Economic Growth.* Eastford, Conn.: Martino Fine Books.

Roulleau-Berger, L. 2001. *Socialisation du risque et différenciation des mondes: Les jeunes à l'épreuve de la précarisation salariale, habilitation à diriger des recherches.* Lyon, université Lyon-II, October.

Rousseau, J.-J. 1964. *Considérations sur le gouvernement de Pologne et sur sa réformation projetée* (1772). In *Œuvres complètes,* vol. 3: *Œuvres philosophiques et politiques d' "Émile" aux derniers écrits politiques, 1762–1772.* Paris: Gallimard.

Roustang, G. 1998. "Grande transformation ou 'alliage sans formule pré-cise'?" In *La Modernité de Karl Polanyi,* ed. J.-M. Servet, J. Maucourant, and A. Tiran. Paris: L'Harmattan.

Roustang, G. 2002. *La Démocratie au risque du marché.* Paris: Desclée de Brouwer.

Roustang, G. 2006. "Décroissance." In J *Dictionnaire de l'autre économie,* by J.-L. Laville and A. D. Cattani. Paris: Gallimard.

Ruby, C. 1997. *La Solidarité: Essai sur une autre culture politique.* Paris: Ellipses, "Polis."

Runciman, D. 1997. *Pluralism and the Personality of the State.* Cambridge: Cambridge University Press.

Ryan, M. P. 1990. *Women in Public: Between Banners and Ballots, 1825–1880.* Baltimore: Johns Hopkins University Press.

Ryan, M. P. 1992. "Gender and Public Access: Women's Politics in Nineteenth Century America." In *Habermas and the Public Sphere,* ed. C. Calhoun. Cambridge, Mass.: MIT Press.

Sainsaulieu, R., P.-E. Tixier, M.-O. Marty. 1983. *La Démocratie en organization.* Paris: Méridiens-Klincksieck.

Salamon, L. M. 1987. "Partners in Public Service: The Scope and Theory of Government—Nonprofit Relations." In *The Nonprofit Sector: A Research Handbook,* ed. W. W. Powell. New Haven, Conn.: Yale University Press.

Salamon, L. M. and H. K. Anheier. 1996. *Social Origins of Civil Society: Explaininig the Nonprofit Sector Cross-Nationally.* Baltimore: Johns Hopkins University, Institute for Policy Studies.

Salamon, L. M. and H. K. Anheier. 1997. *Defining the Nonprofit Sector: A Cross-National Analysis.* Manchester, UK: Manchester University Press.

Salazar, G. 1989. *Labradores, peones y proletarios: Formacion y crisis de la sociedad popular chilena del siglo XIX.* Santiago, Chile: SUR.

Salazar, G. 1991. "Empresariado popular e industrializacion: la guerilla de la mercadores (Chile, 1830–1885)." *Proposiciones* 20.

Salmon, A. 2009. *Moraliser le capitalisme?* Paris: CNRS éditions.

Santana Junior, G. 2005. *A Economia solidaria face a dina- mica da acumulaçao capitalista: Da subordinaçao a un novo modo de regulaçao social.* PhD diss., Bahia, université fédérale de Bahia.

Sarria Icaza, A. M. 2005. "Politiques publiques et économie solidaire au Rio Grande do Sul." In *Action publique et économie solidaire,* ed. J.-L. Laville, J.-P. Magnen, G. C. de França Filho, and A. Medeiros. Toulouse: Érès.

Sarria Icaza, A. M. 2008. *Economia solidaria, accion collectiva y espacio publico en el sur de Brasil.* PhD diss., Louvain-la-Neuve, université catholique de Louvain, Presses universitaires de Louvain.

Sarria Icaza, A. M., and L. Tiriba. 2006. "Économie Populaire." In *Dictionnaire de l'autre économie,* by J.-L. Laville and A. D. Cattani. Paris: Gallimard.

Sauviat, C. 1994. "Le conseil: un 'marché-réseau' singulier." In *Relations de services, marchés de services,* ed. J. de Bandt and J. Gadrey. Paris: CNRS.

Savoye, A. 1994. *Les Débuts de la sociologie empirique.* Paris: Méridiens-Klincksieck.

Say, J.-B. 1814. *Traité d'économie politique* (1803), 2d ed. Paris: Deterville.

Say, J.-B. 1832. *J.B. Say, Cours complet d'économie politique,* vol. 1, ed. C. Bonneuil and J.-B. Fressoz. Brussels, Melène, 2013.

Scholnik, M. 1984. "Les organisations économiques populaires et la vie quotidienne." *Nouvelles de l'écodéveloppement* 31 (December): supplement, *MSH Informations.*

Schumpeter, J. A. 1943. *Capitalism, Socialism, and Democracy.* London: Unwin University Books.

Scott, J. C. 1976. *The Moral Economy of the Peasant.* New Haven, Conn.: Yale University Press.

Seibel, W. 1990. "Government/Third Sector Relationships in a Comparative Perspective: The Cases of France and West Germany." *Voluntas* 1, no. 1.

Sen, A. K. 1987. *On Ethics and Economics.* London: Basil Blackwell.

Sen, A. K. 1999. *Development as Freedom.* New York: Anchor Books.

Servet, J.-M. 1999. *Une économie sans argent.* Paris: Seuil.

Servet, J.-M. 2006. *Banquiers aux pieds nus. La microfinance.* Paris: Odile Jacob.

Servet, J.-M. 2007. "Le principe de réciprocité chez Karl Polanyi: Contribution à une définition de l'économie solidaire." *Tiers Monde* 190 (April–June), special issue, "L'économie solidaire: des initiatives locales à l'action publique."

Servet, J.-M. 2010. *Le grand renversement: De la crise au renouveau solidaire.* Paris: Desclée de Brouwer.

Servet, J.-M. 2013. "Le principe de réciprocité aujourd'hui: Un concept pour penser et comprendre l'économie solidaire." In *Socioéconomie et démocratie: L'actualité de Karl Polanyi* by I. Hillenkamp and J.-L. Laville. Toulouse: Erès.

Sewell, W. H. 1980. *Work and Revolution in France: The Language of Labor from the Old Regime to 1848.* Cambridge: Cambridge University Press.

Sewell, W. H. 1983. *Gens de métier et revolutions.* Paris: Aubier-Montaigne.

Simmel, G. 1978. *The Philosophy of Money.* New York: Routledge.

Singer, P. 2006. "Économie solidaire." In *Dictionnaire de l'autre économie,* J.-L. Laville and A. D. Cattani. Paris: Gallimard.

Singer, P. 2010. "Solidarity Economy." In *The Human Economy: A Citizen's Guide,* ed. J.-L. Laville, A. D. Cattani, and Keith Hart. Cambridge: Polity.

Sismondi, S. de. 1827. *Nouveaux Principes d'économie politique, ou de la richesse dans ses rapports avec la population,* 2d ed. Paris: Librairie Delaunay.

Smith, A. 1994. *Wealth of Nations.* London: Methuen.

Smith, A. 2002. *Theory of Moral Sentiments.* Cambridge: Cambridge University Press.

Smouts, M.-C. 1988. *Les Nouvelles Relations internationales.* Paris: Presses de Sciences Po.

Sola, P. 1978. *Els ataneus obrers i la cultura popular a catalunya (1900–1937).* Barcelona: La Magrana.

Soto, H. de. 1987. *El Otro Sendero.* Buenos Aires: Editorial Sud Americana.

Sousa Santos, B. de. 2002. *Produzir para viver: os caminho de produçao nao capitalista.* Rio de Janeiro: Civilizaçao Brasileira.

Sousa Santos, B. de. 2004. "A Critique of Lazy Reason: Against the Waste of Experience." In *The Modern World System in the Longue Durée,* ed. I. Wallerstein. London: Paradigm Publishers.

Sousa Santos, B. de. 2011. "Epistémologie du Sud." *Études rurales* 187 (January–June).

Sousa Santos, B. de. 2016. *Epistemologies of the South: Justice against Epistemicide.* Abingdon, UK: Routledge.

Steinberg, R., and B. H. Gray. 1993. "The Role of Nonprofit Enterprise in 1993: Hansmann Revisited." *Nonprofit and Voluntary Sector Quarterly* 22.

Steiner, P. 2005. *La Sociologie économique.* Paris: La Découverte.

Sue, R. 1997. *La Richesse des hommes: Vers l'économie quaternaire.* Paris: Odile Jacob.

Tassin, É. 1992, "Espace commun ou espace public? L'antagonisme de la communauté et de la publicité." *Hermès* 10, issue on "Espaces publics, traditions et communautés."

Taylor, M. 2004. *The Welfare Mix in the United Kingdom.* Cheltenham, UK: Edward Elgar.

Thane, P. 1982. *The Foundations of the Welfare State.* Harlow: Longman.

Thelwall, J. 1796. *The Rights of Nature.* London: H. D. Symonds & J. March.

Théret, B. 1999. "Vers un socialisme civil? L'épreuve de la contrainte démocratique de la différenciation de la société." In *Capitalisme et socialisme en perspective. Évolution et transformation des systèmes économiques,* ed. B. Chavance, E. Magnin, R. Motamed-Nejad, and J. Sapir. Paris: La Découverte.

Thériault, J.-Y. 2001. "De la critique de l'État-providence à la reviviscence de la société civile: le point de vue démocratique." In *L'État aux orties? ed.* S. Paquerot. Montreal: Écosociété.

Thompson, E. P. 1966. *The Making of the English Working-Class.* New York, Vintage Books.

Thompson, E. P. 1988. *La Formation de la classe ouvrière anglaise.* Paris: Seuil-Gallimard.

Titmuss, R. 1974. *Social Policy.* London: Allen & Unwin.

Tocqueville, A. de. 1843. *Democracy in America,* 4th ed. Philadelphia: Cowperthwaite.

Tönnies, F. 1987. *Gemeinschaft und Gresellshaft.* Leipzig: Fue's Vorlag (R. Riesland)

Touraine, A. 1981. *The Voice and the Eye.* Cambridge: Cambridge University Press.

Touraine, A., S. Hegedus, M. Wieworka, M. 1980. *La Prophétie antinucléaire.* Paris: Seuil.

Touraine, A., M. Wieworka, and F. Dubet. 1984. *Le Mouvement ouvrier.* Paris: Fayard.

Trouvé, H. 2003. "Fondements théoriques et analyses des productions associatives: une convergence inachevée." *Cahiers de la MSE,* no. 2003.135.

Vaillancourt, Y. 2008. "Note de recherche sur l'apport de l'économie sociale dans la coproduction et la coconstruction des politiques publiques." *Cahiers de LAREPPS-Cahiers du CRISES et de l'ARUC-ISDC.* Montreal.

Vaillancourt, Y. 2015. "La coconstruction des politiques publiques." In *Associations et action publique,* ed. J.-L. Laville and A. Salmon. Paris: Desclée de Brouwer.

Vatin, F. 2007. *Le Salariat: Théorie, histoire et forms.* Paris: La Dispute.

Verley, P. 1999. "Économie de marché: une construction historique." *Alternatives économiques,* no. 166 (January).

Verschave, F.-X. 1994. *Libres Leçons de Braudel: Passerelles pour une suite non excluante.* Paris: Syros.

Vidal, A. C. 1992. *Rebuilding Communities: A National Study of Urban Community Development Corporations.* New York: Community Development Research Center, Graduate School of Management and Urban Policy, New School for Social Research.

Vienney, C. 1980. *Socio-économie des organisations cooperatives,* 2 vol. Paris: CIEM.

Vienney, C. 1994. *L'Économie sociale.* Paris: La Découverte.

Viveret, P. 1989. "De la révolution de l'intelligence à la régulation des passions/" *La Lettre de l'économie sociale,* January.

Viviani, M. 1995. *Tools of Cooperative Identity—Fixing Values in Turbulent Conditions: The Case of Lega della Cooperative.* Manchester: ICA Conference Papers.

Walras, L. 1990. *Études d'économie sociale: Théorie de la répartition de la richesse sociale.* Lyon-Paris: Centre Auguste et Léon Walras-Economica.

Walras, L. 2010. *Studies in Social Economics,* trans. J. van Daal and D. A. Walker. New York, Routledge.

Walzer, M. 1991. "The Idea of Civil Society: A Path for Social Reconstruction." *Dissent* 39 (Spring): 293–304.

Walzer, M. 2000. "Sauver la société civile." *Mouvements,* no. 8.

Wanderley, F. 2015. *Desafios teoricos y politicos de la economia social y solidaria: Lectura desde America Latine.* La Paz: Plural editores.

Weaver, R. K., and B. A. Rockman. 1993. *Do Institutions Matter? Government*

Capabilities in the United States and Abroad. Washington, D.C.: The Brookings Institution.

Webb, B., and S. Webb. 1914. "Cooperative Production and Profit Sharing." *New Statesman,* special supplement.

Weber, M. 1991. *Histoire économique: Esquisse d'une histoire universelle de l'économie et de la société.* Paris: Gallimard.

Weber, M. 1995. *Économie et Société: Les catégories de la sociologie.* Paris: Plon, "Pocket," t. I.

Weber, M. 2001. *The Protestant Ethic and the Spirit of Capitalism.* Trans. Talcott Parsons. London: Routledge.

Weisbrod, B. 1975. "Towards a Theory of the Boluntary Non-profit Sector in a Three-Sector Economy." In *Altruism, Morality and Economic Theory,* ed. E. Phelps. Russel Sage Foundation. Reprinted in S. Rose-Ackerman, ed., *The Economic of Nonprofit Institution. Studies in Structure and Policy.* New York: Oxford University Press.

Weisbrod, B. 1977. *The Voluntary Nonprofit Sector.* Lexington: Lexington Books.

Wievorka, M. 2003. *Un autre monde est possible.* Paris: Balland.

Worms, R. 1898. "L'économie sociale." *Revue internationale de sociologie.*

Wright, E. O. 2010. *Envisioning Real Utopias.* London: Verso.

Yeo, S. 2001. "Making Membership Meaningful: The Case of Older Cooperative and Mutual Enterprises in Britain." In *Membership and Mutuality,* ed. N. Deakin. London: London School of Economics.

Yépez del Castillo, I., and S. Charlier. 1999. "Les logiques plurielles des acteurs dans les initiatives économiques populaires." In *L'Économie sociale au Nord et au Sud,* ed. J. Defourny, P. Develtère, and B. Fonteneau. Brussels: De Boeck.

Young, D. 1981. "Entrepreneurship and the Behavior of Nonprofit Organizations: Elements of a Theory." In *Nonprofit Firms in a Three-Sector Economy,* ed. M. White. Washington, D.C.: Urban Institute.

Yunus, M. 2008. "Creating a World without Poverty: Social Business and the Future of Capitalism." *Global Urban Development* 4, no. 2.

Zaoual, H., ed. 1996. *Organisations économiques et cultures africaines.* Paris: La Découverte.

Zelizer, V. A. 1988. "Beyond the Polemics on the Market: Establishing a Theoretical and Empirical Agenda." *Sociological Forum* 3, no. 4.

Zelizer, V. A. 1994. *The Social Meaning of Money.* New York: Basic Books.

Zinn, H. 1980. *A People's History of the United States.* New York: Harper & Row.

Index

Page numbers in italics refer to figures.

Jean-Louis Laville is professor at the Conservatoire National des Arts et Métiers, Paris, where he holds a chair in Solidarity Economy. He is coeditor of *The Human Economy*; *The Third Sector in Europe*; *Civil Society, Third Sector, and Social Enterprise*; and *Theory of Social Enterprise and Pluralism*.

Stephen Healy is senior research fellow at the Institute for Culture and Society, Western Sydney University, and co-convenor of the Urban-Futures research group. He is coauthor of *Take Back the Economy: An Ethical Guide for Transforming Our Communities* (Minnesota, 2013).

Maliha Safri is professor of economics at Drew University.